The African Renaissance
History, Significance and Strategy

WASHINGTON A. J. OKUMU

Africa World Press, Inc.

P.O. Box 1892
Trenton, NJ 08607

P.O. Box 48
Asmara, ERITREA

Africa World Press, Inc.

P.O. Box 1892

Trenton, NJ 08607

P.O. Box 48

Asmara, ERITREA

Copyright © 2002 Washington A.J. Okumu

First printing 2002

Book and cover design: Roger Dormann

Library of Congress Cataloging-in-Publication Data

Okumu, Washington A.J. (Washington A. Jalango)
The African Renaissance: the history, significance, and strategy /
Washington A.J. Okumu.
p. cm.
includes bibliographical references (p.) and index.
ISBN 1-59221-012-0 -- ISBN 1-59221-013-9 (pbk.)
1. Africa--Politics and government--1960- 2. Africa--Economic
conditions--1960-I. Title.
DT30.5 . 038 2002
960.3--dc21
2002010317

Washington A.J. Okumu is also the author of
Lumumba's Congo: Roots of Conflict.

Contents

Appendices

List of Figures

List of Abbreviations

AAU	Association of African Universities
ACBF	African Capacity Building Foundation
AFRAND	African Foundation for Research and Development
AITROP	African Institute for Training and Research on Peace
ARI	African Renaissance Institute
ARIPO	African Regional Industrial Property Organization
AU	African Union
COMESA	Common Market for Eastern and Southern Africa
DAC	Development Assistance Committee of OECD
DESSA	Distressed Expatriate Scholars from Africa
DFID	Department for International Development (for the UK)
DRC	Democratic Republic of Congo (formerly Zaire)
FDI	Foreign Direct Investment
FPI	Foreign Portfolio Investment
GDP	Gross Domestic Product
GNP	Gross National Product
HIPC	Heavily Indebted Poor Countries
HIV	Human Immunodeficiency Virus
IMF	International Monetary Fund
IOM	International Organization for Migration
MAP	Millennium African Recovery Programme
MMD	Movement for Multiparty Democracy (Zambia)
NAI	New Africa Initiative
NAM	Non-Aligned Movement
NEPAD	New Partnership for Africa's Development
NGO	Non-Governmental Organization
OAU	Organization of African Unity
ODA	Overseas Development Organization
OECU	Organization for Economic Cooperation and Development
PIFA	People's Investment Fund for Africa
PTA	Preferential Trade Area of Eastern and Southern Africa
RUF	Revolutionary United Front (Sierra Leone)
TCDC	Technical Cooperation among Developing Countries
TOKTEN	Transfer of Knowledge Through Expatriate Nationals
UNCTAD	United Nations Conference on Trade and Development
UNDP	United Nations Development Programme
UNECA	United Nations Economic Commission for Africa
UNHCR	United Nations High Commissioner for Refugees
UNICEF	United Nations Children's Fund
UNIDO	United Nations Industrial Development Organization
WTO	World Trade Organization

Dedication

This book is dedicated to the late Mwalimu Julius Kambarage Nyerere, the quintessential African democratic socialist, African statesman and former president of Tanzania, and a member of the Council of Elders of the African Renaissance Institute (ARI), in appreciation of his wisdom and foresight in supporting a wonderful African dream that he believed would become a reality. We must not let him down.

Acknowledgments

The African Renaissance is a work of reflection, written as the culmination of my thoughts regarding the future of Africa and its people. My interest in this subject had earlier led me to undertake what seemed, at that time, fruitless research into the history of the European Renaissance and the lessons it held for Africa. I was living in London between 1986 and 1993, but on returning to Africa my thoughts were refocused and my enthusiasm rekindled as Thabo Mbeki, now the president of South Africa, began to articulate and to popularize the idea of creating an African Renaissance.

There are several African leaders to whom I am most grateful for encouraging me to put pen to paper and to write this book for the benefit of Africa, but also for the wider world in the hope of facilitating a true understanding of the aspirations of the African people. Preeminent among those leaders is Nyerere, who personally offered me encouragement when I began work on this project. His unflinching support for Mbeki's idea of the African Renaissance, his willingness to put his personal prestige behind the African Renaissance Institute (ARI) and to serve, together with his friend and colleague, former South African president, Nelson Mandela, and with others in the ARI Council of Elders, was an immense inspiration to many of us.

On the professional and intellectual side, I want to record my thanks especially to my long-standing friend and colleague, Michael Schluter, chairman of the Relationships Foundation in Britain, for extended discussions and advice on the themes of this book, for his patience, tolerance, and affection and sometimes for his acutely productive disagreement. He painstakingly read the whole manuscript and offered valuable advice, some of which I politely rejected.

I am also grateful to that renowned African scientist, president of the African Academy of Sciences and former director of the International Center for Insect Physiology and Ecology, Professor Thomas Risley Odhiambo, who first read the manuscript in its early, raw form and who generously supported and encouraged its publication, recommending it to ARI's executive board. Jeremy Ive also offered valuable advice.

For creative inspiration and editorial skill, I owe my heartfelt thanks to Nicola Morgan, who discovered a number of errors and made me aware of my intellectual limitations, and who forced me to be brutally selective of the final material. Whatever errors and omissions remain, however, are entirely my own responsibility. To my personal secretary, Grace Ndungu, I will always be grateful for putting up with my frequent mood changes and occasional tantrums, and for typing the entire manuscript several times.

Last, but not least, I owe a great debt of eternal gratitude to my wife, Rispah Achieng' Okumu, for having provided a congenial and peaceful atmosphere at our home in Nairobi and at our farm at Dala Kwe at Sakwa, Nyang'oma Catholic Mission, Bondo, in which I was able to thrive intellectually and thus to write this book.

Professor Washington A.J.Okumu
Nairobi and London.
24th June 2002.

1
Introduction:
The Rationale and Meaning
of Renaissance

1.1. Frequently Asked Questions

Irealize what a challenging, if not downright impossible,
task it is to write a book on such an important subject as
the African Renaissance in the twenty-first century; however, wherever one travels in Africa today one is frequently
confronted by many questions in that regard: We have heard so
much about the African Renaissance, but what exactly does it
mean? Has a book or an article ever been written about it? We
hear that Thabo Mbeki, South Africa's president, has spoken a
great deal about it: Is it true that it is mainly his brainchild? We
hear about the establishment of the African Renaissance Institute: Where is it located and what does it do?

The British Broadcasting Corporation, the Western media,
and international commentators say that the concept is still-
born, because it is ill-defined and lacking direction. How can
Africa propose a Renaissance when ethnic and civil wars rage
throughout the continent; when Africa is burning; when in

countries like Somalia, with its extensive clans and sub-clans, the concept of a modern state is non-existent, and when most African leaders are still so dictatorial and corrupt? Indeed, how could Africans ever embrace the concept of an African Renaissance, even if it were explained to them?

What role can the Organization of African Unity (now the African Union) play in promoting an African Renaissance, given the fact that it has totally failed to bring peace to even one of the warring African nations? Nearly every African president has become a peacemaker, regardless of whether their own regimes are in total chaos. What can the African Renaissance possibly do about all these problems?

Most of these questions are quite legitimate and must be candidly addressed if the term "African Renaissance" is not to mean all things to all men. In fact, these questions are reminiscent of the sort of scepticism which was rampant in the early 1960s, when the notion of African socialism was so popular in the continent, embraced by all and sundry. This led the former prime minister of Senegal to comment: "It is becoming good form, in the developing countries, to call oneself a socialist and the word attracts, day by day, more of a mystical overtone affording specialists in social psychology a limitless field for study." (Friedland and Rosberg 1966; Hadjor, 1993, p. 15).

During that period, and faced with the daunting tasks of nation-building and economic development, many African leaders looked for ideological support; and so socialism became an ideal instrument for winning popular backing for the politics promoted by the new African leaders and their governments. Socialism was thus cynically manipulated in an attempt to win legitimacy for Africa's new governments. As Modibo Keita, the former president of Mali, warned: "If we are not careful, the word 'socialism' will be emptied of its meaning and bourgeois systems of the most reactionary kind will be able to camouflage themselves under the sign of social-

2

ism" (Mohiddin 1981, p. 15).

I would like to state, quite categorically, that the idea of an African Renaissance must not be perceived as empty rhetoric to be manipulated cynically by the enemies of African liberation, progress, and economic development. Neither should it ever be viewed as a form of propaganda. That is why I attempt to answer these and other questions here.

It will be evident throughout this book that I have given authoritative historical evidence and background to the analysis and the answers to the questions above, in order to avoid being irresponsibly subjective, as have been some critics of the African Renaissance. This is because of my firm belief in the African tradition; that without a knowledge of history or his links to the past, man is a social amnesiac, both intellectually and therefore to some extent emotionally rootless. The great British statesman Sir Winston Churchill once said: "The farther backward you look, the farther forward you are likely to see." (Dualeh 1994, p. 2).

1.2. The European Renaissance Model

"Renaissance" is derived from the Latin word *renascor*, which means "to be born again". In its original conception in the European context, the idea of Renaissance was concerned primarily with culture. According to the *Oxford English Dictionary*, the word "Renaissance" refers to a period in European history between the fourteenth and sixteenth centuries, when there was a great revival of literature, painting, science, commerce and art. Based on ancient Greek learning, the Renaissance saw the revival of Greek and Roman art, culture, and letters. It was a period of great developments, of a new style of art and architecture that represented a new birth or renewal of nations and their peoples. Every secluded corner or recess of

3

society was revolutionized; whatever was old and archaic was renovated and revised. Everything was renascent, springing up anew, being reborn.

The Renaissance was a turning point in European culture and civilization—a time of almost unprecedented creativity and optimism. It was also a time of intellectual curiosity, humane scepticism, and sensitivity. That is why the word "Renaissance" was considered by many scholars as the most glorious piece of shorthand in European historical language, accurately describing a great movement in their rich history.

A recent book by Professor Peter Burke of the University of Cambridge (Burke 1998) has given a unified and comprehensive account of the European Renaissance, making some distinctively illuminating remarks from which, I believe, the proponents of an African Renaissance could usefully learn.

First, Burke points out that the Renaissance was not an event or a period, but a European cultural movement whose response in different countries was shaped by local social and political structures (Burke 1998, pp. 1–2). Although this movement involved innovation as well as renovation, the most important point to bear in mind was its "enthusiasm for antiquity and the revival, reception and transformation of the classical tradition". In order to explain its real importance and significance in the transformation of society, the terms "rebirth", "revival", and "restoration" were used over and over again. Burke further stresses that "the history of the Renaissance may be regarded not only as the history of an enthusiasm and the history of a movement, but also as the history of a metaphor which many individuals and groups tried to enact" (Burke 1998, p. 16).

The second point Burke makes is that Western European culture can be viewed as "one culture among others, co-existing and interacting with its neighbors, notably Byzantium and Islam, both of which had their own 'Renaissance' of Greek and

Roman antiquity." (op.cit. p. 3). In Africa too, we have our own African culture, dating back to antiquity, and similarly we should therefore view it as continuing to coexist with other cultures as we try to borrow and assimilate ideas from the European Renaissance.

Third, Burke highlights an issue that I believe will be of central importance in an African Renaissance, i.e. the idea of "reception", which he describes as, "an active process of assimilation and transformation, as opposed to a simple spread of classical or Italian ideas", and again, "receiving ideas creatively means adapting them to a new context" (Burke 1998, p. 9).

This concept of reception differs from other models for the spread of ideas, and in view of the importance of this distinction for our situation in Africa, it is useful to quote directly from Professor Burke:

> The traditional account of the Renaissance outside Italy not only uses certain recurrent metaphors or models but is also shaped by them. There is the impact model, for instance, in which the movement "penetrates" one region after another. There is the epidemic model, in which different parts of Europe "catch" the Renaissance by a kind of contagion. There is the commercial model of "borrowing", debts, imports and exports—some literal, as in the case of paintings and books, others metaphorical, as in the case of ideas. Most common is the hydraulic model, according to which the movement is viewed in terms of "spread", influence, channels and absorption. (ibid. pp. 5–6)

In the African context, therefore, our reception of the ideas that animated the Renaissance movement in Europe should be considered from the standpoint of receiving the messages of antiquity in a creative manner, transforming what we have appropriated. As Burke says, "Reception was the complete opposite of tradition; the latter is a process of handing over, the former of receiving. It was more or less assumed that what was received was the same as what was given, not only in the case of material objects but also in that of immaterial goods such as ideas." (ibid. p. 6).

In the longer term, these ideas permeate into the institutions and habits of society.

Alongside the key concept of reception, "the cultural, social and political surroundings of a text, image, idea or institution" are crucial (ibid. p. 9), and therefore Burke goes on to consider the role of contexts, networks, and locales, as well as centers and peripheries in the spread of ideas. In other words, one can conceive of a brilliant idea, but how is that idea dispersed throughout society, disseminated and then domesticated so that it becomes an integral part of that society? These issues will be reconsidered under 1.5 below.

1.3. African Distinctives

It must be clearly understood that an African Renaissance does not mean imitating or blindly copying everything European. In this context let us consider some of the most distinctive aspects of Africa's identity and cultural glory.

What should Africa celebrate in regard to its identity that it is not celebrating now? At present, in my view, Africa too often regards itself as the poor relation, in economic and intellectual terms as compared with the rest of the world—in particular with Europe and the United States for obvious historical reasons. Instead, therefore, of celebrating its own identity, Africa craves to be like Europe or America, or even like Asia. The question therefore becomes: does Africa really want to be like

Western countries?

In countries like Britain, France, and the U.S., for example, there are certain aspects of behavior that are still repugnant to African people, such as neglect of, and lack of respect for, the elderly, and for parents in particular. In Africa, age is regarded as an accumulation of wisdom over the years and is therefore given great respect, and so too are parents.

Second, the high levels of child abuse and child neglect in the West is still largely anathema in Africa, although we are beginning to see these problems in urban areas due to poverty and the encroachment of Western civilization and influence. Third, the perception of marriage as "serial monogamy" in the West is unheard of in Africa. The high degree of social exclusion, the lack of willingness to show hospitality and to visit each other's homes, and the absence of sharing possessions and money with the needy are characteristics that have not yet begun to appear in Africa. Social inclusion, hospitality, and generous sharing are some of the cultural traits that Africa must retain. These should not discourage an ethic of hard work or produce a culture of dependency in the extended family. People can be motivated to work for their family, not just for themselves; everybody needs a sense of responsibility to contribute to the welfare of the family group.

Wholescale embracing of the idea of an African Renaissance should not necessarily bring about abandonment of our special African identity collectively or as individual nations, any more than the European Renaissance made the Europeans abandon their national European identities. This brings me to the subject of African cultural glory. I believe that Africa's greatest strength lies in the way it handles many aspects of personal relationships. The Zulu concept of "ubuntu"—meaning "personhood"—is found in many other African ethnic groups. It suggests that it is through relationships that people discover who they are, how they should lead their lives, and what life is for. The values that a person learns from their relationships give content to a person's understanding of proper behavior towards others. Africa's strength still lies in those areas where the wealthy West is weakest.

This includes, for example, the following areas of human behavior:

First, accepting others on the basis of blood ties rather than on the basis of wealth or status, thus preventing social exclusion and giving the handicapped, the mentally ill, the very old, and the very young a place of respect within the community.

Second, providing a welfare system that does not depend on state handouts but on the generosity of relatives and friends, mediated in such a way as to avoid both paternalism and dependency.

Third, a sophistication in listening to the views of others and thereby discerning motives, feelings, and goals with greater accuracy and perception than the often superficial approach of Western conversation.

Fourth, exhibiting cheerfulness in the midst of adversity and suffering, drawing strength not from financial resources but from the network of committed support relationships. (Indeed, the old American "Negro spirituals" and the South African black "toy-toy" dances derived their inspiration and strength from the racial slave persecution in America and the apartheid system in South Africa respectively.)

Fifthly, a value system which shows respect for marriage and for the role of elders in society, especially parents; showing a sense of duty for the care of relatives who are financially impoverished; and showing a willingness to share resources and show hospitality even to the point of significant financial self-sacrifice.

Today, such characteristics are described in terms of "cultural capital" and "social capital". According to Robert Wuthnow, "Cultural capital, following Bourdieu, refers to the artistic, musical, literary, or intellectual resources that give people a shared identity and often serve to distinguish them from others. It is an important factor in people's sense of self-worth, personal confidence, optimism about human nature, and willingness to trust others." ("How Religious Groups Promote Forgiving: A National Study," *Journal for Scientific Study of Religion*, Vol. 21 (3), 2000, pp. 125–139). Cultural values give content to social vision. To seek merely economic goals is to deaden the soul of a people, a nation or a continent. Art and design, poetry and music, education and social welfare all derive their inspiration from the dreams that a society holds for its future.

On the other hand, again according to Robert Wuthnow in the same article, "social capital can... refer to the resources generated by activities specifically concerned with creating intimate, informal, or personal bonds among group members. Such ritualised activities as eating together, singing together, and having parties are likely to generate such bonds. They do so by giving people opportunities to talk informally, to express humour, and to focus on collective activity." Wuthnow goes on to argue that social capital enhances social skills, generates trust, and links people with positive role models.

Professor Richard Rose defines social capital as "informal social networks and formal organizations used by individuals and households to produce goods and services for their own consumption, exchange or sale." As he says, "It is thus about getting things done...." (This report was prepared as part of the World Bank's Social Capital Initiative at Strathclyde University, November 1997.) However, this again confuses means and ends. Relationships are the essence of social capital, but instead of seeing economic activity as the means of providing human welfare and well-being, it is now the relationships that are used to serve materialistic goals. Professor Rose concludes, "If social capital does not directly or indirectly affect the production of goods and services and the avoidance of poverty, then whatever its academic interest, it is not relevant to policy makers." What about its linkage to cultural expression, conflict prevention and mediation, health, education, personal motivation and aspiration...? This is materialism taken to its logical conclusion, a confusion of means and ends.

1.4. Defining the African Renaissance

In Africa, the idea of the African Renaissance has been around since 1996, but many areas of the continent still do not have the slightest understanding of it! It is not that they do not want to understand the rationale and meaning of the movement. The point is that most people cannot lay hands on a compact document that clearly and concisely articulates the intellectual basis of the movement. Apart from the original speeches of president Thabo Mbeki of South Africa—undoubtedly the continent's leading champion of this idea—what writing there is remains scattered in newspaper articles, journals, monographs, and pamphlets, making a general synthesis a difficult undertaking. The African Renaissance Institute in Gaborone might undertake that task, but since it is still a young organization, it has neither the physical nor the financial resources necessary. It requires not only the support of one or two African governments in both material and physical terms, but that of many more governments elsewhere on the continent, not to speak of the international financial community that might be sympathetic to Africa. These issues, particularly the required support from the West and other countries that would like to identify themselves with the African Renaissance movement, have been dealt with specifically in Chapter 7.

With such a complex subject as the African Renaissance, it is a daunting task to give a simple and yet comprehensive definition in one sentence, paragraph, or page. Nevertheless, we must define what we mean by an African Renaissance. "Renaissance" is not exclusively or primarily concerned with economic growth, as is often perceived, although it may contribute to bringing that about. Just because South Korea has experienced rapid economic growth in the forty years since the Korean War in 1950 does not mean that it is appropriate to speak of a "Korean Renaissance". Nor could one say that there has been an "Asian Renaissance".

It is in this context that we need to critique the use of the word "development" to obtain absolute clarity as to the nature of the economic and social development to which Africa would aspire in the context of the "Renaissance" movement. Prior to the 1970s, development was generally seen as a purely economic phenomenon. Discussion focussed on growth of *per capita* GDP and relatively little attention was given to problems of poverty, unemployment, and income distribution. Only gradually during the 1960s did attention shift from a focus on heavy industry, as the key to getting the economy moving, towards a realization that agriculture was the key sector, and that a "green revolution" was needed to bring about economic transformation in a largely rural economy.

By the early 1990s the debate had moved on. The World Bank summarized a broader view of what was involved in development in the following areas:

> The challenge of development...is to improve the quality of life. Especially in the world's poor countries, a better quality of life generally calls for higher incomes—but involves much more. It encompasses as ends in themselves better education, higher standards of health and nutrition, less poverty, a cleaner environment, more equality of opportunity, greater individual freedom and a richer cultural life. (World Bank, *World Development Report*, 1991, p. 4)

This wider definition is clearly a great advance on the narrower discussion of the economic issues in the 1950s. However, in my view it still fails to take adequate account of relational factors.

For some time, Africa has been referred to as a "developing continent", and Britain and America as "developed countries." This is, of course, reducing the term "development" to a purely financial or economic meaning, a form of reductionism that implies that only the material things of life matter. If Britain is a "developed" country, and Africa aspires to be like Britain, does that mean that Africa wishes to mimic Britain on issues like child abuse, divorce rates and treatment of the elderly? The great arrogance of the West is exemplified and explicit in its reference to low-income countries as "less-developed countries." A much more satisfactory terminology would be a reference to "low-income countries" and "high-income countries", omitting a reference to development altogether.

Pure quantitative growth in and of itself does not produce development. There are examples of countries in the so-called Third World that have grown financially without major changes in everyday life. For example, oil-rich countries in the Middle East such as Saudi Arabia and Kuwait have high per capita incomes. Yet this wealth has remained in the hands of a small elite and much of the country lives as before. Statistically, these countries are qualified as "developed", but closer inspection of them shows great resistance to change. That is why it is dangerous to treat development as a purely quantitative process—one that can be measured by a series of indices such as economic growth figures, the number of telephones, and the rate of literacy. We in Africa should not therefore fall into the trap of reducing the concept of development as a process of change to a mere series of numbers. The African Renaissance movement must consider the development it wants to bring about as a process of social transformation that implies not just quantitative but qualitative change.

Western arrogance towards Africa in measuring Africa's well-being and performance by financial rather than relational criteria is in itself a measure of the West's cultural impoverishment. This ethnocentric Western view of Africa's development is something we totally reject in the context of our Renaissance. As long as Africa buys into the Western materialistic worldview uncritically in its definition of "development" it will continue to feel inferior and inadequate, and there will be no renaissance. A country is more than its GNP; values and culture are the qualities that give a nation its true identity and determine its long-term place in the world. That is why I agree strongly with Robert F. Kennedy on this important issue:

> ...the Gross National Product does not allow for the health of our children, the quality of their education, or the joy of their play. It does not include the beauty of our poetry or the strength of our marriages... it measures everything, in short, except that which makes life worthwhile. And it tells us everything about America except why we are proud that we are Americans. (Address, University of Kansas, Lawrence, Kansas, 18 March 1968)

In summary, we can define "development" as the process of a country moving towards greater inclusion, health, opportunity, justice, freedom, fairness, forgiveness, and cultural expression. Wherever I refer to "development" in this book, the term is meant in this sense. However, the reader should be forewarned that where other authors are quoted, they may well be using a narrower understanding of the word.

The eight factors within my definition can be expanded as follows.

"Inclusion" refers to political, economic, and social inclusion. The goal in society should be to ensure that every person in the population can participate fully in political, economic, and social life, unless they are in a dependant status owing to age or infirmity. Political leaders of such a society must genuinely abandon the prevalent hypocritical attitude of saying one thing publicly to people and doing exactly the opposite, e.g. by excluding from the levers of economic and political power members of society who are not from their own ethnic origin. Such a society cannot develop and will remain backward until everyone, men and women, becomes part and parcel of the development process.

"Health" means not just the absence of disease, but should be understood in the positive sense of well-being in body, mind, and spirit, and with sound nutritional status. This will require the provision of adequate health facilities in rural areas, with the establishment of dispensaries and hospitals that are properly staffed by nurses and doctors and easily accessible to poor rural communities.

"Opportunity" includes access to education for everyone in the society to achieve literacy, numeracy, and at least primary education, access to healthcare, the opportunity to work, the opportunity to participate in political and economic decisions affecting daily life, the opportunity to develop musical and artistic talent, and the opportunity to become acquainted with people from outside the immediate locality in which they are born. This will foster cohesion in society and render differences, divisions, and suspicions based on ethnicity a thing of the past.

"Justice" would be assessed not only by the objectivity and freedom of operation of the courts, but by whether the justice system succeeds in rebuilding relationships between the offender and the victim, and between the offender and wider society. To facilitate such a just system to operate freely and fairly, the executive branch of government must not be allowed to infiltrate and interfere with the judiciary as is often the case

14

in Africa. Debate about the separation of powers between the legislature, judiciary, and executive branches of government must not be theoretical and meaningless but genuine and enforceable by the rule of law.

"Freedom" includes freedom from fear, oppression, discrimination, hunger, and malnutrition; it also includes freedom for cultural expression, pursuit of personal and family goals, to nurture children, to provide for our elders, and to understand the wider trends affecting local, national, and global society.

"Fairness" would be measured not just in terms of differentials in wealth and income between individuals or sections of society, but in the distribution of property and in access to jobs in both the public and private sectors.

"Forgiveness" occurs when a person stops repeating the story of the hurt and releases the other party from the perception of guilt for their part in the offence. Sadly, it does not always bring about reconciliation in the sense of the other party also exercising forgiveness regarding a perceived offense. However, forgiveness is a fundamental precondition for a society to be able to develop its social, political, and economic institutions.

Finally, "cultural expression"—as the word "renaissance" reminds us—is the way a society demonstrates its beliefs and values through literature, music, art, and drama, which contributes to moulding its unique identity. The form, quality, and diversity of cultural expression are a measure of a society's development, and one of the cardinal principles of the African Renaissance is to promote African culture.

Considering everything I stated above, our proper conception of development should be seen in the context of the appropriate improvement of the well-being of the African people. General improvement in the lives of men and women in Africa will require that African society become more and more capable of understanding, of coexisting with, and of sometimes controlling, the forces of nature through scientific and technological advancement. Improvements in agriculture and in industry should ensure that African societies cease to be the victims of the elements and cope with changes in climate and other natural conditions. In the age of the African Renaissance, it will matter little how much information we may possess about development if we have not grasped its inner meaning. This is the cruel choice facing the African people. Professor Paul P. Streeten states that "development must be redefined as an attack on the chief evils of the world today: malnutrition, disease, illiteracy, slums, unemployment and inequality" (Quoted from Michael P. Todaro 1985, p. 61). In other words, development should not be measured only in terms of "aggregate growth rates", but also in terms of, "jobs, justice and the elimination of poverty."

Soedjatmoko, the former rector of the United Nations University in Tokyo, has said:

> Gone are the early naive illusions of development as an endeavour in social engineering toward a brave new world. Multiple goals have now replaced the initial single focus. There is now a greater understanding of the profound interaction between international and national factors in the development process and an increasing emphasis on human beings and the human potential as the basis, the means, and the ultimate purpose of the development effort." (Quoted from Todaro, ibid., p. 61)

And the father of modern economics himself, Adam Smith, wrote in 1776: "No society can surely be flourishing and happy, of which by far the greater part of the numbers are poor and miserable." (See Todaro, Ibid., p. 137.) Africa and its leaders had better heed these wise and far-reaching thoughts. If they do, the greatest beneficiary will be the African Renaissance.

1.5. Spreading the Renaissance Idea

Having discussed some of the issues arising from a definition of the African Renaissance, and wanting to present our renaissance as a movement rather than as an event or a period, I consider the question of the mechanisms of spreading this idea to be of paramount importance.

The big questions we must ask ourselves in Africa are: How do we intend to inculcate the idea of Renaissance into the bloodstream of African sociocultural and political life? How do we expect the African population to imbibe and to accept the idea of Renaissance? How do we intend to spread the idea and, more particularly, through which channels, networks, or groups?

In order to answer these questions, we in Africa must consider the contextual framework in which the idea of the Renaissance is received, that is, "the cultural, social or political surroundings of a text, image, idea, institution or whatever which may require re-contextualization, relocation or domestication." (Burke 1998, p. 9). The domestication of the "Renaissance" in the African context will require its "social diffusion, its incorporation into everyday practices and its effects on both material culture and mentalities". (ibid., p. 14). A consideration of the locales and networks of its reception in Africa will have to concentrate on the identification and examination of the channels, networks, or groups through which the process of reception will take place.

We, of course, already have the African Renaissance Institute (ARI) which has its headquarters in Gaborone, Botswana. It will necessarily form the center, in terms of the formulation of programs and ideas that will activate the Renaissance concept and ensure that it will spread throughout Africa.

While in the case of the European Renaissance the monastery, a traditional site for study, played a significant role in this regard, in Africa we plan to utilize universities, churches, receptive political parties, professions, women's organizations, law societies, national teachers' organizations, trade unions, youth organizations and any other available networks for this purpose.

Already, the ARI plans to make this a thorough-going mass movement in the whole of Africa by establishing and mobilizing regional, national, and local chapters throughout the continent. Through its interlocking and interdependent regional directorates and sectoral commissions responsible for various multidisciplinary aspects of its work, it will buttress the above institutions with appropriate professional support. Other channels of communication such as scholarly correspondence will also be used. This implies that the reception and spread of ideas of the African Renaissance will not depend solely on physical contact, but also on Internet communication, scholarly journals, monographs, and similar media.

One other important consideration for Africa is what Professor Burke has referred to as "centers and peripheries". "The emphasis on the receiver also implies a concern with the interaction between an international movement and local conditions (whether cultural, social or political)" (op.cit, p. 12). In the case of Africa, where is the "center" of the movement, and where is the "periphery"? At the moment South Africa will necessarily play a central role in the development of the idea of the African Renaissance, due to the acknowledged leadership that President Mbeki has provided. What, however, will count as periphery on the continent will vary according to the period and also the art or discipline under consideration. These matters will be dealt with in greater detail in Chapter 8.

1.6. Preconditions for an African Renaissance

As we have briefly recounted above, the idea of renaissance derives from the European renewal of the fifteenth and six-

18

teenth centuries, a period of great artistic and intellectual achievement. From the African standpoint, reference to the European experience is important because although the idea of an "African Renaissance" will include economic renewal and political change, we must bear in mind that the preconditions and motivation for political and economic renewal derive from the same social forces that give rise to cultural renewal. However, it is vital not to equate the idea of Renaissance only with economics, for that is the Western materialistic fallacy.

Many sceptics have questioned comparing the concept and meaning of the African Renaissance with that of the European historical process, contending that a society ruled by a corrupt and immoral leadership is not conducive to the emergence of men and women of intellectual curiosity as arose during the European Renaissance. Such a deep and profound transformation of society cannot occur under primitive leadership with scant education and little understanding of our contemporary world; a world that has not only seen man land on the moon and begin exploring the possibility of finding life on Mars, but a world that has also just achieved, as I write, a major scientific breakthrough with the completion of the first rough map of the human genetic code known as the human genome.

Former American President Bill Clinton captured the mood of the scientific world when he said: "Today we are learning the language in which God created life. We are gaining ever more awe for the complexity, the beauty, the wonder of God's most divine and sacred gift."(quoted in the *Daily Nation*, Nairobi, 27 June 2000). He called the achievement "a day for the ages", likening it to Galileo's celestial searching and the mapping of the American wild by explorers Lewis and Clark. (Note that the Italian astronomer Galileo, together with Nicolaus Copernicus, whose theory of the universe he tried to improve, were both the products of the European Renaissance.)

British Prime Minister Tony Blair joined President

Clinton, saying: "Let us be in no doubt about what we are witnessing today; a revolution in medical science whose implications far surpass even the discovery of antibiotics, the first great technological triumph of the twenty-first century." (quoted in the *Daily Nation*, Nairobi, 27 June 2000).

Indeed, this is a mind-boggling scientific discovery and it can only occur in a society where intellectual activity and the quest for truth are untrammelled. To be able to decode over 3.1 billion subunits of DNA, the chemical letters that make up the recipe of human life, is no mean achievement. That is why a sceptical Western world is asking whether we in Africa realize the preconditions that are necessary for us to achieve an African Renaissance.

At an individual level, renaissance perceived as rebirth, rediscovery, renewed commitment and achievement, usually begins with a fresh sense of personal identity, which leads to a sense of well-being. This, in turn, results in renewed motivation as epitomized in Frank Lake's "dynamic cycle" (Lake 1966, p. 163). I believe that the same dynamic operates also at the level of society. Renaissance, therefore, must begin with a fresh sense of the purpose and meaning of life as the basis of cultural identity. This will lead on to a sense of well-being, renewed motivation, and then achievements: first, in the arts and culture; then, in science, technology, commerce, and in politics. However, in the particular case of present-day Africa, the process could move much faster because we are now living in the twenty-first century, benefiting from scientific and technological breakthroughs undreamed of during the age of the European Renaissance. Africa does not need to re-invent the wheel, and Japan in particular has shown us the way.

It seems that popular phrases such as "Afro-pessimism" and "African fatigue", which came into vogue after the end of the cold war in 1989 in relation to the involvement between the West and Africa in economic terms, have been replaced by a more fundamental malaise. The West wonders whether Africans and their leaders are aware that the international community is increasingly weary of involvement with our problems. Nowadays whenever Africa is mentioned, people immediately think of ethnic wars caused by greedy and predatory leaders who do not want to relinquish power, let alone allow their citizens political freedom and economic prosperity. (see section "Africa's Big Men" and "Strong Men" in Chapter 3).

At the outset I would like to state that African leaders in the forefront of advocacy for the African Renaissance are fully aware of these criticisms from honest and well-meaning individuals from the West. (But not all African leaders, I must add quickly!) That is why this book attempts to face these concerns and criticisms head-on. In no way does it attempt to justify the behavior of some of our past and present leaders; rather it attempts to foster a better understanding of Africa's dilemmas.

No one can hope to gain a true understanding of Africa and its hopes for renaissance without first looking back at the continent's history (as I shall do in Chapter 2) and without considering some of the problems besetting modern-day Africa (see Chapters 3 and 4). The basis for our belief in the viability of an African Renaissance will be explained fully in Chapter 5, before we explore the practical policies through which it can be achieved, in Chapters 6 and 7. Chapter 8 provides a brief summary of some of the main conclusions of the book.

2

African History: Roots of Poverty

2.1. Cradle of Mankind—yet the Poorest Continent

There is no denying that the world is used to thinking of Africa as a backward and "primitive" continent; so much so that Africa is always associated with everything negative, and therefore designating Africans as inferior to other races in the world. The renowned British historian and the world's leading expert on African historiography, Professor Basil Davidson, has traced the origin of this European conception of Africans as inferior. He believes it began in 1440, after the advent of the Atlantic chattel slavery, which thoroughly, and almost permanently, dehumanized black people (Davidson 1994, pp. 42–64). From that time onwards, the earlier acceptance of a "different but equal" relationship between the races vanished and was replaced by an attitude that has taken the "different" as being deviant by nature and therefore necessarily inferior—humanly, i.e. inherently or congenitally.

If one listens to various world broadcasting systems, every news item emanating from Africa has to do with poverty, malnutrition, poor sanitation and hygiene, or pestilence and disease of all kinds. Medical experts have estimated that at any one time there are over 500 disease-causing germs in the air in Africa, compared to Europe's 140. Africa is where diseases such as malaria, yellow fever, bilharzia, river blindness, sleeping sickness, ebola and HIV/Aids reside, relegating the continent to a place of fearful disadvantage.

The Gross National Products (GNP) of fifty-three African countries collectively totals approximately one-eighth of that of the United States of America. Average GNP per capita in Africa is only one-sixteenth of that in the United States. In other words, Africa is a poor continent in material terms and Africans have grown tired of being reminded of this time and again, because they now know why they are poor. Africans are aware that their continent is perhaps one of the richest in the world in terms of its abundant natural resources, an issue we will examine in Chapter 5. The main question, then, is: Are there other factors that have contributed to this endemic African poverty? Why is it that Africa, now universally acknowledged as the cradle of civilization, continues to be the poorest continent on earth?

Remarkable advances in archaeological techniques, such as the application of radiocarbon dating and other ingenuities, have greatly improved the understanding of Africa's historiography and its position in the world. While Africa is considered the cradle of mankind, Egypt is thought to be a center of early civilization. Let us understand that the word civilization refers to "human societies which have attained a high level of cultural and technological achievement together with complex social and political development" (Reilly 1988, Vol.1., pp. 52–57). According to this definition, the countries of the so-called

Third World had civilizations spannning the time from the beginnings of recorded history and continuing till after European colonization. Some were empires with a unified political organization encompassing diverse ethnic groups over a wide area. In the case of Africa, the old civilizations of Ghana, Mali, Songai, Zimbabwe, and Axum existed at the same time as the Roman Empire, whereas those of Egypt, Sumeria, and Indus (Harappan), the so-called "river valley civilizations", are much older than any other in the world.

Africa south of the Sahara also had its own cradle of civilization in the Ghana, Songhai, Benin, Ife, and Mali empires, stretching as far back as C.E. 700 when Timbuktu played a crucial role in the development of trade and knowledge. Of the empire of Ghana, Ahmad Yaqubi wrote in C.E. 871, "There is the Kingdom of Ghana, whose King is also very powerful. The gold mines are in his country, and a number of kings obey his rule" (Davidson 1994, p. 27).

In 1332, during the early phase of the Italian Renaissance, Ibn Battuta, the renowned Moroccan Arab traveller, travelled the East Coast of Africa, and not long afterwards the Portuguese explorer Duarte Barbosa noted two well-established Swahili centers of civilization, where trade was already flourishing: the city of Kilwa with its "many handsome houses made of stone and mortar, with many windows such as our own houses have", and Mombasa, another northern Swahili city, which he described as "a place of much traffic with a good harbour where are always moored boats of many kinds, and also great ships" (cited in Davidson 1994, p. 35).

Basil Davidson himself writes:

> ...one can visit old Swahili houses in one or two old towns such as Lamu on the Kenya coast, merchants' houses for the most part, and stand in some awe at the comfort of those who had desired and built them

...here was another great intercontinental trading
system of medieval times... (Davidson 1994, p. 35)

The next chapter notes some of the fundamental short-
comings of Africa today, i.e. relating to its poverty, poor leadership, and lack of development of human resources. This,
however, does not address the fundamental question: What
caused the ruin of Africa's past glories, and also the suspension
of its economic development?

From the knowledge that is now at our disposal, it is quite
clear that Europe's pillage of the Third World, particularly of
Africa during the Atlantic Slave Trade era, ushered in its wake
pernicious, disruptive and destabilizing forces affecting the
economic development of this continent.

It is, of course, a fact of history that many great empires
have accumulated wealth through the plunder of civilizations
which they could subdue. Alexander, for example, is believed
to have collected booty worth about 80 million British pounds
sterling (at late nineteenth-century prices) from Asia in 323
B.C.E. The worldwide expansion of European control, beginning in C.E. 1492, was not unique in this respect, but
Europe's explorers, merchants, rulers, and settlers brought
new mechanisms of plunder and carried it out on a much larger scale than their predecessors.

The essence of "pillage" or "plunder" is the accumulation
of resources with little or no exchange; resources, goods, and
labor are taken by force, as during the slave trade. There is no
regard for the subsistence needs of those whose labors accumulated or created the plundered goods, nor is there regard
for those left behind after a labor force has been extracted.

Dramatic population declines in many areas reflected the
brutality of labor conditions (along with the spread of European diseases and conscious attempts to wipe out indigenous
populations). With these clear examples of pillage we can

include two major "trades" that depended on the use of force or drugs: the Dutch spice trade and the (primarily British) opium trade. In addition, the plunder during British rule, drained the Bengals' wealth through harsh taxation.

It has been estimated that in total the various forms of European plunder of the Third World must have concentrated the equivalent of more than 850 million pounds sterling at late nineteenth-century prices (the equivalent of £60 billion at 1991 prices) of financial resources in Europe (Thomas *et al.* 1994, p. 23). While this pillage covered the extraction of silver and gold from the Americas, the profits of trade from the Dutch East Indies, India's "tribute" to Britain—opium and tea—and the "opening" of China, it is the slave trade and slave production that affected Africa most directly and more than any other Third World region.

2.2. The Atlantic Slave Trade

The Atlantic Slave Trade began around 1440, the same time as the second phase of the Italian Renaissance and its spread throughout Europe. The slave trade was the largest intercontinental forced migration of wageless labor from one society to another, a development that followed racial lines, with the African slaves referred to as "ebony" or "black" cargoes. The main slavery routes are shown in Figures 1 and 2. It resulted not only in the growth of a sizeable black population in the so-called "New World", but it was also a complex economic process centered on the production of tropical crops in the agricultural plantations of Brazil, North America, and the Caribbean. Africa as a source of wageless labor, and Europe as a source of managerial and commercial direction, composed this economic complex.

27

Figure 1. Map of International Slave Routes

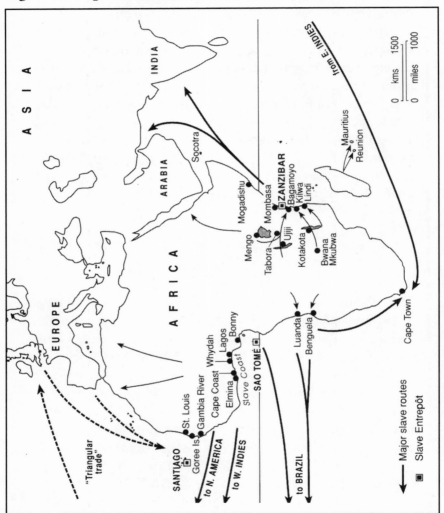

Source: I.L.L. Griffiths, *The Atlas of African Affairs,* 2nd edition
(Routledge: London, 1994), p. 47

Figure 2. The Atlantic Slave Trade

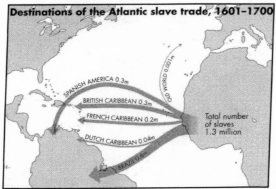

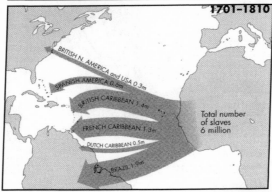

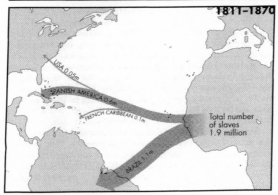

Source: Alan Thomas *et al, Third World Atlas,* 2nd edition
(Open University Press: Buckingham, 1994), p. 34 & 35

Figure 2. The Atlantic Slave Trade *(cont.)*

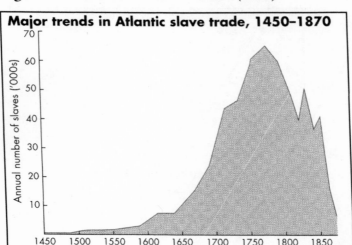

It was Dr. Eric Williams, the former prime minister of Trinidad and Tobago, in his renowned book, *Capitalism and Slavery*, who wrote that the Industrial Revolution in England in the eighteenth and nineteenth centuries was financed by profits from Liverpool slave-traders (Williams 1993, pp. 51–84). This might be an exaggeration, but the fact remains that during the period of the slave trade, 1440–1870, millions of Africans were shipped to Europe, the Caribbean, North and South America by Spanish, Portuguese and British "merchants in human beings", who thereby created an economic system which has been termed "the South Atlantic System". It was an economic system based on the utilization of cheap African slave labor producing tropical crops in the Americas for export to, and consumption in, Europe. Sugar was the main slave crop. Processing sugarcane—the most nearly "industrial" crop for several centuries—required careful timing of labor tasks and a large, disciplined labor force. Until the beginning of the eighteenth century these requirements could be most cheaply met by using slave labor.

The exact statistical information listing the numbers of African slaves shipped to the New World between 1440 and the 1880s varies considerably, but the latest study by a Nigerian professor in an American university puts the figure at slightly over 12 million (Falola 1995, pp. 10–11). Alan Thomas, however, has said that in total the Atlantic Slave Trade carried some 9.6 million Africans to the Americas. A much smaller trade in African slaves to Arabia flourished simultaneously. In any case, these figures are substantial relative to the population figures of those times and also considering the fact that many Africans died on the way, either through sickness, disease, or revolt against their masters, and were summarily thrown into the Atlantic Ocean. We shall never know the exact numbers.

Whatever the figures, Alan Thomas writes in the following terms about the profitability of the African slave trade to the Western world:

> It is estimated that the eighteenth century British and French slave trades created profits of the order of 75 million and 50 million pounds sterling respectively, and together constituted approximately one-third of the total slave trade. Profits from the use of slave labor in production, primarily of sugar, in the British West Indies are estimated at 200–300 million pounds sterling. Again, this is only part of the whole; production methods relying on slave labor were used more extensively and for a longer period in Brazil. (Thomas 1994, p. 29)

We should, however, bear in mind that the above statistical figures refer to eighteenth-century values. Their equivalents in modern values are, needless to say, significantly higher. It should also be noted that only the African continent was affected by the slave trade in this cataclysmic manner; the other countries of the Third World were spared this ordeal. Interestingly enough, it began at more or less the same time as the European Renaissance.

2.3. Arab Slave Trading

We have referred only briefly to Arab involvement in the African slave trade, a subject that has been suppressed, so much so that it is very difficult to discover any literature on the issue. The main reason, in my view, is that some people representing these two races—Arabs and Africans—would like to believe that slavery was a vice in which only the Europeans engaged. After all, the two races share the same continent and belong to the same geopolitical and geoeconomic organizations, except those in Arabia.

As a matter of fact, the establishment of the first politically united continental organization—the African Union—has been championed and spear-headed by an Arab leader. Although President Kwame Nkrumah of Ghana was the first African leader passionately to advocate establishment of a continental "African Union government", he failed, not only because of wrong timing due to the maelstrom of the cold war—but also because he did not command the massive financial resources required to implement such a grandiose idea. Instead, the African and Arab leaders of the early 1960s opted for the more limited Organisation of African Unity (OAU). Africa should therefore be grateful to Col. Muammar Gaddafi for having taken this wise initiative and for providing the bulk of the resources required for its initial launching. Monday, 9 July 2001, will be remembered as an important day in the African calendar, the date when the OAU replaced the African Union at a meeting of the African leaders in Lusaka, Zambia.

This does not, however, absolve the Arabs from their

involvement in the African slave trade. They were just as guilty as the European powers. H.A. Kalambuka, an African lecturer at the University of Duisburg in Germany, writes a revealing article on this subject:

> In the year 869 AD, a group of slaves rose in rebellion against the Abbasid empire whose territories now form Iraq, Kuwait, Jordan, Syria, Egypt, Saudi Arabia and parts of Iran. In the end, after 14 years of fighting, they were crushed. Their leader's head was paraded through the streets of Baghdad. Why? The slaves were black. These were the slaves used in the salt flats east of Basra (Iraq), where they drained the marshlands for agriculture and salt extraction. They labored in gangs of between 500 to 5,000 in conditions as inhumane as those that would exist, much later, in the Americas. (Kalambuka 2001, p. 6)

The above revelation would appear to indicate that the trade in slaves in East Africa by the Arabs—the Arabian slave trade—began many centuries earlier than the Atlantic Slave Trade, and that it was just as brutal. Kalambuka notes that according to Arabic sources, these slaves were mainly obtained from East Africa through capture, purchase, or tribute from vassal states. Most East Africans have read little, if anything, about the trade that delivered millions of blacks to the Middle East, a commerce established centuries before Europeans joined it in the mid-1400s. Kalambuka continues: "Obscurely documented, East Africa's slave trade history is apologetic about Arab slavery, and therefore conceals distortions. It extols the importance of ivory without mentioning the slaves who transported the tusks from the interior to the coast, and who were sold along with the ivory."

Kalambuka quotes Lovejoy's estimate of 2.4 million slaves

traded on the East African and Red Sea coasts between C.E. 800 and 1600.

"In fact Arabs probably transported more slaves to Morocco, Turkey, Arabia and India than the estimated 15 million West Africans shipped to the Americas....D. Clarke's recent book *Slaves and Slavery* (1998), is more realistic. He says that at its peak in the nineteenth century alone, the trade took 1.2 million slaves to Arabia and another 4.1 million across the Red Sea to the Persian Gulf and India. On the Indian Ocean and Red Sea floors lie the bones of millions of blacks". (P Lovejoy, *Transformation in Slavery*)

Even more recently, Ronald Segal, in *Islam's Black Slaves: A History of Africa's Other Black Diaspora* (2001) has estimated that the Islamic world enslaved a total of more than 10 million black Africans, not many fewer than the number who were shipped to the New World. The historical pictures shown in Figures 3 and 4 illustrate in a small way the realities of this degrading experience.

British missionary explorer Dr. David Livingstone documented the atrocities visited on pregnant women slaves by Arabs as they plodded to the east coast for auction. Kalambuka commented that the insignificant role that Africans in the Middle East diaspora play today is because of the large proportion of slaves castrated and imported as eunuchs, precluding them from having offspring. (See *Daily Nation*. op. cit.)

It has also been noted that the Arabs glorified war, and that many Africans perished in military service. Women remained in harems as slaves until death, as neither casual mating nor marriage were permitted. Because they came from distant shores and lacked natural immunity, many slaves died from endemic, as well as epidemic, diseases. This caused a steady demand for

Figure 3. British Attack on a Slaving Dhow

Source: J.O. Sagay & D.A. Wilson, *Africa: A Modern History (1800–1975)*
(Evans Brothers: London, 1978), p. 176

Figure 4. Arab Slavers Attacking an African Village

Source: J.O. Sagay & D.A. Wilson, *Africa: A Modern History (1800–1975)* (Evans Brothers: London, 1978), p. 184

replacements, thereby fueling the genocide against Africans.

This brings us to one of the most important points about the relationship between Arabs and Africans, namely, the question of racism. It has been claimed that the Arabs never practiced racism against the Africans in the way the white European races did. However, the following quotation points to the contrary:

As late as the nineteenth century, western travellers in the Middle East constantly noted the high death toll among black slaves. Unfortunately, lies such as the one peddled by S. Foreman in his *History and Life* prevails in the African-American psyche—that "there was little racism in the Arab world." Such beliefs were reinforced by the messianic influence of Malcolm X, who states, in *The Autobiography of Malcolm X*, that "America needs to understand Islam, because this is the one religion that erases from its society the race problem." (*Daily Nation*, op.cit, p. 6)

However, commenting on the prevalent human trade in Arabic cities, the fourteenth-century Arab traveller and historian Ibn Khaldun observes that "therefore, the Negro nations are, as a rule, submissive to slavery because they have little that is essentially human and have attributes that are quite similar to those of animals" (*Daily Nation*, ibid, p. 6). The rise of the Arab influence reinforced the institution of slavery, not only by recognizing and protecting basic inequality between master and slave but also by allowing its potentates to own slaves. In the Bible, the Veda, or the Qur'an, galaxies of verses have been misused to give impetus to a religious perpetuation of slavery. Nevertheless, race outranks religious doctrine, mostly among those who pioneered the global reorientation of slavery to mean anti-Negritude—the Arabs. Is it not black slaves who built the expanded pilgrimage site at Mecca? Even today, are not black slaves in the Islamic republics of Mauritania and Sudan still being traded? Are not desperate East Africans being duped into neo-slavery in the Middle East because of the harsh economic conditions in their countries?

In fact, it has been said that European slave traders never chased and captured blacks; much of the trade was carried out by Arab middlemen and African chiefs. Innocently, some African tribal chiefs sold off their people to both the Arabs and Europeans. We say innocently because most were already slaves. A few societies had slaves, but the slaves had some legal rights, such as permission to marry nonslaves, integration into the families of their masters, and freedom for their children. Invading Arabs would typically raid and kidnap blacks. They sometimes set fire to a village by night and captured the inhabitants as they tried to escape. That involved an unforgettable wanton slaughter of many innocent blacks.

It has been necessary, therefore, that when we are writing about the Atlantic Slave Trade, we should put into proper historical perspective this whole unfortunate episode of cruelty to fellow human beings. It is not only the Europeans and Arabs who have been involved in the slave trade. The most important fact to note in all this is that the African people have been, by and large, the victims. Lastly, one cannot fail to be disturbed that while by the early nineteenth century the West was committed to ending slavery, only in 1962 was slavery ostensibly abolished in Saudi Arabia, and for the fourth time, in Mauritania in 1980. It is still reported to be going on in Sudan up to the present day!

2.4. The "Scramble for Africa"

2.4.1. New Imperialism
The other most important historical event, apart from the

Atlantic Slave Trade that left an indelible scar on the face of Africa, is the "Scramble for Africa" between 1880 and 1914, which led to the partitioning of the continent by Britain, France, Germany, Belgium, Portugal, and, to a lesser extent, Spain.

The division of Africa into territories ruled by the major European powers was the most striking example of the new imperialism, and several questions have been asked about its origins and motivations. Was the conquest and partition of Africa motivated purely by economic causes, or were other factors at work? Some Western writers, such as Fieldhouse and Laird from Britain (Fieldhouse 1992), have tried to justify this new imperialism by saying that the expansion of Britain in the middle of the nineteenth century was that of a world power claiming to want no more imperial responsibilities, yet reluctantly acquiring territories "in a fit of absent-mindedness." Was this really a case of "a metropolitan dog being wagged by its colonial tail?" Or was it perhaps a many-headed dog, for imperialism did not originate from one source only.

There is no doubt that British imperialism was linked to material financial interests, as Lord Lugard wrote: "The partition of Africa was, as we all recognize, due primarily to the economic necessity of increasing the supplies of raw materials and food to meet the needs of the industrialized nations of Europe" (Reilly 1988, p. 172). The scale of this economic pillage was enormous. Some estimates of the size and direction of these transfers of wealth as a result of European colonial power are shown in Figure 5.

André Gide, the French writer, asked: "What have these big companies done for the country? Nothing. The concessions were given with the hope that the companies would develop the country. They have exploited it, which is not the same thing as development; they have bled and squeezed it like an orange whose skin is sooner or later discarded" (ibid. p. 172).

Figure 5.
Transfers of Wealth to Europe, 16th to 19th Centuries

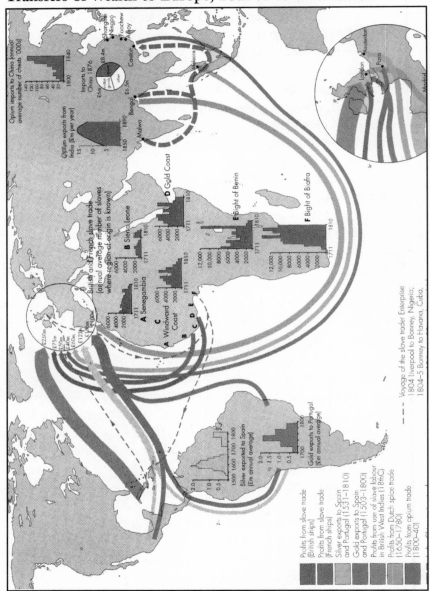

Source: Alan Thomas *et al*, *Third World Atlas*, 2nd edition
(Open University Press: Buckingham, 1994), p. 29

40

2.4.2. The Age of Exploration

The transition from the free-trade imperialism of the early nineteenth century to the global colonialism of the latter part of the century was demonstrated most dramatically on the continent of Africa and particularly by the activities of Sir Henry Morton Stanley.

In 1872, Stanley found David Livingstone at Ujiji on the banks of Lake Tanganyika. This meeting is still considered one of the most memorable episodes of African exploration. Livingstone's explorations in Malawi led to Scottish missionaries settling there—hence the great link that existed between the first president of Malawi, Dr. Hastings Kamuzu Banda, and Scotland and its institutions. (He had studied medicine at the leading Scottish University of Edinburgh.) Livingstone died at Ilala in 1873.

H.M. Stanley became one of the greatest European explorers of Africa, circumnavigating Lake Victoria (the second largest freshwater lake in the world—after Lake Superior in America) and then Lake Tanganyika. Other distinguished European explorations included those of James Bruce (1766); Mungo Park (1796) and (1806); Clapperton, Oudney and Lander (1823–30); and René Caille (1827). Meanwhile, Burton, Speke, Grant and Baker were busy on the East coast of Africa around Zanzibar, Lakes Tanganyika, Victoria and Albert, and the River Nile. Reports from major expeditions by Stanley and others paved the way for the "Scramble for Africa".

2.4.3. The Age of Partition

In 1870 Stanley appeared on the Congo river, but this time he was functioning as an agent for King Leopold of Belgium rather than as an explorer. The age of exploration had given way to the age of African partition. By the First World War the great powers of Europe had divided among themselves the entire

continent, the only exception being Liberia and
Ethiopia. With the partition of Africa, the way was
clear for the economic penetration of the continent—for the full-scale integration of Africa into the
global market economy. (Stavrianos L.S., quoted in
Reilly 1988, p. 172)

During the early nineteenth century the trade in African
slaves was gradually replaced by a flourishing trade in West
African commodities—palm oil, palm kernels, groundnuts,
gold, timber, ivory, and cotton. The terms of trade were favorable for West Africa until the 1850s, when economic conditions deteriorated sharply. The resulting economic tensions
between European companies and African traders, combined
with changing diplomatic relationships between the great
powers, precipitated a scramble for African lands and the
speedy partitioning of the continent.

After the 1850s, palm-oil prices dropped considerably
because of competition from burgeoning oil fields opened in
the United States in 1860; from groundnuts imported from
India; and from Australian tallow transported profitably to
western Europe after the opening of the Suez Canal in 1869.

The effect of this growing competition was accentuated by
the shrinking European demand for oils and fats during the
Great Depression of the nineteenth century. European firms
now received lower prices in Europe for their West African
goods and tried to pass on the reduction to the African producers. This initiated an economic power struggle in which
each side indulged in malpractices, such as diluting the palm oil
and misrepresenting the quality and length of cloth. Demarca-
tion disputes also arose over their respective functions and
areas of operation. Some European firms established bases
inland to buy commodities more cheaply from the producers
by eliminating the African middlemen, and the latter often

responded by destroying the company bases. Conversely, some African wholesalers tried to bypass the companies by selling directly in Europe, and they also attempted to keep up prices by withholding supplies.

European firms called on their governments to use force to beat down what they considered to be unreasonable obstructionism by African growers and merchants. Colonial officials often supported this demand for an active policy, viewing it as a means for advancing their own careers. Furthermore, activism was becoming more feasible and appealing, with the vastly increased power made available to Europeans by the industrial and scientific revolutions.

Advances in tropical medicine, especially the use of quinine for combating malaria, freed Europeans from the staggering mortality rates they had hitherto suffered. West Africa ceased to be called the "white man's grave," referring to the scourge of malaria. Also, the advances in weaponry—guns and other superior arms made possible during the Industrial Revolution's technological progress—shifted the military balance of power decisively against the Africans. The advent of repeating rifles and machine guns rendered the Africans almost as badly outclassed as the Aztecs and Incas had been by Spanish muskets. Other engineering advances effected during the Industrial Revolution, including river steamers, railways, and telegraphic communications, also facilitated penetration into the African continent.

The increased power available to Europeans stimulated demand to make use of it to gain certain objectives. One was to lower the cost of goods reaching the coast by eliminating African middlemen and the tolls levied by African states. Another was to build railways into the interior, which they believed would transform the economy of Africa, as it had that of Europe. The most far-reaching objective was outright annexations, urged in order to assure law and order, to maximize business opportunities, and to discourage European rivals. To rationalize their demands, the new merchants who wished to penetrate inland (as against those who wanted to safeguard their traditional operations on the coast) began using phrases such as "the regeneration of Africa," "the redemption of the savage," and "the preaching of the Gospel on the Banks of the Niger."

Nevertheless, the battle between the two groups was predominantly economic not ideological. As far as the British government was concerned, it was ready to protect its merchants in whatever regions they extended their operations. William Wylde, Foreign Office official, wrote in 1876: "Where there is money to be made, our merchants will be certain to intrude themselves and ...if they establish a lucrative trade, public opinion in this country practically compels us to protect them"(Reilly 1988, Vol. 2, p. 174).

The most outstanding among the annexationists in West Africa was Sir George Goldie, who admitted: "My dream as a child was to colour the map red. With old established markets closing to our manufacturers, with India producing cotton fabrics not only for her own use but also for export, it would be suicidal to abandon to a rival power the only great remaining undeveloped opening for British goods". (Reilly 1988, Vol. 2, p. 174).

In order to carry out this policy Goldie found his opportunity in the Niger Valley, where in 1879, under his direction and management, he brought together a number of British companies that were hitherto engaged in fierce competition and formed the United African Company. The group later absorbed French competitors in the upper Niger and was renamed the National African Company. With his customary vigor, Goldie set out to gain mastery over the Niger delta and to present the British government with a *fait accompli*. He established over 100 trading posts in the interior, backing them up with some 237 treaties, which his agents had concluded with African chiefs by 1886.

These documents invariably ceded to the African National Company "the whole of the territories of the signatories," along with the right to exclude foreigners and to monopolize the trade of the involved territories. To deal with those African leaders who were unwilling to submit, the company constructed twenty gunboats of shallow draft that were capable of navigating the Niger River during the dry as well as the rainy season. Attacks upon company posts were countered by devastating naval bombardments. Thus, the African National Company became the *de facto* government of the Nigerian hinterland before it was claimed by Britain at the 1884–5 African Conference in Berlin, Germany.

It was not only West Africa that was partitioned between 1880 and 1900. During those same decades other parts of the continent were also annexed, even though they were not generating any large-scale trade of the sort that was causing friction in West Africa. It is also necessary, therefore, to take into account the background forces engendered by the Industrial Revolution that culminated in the partitioning, not only of Africa, but also virtually the entire globe. Entire continents were subjected either to outright colonial status or, as in Africa, India, and South-East Asia, subjected to semicolonial status, as in the Ottoman, Persian, and Chinese empires as well as all of Latin America.

In the case of Africa, the partition process was triggered by new intruding powers that annexed choice but unclaimed African regions, thereby precipitating a chain reaction of pre-emptive partitioning by all the great powers.

King Leopold of Belgium initiated the process by hiring Stanley to acquire territory in the rich Congo basin. By 1879–80, Stanley gained title to over 9,000 square miles (more than seventy-six times the entire area of Belgium) from local chiefs who could not comprehend the meaning of the scraps of paper they were signing in return for baubles, such as cases of gin and rum, and brightly colored coats, caps, and handkerchiefs. With their communal landholding traditions, the notion of selling title to tribal lands was as preposterous to these chiefs as it would be for an American city mayor to sell title to the city's courthouse or to city hall, and yet this was done all over Africa—not only by Stanley for Belgium but also by Count de Brazza for France (north of the Congo), by Karl Peters for Germany in East Africa, and by other adventurers in the service of other foreign powers.

The race or the "Scramble for Africa" was now earnestly under way, so the Berlin Conference was held in 1884–85 by the major European powers, under the chairmanship of German Chancellor Otto von Bismarck, to set down ground rules for the acquisition of African colonies. It was agreed that notice of intent should be given, that claims had to be legitimized by effective occupation, and that disputes were to be settled by arbitration. This treaty cleared the way for the greatest land-grab in history. By it the European powers constructed the rules for the "great game of scramble" (Griffiths 1987, p. 44). A free trade zone was declared in Central Africa, including the entire "Congo Free State."

In 1879, the only colonies in Africa were those of France in Algeria and Senegal, of Britain along the Gold Coast (now Ghana) and at the Cape in South Africa, and of Portugal in Angola and Mozambique (see Figure 6). By 1914, the entire continent had been partitioned, except for Ethiopia and Liberia, and there has been little change in Africa's political map since (see Figure 7). Independent Africa ratified its countries' boundaries in the charter of the Organization of Africa Unity (OAU) signed in Addis Ababa in May 1963.

The following table indicates how the European colonial powers had divided African lands between them by 1914.

Table 1. Colonial Division of Africa in 1914

Colonial power	Territories*	Sq. Miles
1 France	Tunisia, Algeria, Morocco, French West Africa, French Congo, French Somaliland	4,086,950
2 Britain	Union of South Africa, Basutoland, Bechuanaland, Nyasaland, Rhodesia, British East Africa, Uganda, Zanzibar, Somaliland, Nigeria, Gold Coast, Sierra Leone, Gambia, Egypt, Anglo-Egyptian Sudan	3,701,411
3 Germany	East Africa, South-West Africa, Cameroon, Togoland	910,150
4 Belgium	Congo State	900,000
5 Portugal	Guinea, West Africa, East Africa	787,500
6 Italy	Eritrea, Italian Somaliland, Libya	600,000
7 Spain	Rio de Oro, Mini river Settlements	79,800
8 Independent states	Liberia, Ethiopia	393,000
Total		**11,458,811**

*Note: Colonial names have been retained for purely historical purposes, and also because some new colonies were acquired, or changed hands, after World War II. (Source: Stavros 1971, p. 380).

Figure 6.
Colonial Possessions in Africa at the Time of the Berlin Conference

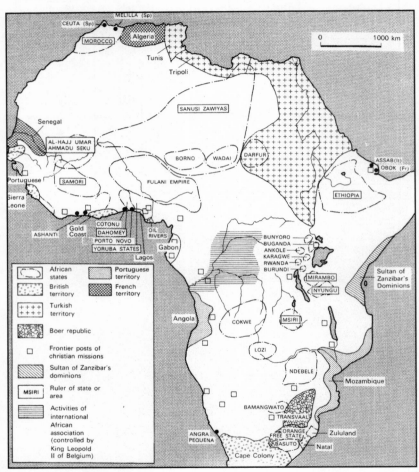

Source: J.O. Sagay & D.A. Wilson, *Africa: A Modern History (1800–1975)* (Evans Brothers: London, 1978), p. 193

Figure 7. Colonial Africa after the Scramble

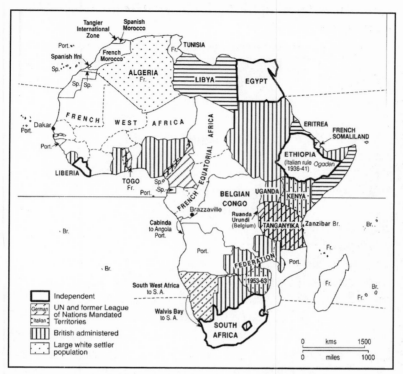

Source: I.L.L. Griffiths, *The Atlas of African Affairs,* 2nd edition
(Routledge: London, 1994), p. 53

In order for us to appreciate the full complexity of the
European colonial powers' pillage of Africa and its implications
for the future of the continent, it has been necessary to give, in
one place, an adequate but concise analysis of these momentous events, so that no one can question our impatience to
achieve as soon as possible the regeneration of African society
in terms of its economic development.

In summary, therefore, it is clear that in the history of
European expansion, the partition of Africa stands out as an
episode of high drama. Seven European powers took simulta-

neous military action and in just over twenty years Africa was carved up and completely subjugated. Until 1880, title of Africa was under direct European control or rule. In what is now South Africa, Britain possessed the Cape Colony and Natal, and the Dutch settlers had established the Boer Republics in the Orange Free State and the Transvaal. In the north, France had conquered Algeria, and there were small European settlements scattered mainly near the coasts.

By 1902, the political boundaries of modern Africa had been defined, and thirty-six of the forty political units into which it had been divided were ruled by Britain, France, Portugal, Germany, Belgium, Italy, or Spain. In 1882, Britain occupied Egypt, partly to defend the Suez Canal and the route to India but primarily to maintain financial control. In the southern part of the continent, in the specific case of South Africa, Britain's acquisition of the Boer Republics in 1899 was in defence of investors' interests in Transvaal gold, which had been discovered in 1886, as much as for the Cape sea routes. Britain's stake in controlling these resources was manifest: gold reserves underwrote Britain's capacity to finance free trade on a global scale; British investors supplied 60–80 percent of foreign investment on the Rand in 1899; and economic growth centered on the Transvaal provided a rich and rapidly growing market for British goods. So the generally popular notion bandied about that British colonial and imperialist expansion was conducted in "a fit of absent-mindedness" should be regarded as a self-absorbing joke.

The conquest of west and north Africa was dominated by three French advances: up the Senegal River and down the Niger; into the Sahara desert from the north; and into Central Africa and Gabon. These substantial military interventions occurred in the context of relatively modest strategic ambitions, but they were spurred by intense inter-imperialist rivalry and by an army unwilling to be halted by Muslim resistance.

During this same period, Germany occupied territories in south-west, east, and central Africa. Belgium followed Stanley into the Congo; Italy established a presence in the horn of Africa; Portugal expanded settlements in Angola and Mozambique; and Spain began its occupation of Spanish Sahara.

Historical explanations for the Scramble for Africa, this last rush to complete the seizure of the African continent, cannot therefore be doubted. Economic and material financial interests were supreme. The strategic aims of governments and local rivalry between merchants undoubtedly shaped the immediate pattern. It is important to note, moreover, that the four main European actors involved—Britain, France, Germany and Belgium—had just achieved roughly comparable levels of industrialization, and Africa offered the last chance to extend their political dominion over resources, labor and markets on a large scale.

Thus the European colonial legacy mainly in the latter half of the nineteenth century led to the disempowerment, and indeed in some cases to the destruction, of pre-colonial polities directly or indirectly with the imposition of colonial boundaries, often more a result of the Scramble for Africa (culminating in the Treaty of Berlin of 1885). These boundaries were enshrined in 1963, with the agreement by the newly independent member states of the Organization of Africa Unity, fearing the danger of irredentism, that they should remain unchanged as the inviolable basis of interstate relations within Africa. Struggles, such as those over Western Sahara, have resulted in the immobilization of the OAU, since it has not had the mechanism to resolve the implications of such disputes without the consensual support of all its members—which is almost impossible to attain.

The period of European decolonization, beginning with the independence of Ghana in 1957 and culminating with the transition from minority European-Afrikaner ("white") political hegemony to majority democracy in South Africa in 1994, has only partially addressed the colonial legacy. In some cases it has intensified the problem, with such figures as Mobutu, in what became known as Zaire, Bokassa, in what he called the Central African Empire, Idi Amin in Uganda, and Hastings Banda in Malawi as extreme and notorious examples. The worst excesses of European colonial power were copied and exaggerated, mixed with a lack of restraint that they claimed as indigenous. Obote in Uganda cynically manipulated unresolved tensions from the colonial past with murderous results on a massive scale; and this brutality has been mirrored in many other countries even today. Apart from such dramatic examples, the phenomenon of the old colonial patterns being adopted and replicated in the successor governments has become widespread.

3

Africa Today: From Western Imperialism to African Dictatorship

3.1. Black Renaissance

3.1.1. Independence of Ghana

We have seen that "renaissance" is not a new concept in terms of world history. However, in the context of defining an African economic development paradigm the term had never been used except in a cursory and nontechnical manner by Dr. Namdi Azikiwe, the first president of Nigeria, and by Dr. Kwame Nkrumah, the first president of Ghana. It was Dr. Azikiwe who first wrote about what he termed "Renascent Africa" in the newspaper *Western African Pilot* in 1938, but he never attempted an intellectual exposition of its meaning. We can only assume that he was referring to the birth of African nationalism in Nigeria in particular (of which he and Obafemi Awolowo were the fathers) and in West Africa in general. It was the Osagyefo (as Nkrumah's followers fondly referred to him in Africa—meaning the "savior" or "redeemer", not only of his native country of Ghana but also of the rest of Africa) who attempted to define and popularise what he referred to as the "Black Renaissance."

This received its first exposition in March 1957, in purely political terms, when Ghana attained its independence, the first black African country in the whole continent to do so. The history of Ethiopia and Liberia are entirely different. (Ethiopia was never colonized, except for a short-lived occupation by Mussolini's Italian fascist regime during the Second World War; whereas Liberia was "settled" by freed African-American slaves in 1847 and was then declared independent.)

At the time of Ghana's independence, Nkrumah made an announcement that shattered the confidence of the European colonial powers. Before the vast crowds assembled at the polo ground at Accra on Independence Day he proclaimed, "Our independence is meaningless unless it is linked with the total liberation of the African continent" (quoted in Meredith 1984, pp. 94–5).

3.1.2. Pan-Africanism

In order to give practical realization to this concept, in April 1958 Nkrumah organized the first conference of eight independent African states in Accra. This was the precursor to the founding of the OAU in Addis Ababa, Ethiopia, in 1963.

Under the banner of the All-African People's Conference, described by Nkrumah as the first Pan-African meeting on African soil, the 300 or so African delegates included representatives from various political parties, trades unions, and student organizations' leaders. Among the attendees were Hastings Banda of Malawi, Kenneth Kaunda of Zambia, Joshua Nkomo of Zimbabwe, Patrice Lumumba from that nation that became Zaire and is now the Democratic Republic of the Congo (DRC), Holden Roberto from Angola, Amilcar Cabral from Portuguese Guinea. The conference chairman was Tom Mboya, the young Kenyan trade unionist who became one of Africa's foremost intellectual and articulate nationalist politicians. In his concluding speech he summed up the mood of the conference, telling the colonial powers: "Your time is past. Africa must be free. Scram from Africa" (Meredith 1984, p. 96).

Nkrumah's contribution to the rebirth of African nationalism is best described by the black African American Stokely Carmichael, who later adopted an African name, Nkrumah Toure, obviously in admiration of Kwame Nkrumah and Sekou Toure, presidents of Ghana and Guinea respectively. He said, "The highest political expression of black power is Pan-Africanism and the highest expression of Pan-Africanism is Nkrumahism" (quoted in Hadjor 1988, p. 104). For many African intellectuals, Kwame Nkrumah's ideas provide the most coherent expression of Pan-Africanism and liberation.

In fact, it has been said that Nkrumah's outstanding intellectual achievement was not as a politician or as a philosopher. In both these domains he made important contributions, but it can be argued that his philosophical writings are of limited relevance to Africa, and that as leader of Ghana his political experiment failed to realize its objectives. Nkrumah's main achievement, then, was his ability to synthesize the experience of Africa in the crucial decades of the 1950s and 1960s. His own struggle against colonialism, and afterwards against the forces of neocolonialism, provided him with the necessary experiences for developing African political thought.

In the same way, leaders of the African National Congress such as Nelson Mandela and Thabo Mbeki (and Oliver Tambo, were he still alive) can develop African political and economic thought born of their experiences in the struggle for freedom. Hence their commitment to, and clear understanding of the need for, an African Renaissance. In fact, Nkrumah, during his later years of exile in Guinea, showed in his analysis of the problems of African liberation a keen appreciation of the limited significance of mere political independence (without economic empowerment of the African people) for the former African colonies of European powers. He, therefore, argued constantly that political independence was not the end but a means to real freedom. In just the same way, we are now saying that without the means of achieving economic independence through an African Renaissance, the future of the continent would be bleak indeed.

It has been written that "Nkrumah's attempts to use the institutions left behind by the colonial powers ended in his own political destruction. From the experience of defeat, Nkrumah drew the conclusion that there was an urgent need for a major rethink of the strategy of African liberation" (Hadjor 1988, pp. 88–9). It was this realization that led Nkrumah to analyze and reorient tactics and strategies, concluding that, "It is only through resort to arms that Africa can rid herself of the remaining vestiges of colonialism, and of imperialism and neo-colonialism; and a socialist society can be established in a free and united continent" (Nkrumah 1970; Hadjor 1993, pp. 229–230).

Although the world has greatly changed since Nkrumah wrote these words, and the end of the cold war and the collapse of communism have made the concept of socialism somewhat irrelevant in a world controlled by only one superpower that advocates a different ideological economic orientation, some of the things he spoke of still occur even today. The resort to several armed conflicts in Africa, both of an internal ethnic nature and inter-African in scope, are glaring examples of what Nkrumah meant. There are certain regimes in Africa today that are led by people who are so corrupt that they can only be removed through armed struggle. What is strange is that the West is so preoccupied by its own problems that it can only passively watch some of these African regimes brutalizing their own citizens.

Nkrumah's emphasis on the "resort to arms" was not the

product of some morbid fascination with violence. It represented a recognition of a trend towards the armed suppression of the anti-imperialist struggle in Africa and was therefore not a choice but a necessity under these conditions. This lesson had been learned by the liberation movements in Southern Africa. Today, after the numerous military invasions and interventions in Africa, Nkrumah's message has grown in relevance.

This text dwells on Nkrumah's example because, like Nelson Mandela, he is perhaps one of Africa's most important leaders. Although his role in history is not yet decided and will only be resolved through the outcome of Africa's contemporary crisis, C.L.R. James, a leading black theoretician, considered Nkrumah one of the four great statesmen of the twentieth century, along with such giants as Gandhi, Lenin, and Mao Zedong (Hadjor 1988, pp. 103–4). Nkrumah had a keen perception of the common destiny of the peoples of the Third World. Though he was a Pan-Africanist his vision was internationalist. In many respects it was his understanding of the international character of the class struggle that turned him into such a forceful advocate of Pan-Africanism. His message of liberation, though drawn from the experience of Africa, is profoundly universal; hence, his inspiration of a Black Renaissance in terms of African nationalism.

3.2. "Wind of Change"

Nkrumah's idea of a Black Renaissance was given impetus in purely political terms by events taking place in other parts of black Africa at more or less the same time. In 1956, the Anglo–French Suez adventure caused great division between America under President Dwight Eisenhower and the European powers, which resulted in Britain and France beginning to plan their withdrawal from Africa.

As early as 1942, during the Second World War, Harold Macmillan, then a junior Colonial Office minister, had warned of the danger of violence between Kenya's small white land-owning population and "land-hungry" Africans. His proposed solution involved the government buying up white farms and encouraging white farmers to stay on as managers. "In this way, the whites would get security of their money and employment, the land would be farmed in the most productive way, and the government would be free to allocate land to Africans when the need arose" (Meredith 1984, pp. 112–113). This idea, however, was not pursued until the 1960s, after Kenya had gone through the Mau Mau rebellion (1952–56), triggered primarily by land grievances and hunger among the Kikuyu ethnic community.

In January 1960, Harold Macmillan, then Britain's prime minister, attended a state banquet in Accra at the invitation of Nkrumah and referred for the first time to the "winds of change blowing through Africa". Nkrumah, in his own speech, spoke of this wind as "no ordinary wind, but a raging hurricane". Following that speech, he emerged as the charismatic leader of the Black Renaissance.

Macmillan, for his part, made Britain's thinking regarding the continent quite clear to all his audiences throughout his African tour; but the most definitive of Macmillan's speeches came on 3 February 1960 in Cape Town. Speaking to the two Houses of the old Cape Colony parliament, Macmillan praised the achievements of South Africans in some areas, but spelt out British disapproval of the policy of apartheid, or separate development. However, he coined his most vivid phrase in his description of the rise of nationalism in Africa:

> ...the most striking of all the impressions I have formed since I left London a month ago is of the strength of this African national consciousness. In dif-

ferent places it takes different forms, but it is happening everywhere. The wind of change is blowing
through this continent, and whether we like it or not,
this growth of national consciousness is a political fact.
We must all accept it as a fact, and our national policies
must take account of it. (Meredith 1984, p. 117)

This speech became famously known throughout Africa as
the "Wind of Change Speech." It was the first significant, clear
indication by a leader of a major colonial world power that they
had decided to "scram from Africa," in the words of Tom
Mboya. There was another extremely significant aspect of this
speech, namely that the voice of the oldest nationalist political
movement in Africa, the African National Congress of South
Africa (founded in 1912 after the establishment of the Union
of South Africa in 1910) had hitherto been completely
ignored; and yet a political speech of such vital importance on
African affairs was being made in a country where the black
man's voice was completely suppressed. Africa would never be
the same again, and from that year onwards, one country after
another attained its own independence. The decade of the
1960s witnessed tremendous transformation of the political
map of Africa for good. It was indeed the decade of the Black
African Renaissance in political terms.

In the autumn of 1960, one of the biggest gatherings of
world leaders met during that year's session of the United
Nations General Assembly. It was in that same year that Dr.
Hendrik Verwoerd, the architect of the apartheid policy, had
decided to withdraw South Africa from the British Common-
wealth, for they made it abundantly clear to him that the other
members considered South Africa's continued membership in
the club repugnant to them on account of its racial policies,
they were ready to expel the country. Kwame Nkrumah played
a major role in instigating this tactic.

In Cuba, Dr. Fidel Castro had just come to power the previous year through revolution after a successful guerrilla war that overthrew the Batista regime. The Asia–Africa Conference of April 1955, popularly known as the Bandung Conference (discussed below), the precursor to the establishment of the Non-Aligned Movement in Belgrade, Yugoslavia in 1961, had taken place. It was at the height of the cold war and during the October 1960 session of the U.N. General Assembly meeting, Nikita Khrushchev, the first secretary of the Communist Party of the Soviet Union, took off his right shoe and hit the podium as he was delivering his speech as an expression of his anger with the United States and the capitalist system. Kwame Nkrumah, in his speech, delivered a most eloquent and emotional testimony of the African situation. He said:

> For many years the colonial powers strode through Africa like a colossus from North to South and East to West without any compunction. But today, I, as an African, stand before this august assembly, proclaiming to the world the dawn of a new era.

In talking of the dawn of a new era in Africa, Nkrumah meant the renewal or rebirth of the continent, as newly independent states sprang up one after another. It was a time that Adlai Stevenson, a brilliant American liberal intellectual and two-time presidential candidate (in 1952 and 1956), referred to as the age of rising expectations; the age when democracy, prosperity and self-rule became the bedrock vision of African independence. Today few Africans express satisfaction with the fruits of "*Uhuru*" (which means "freedom" in the Swahili language). Those heady days of anticolonial mobilization, demonstrations, and demands, though only three decades old, seem now a dream from which one has awakened to another historical epoch. What went wrong?

3.3. African Socialism and the Cold War

Mwalimu Julius Nyerere, the former president of Tanzania, made an enormous contribution to giving ideological shape and content to the newly born Africa through his concept of *ujamaa*—African socialism—as enshrined in the Arusha Declaration of 1967, but it did not gain continent-wide influence because of competing ideologies of the cold war. The "cold war" refers to the strategic and political struggle after the Second World War between the then two "superpowers"—the U.S.A. with its Western European allies and the U.S.S.R. with its communist allies. The conflict was based on mutual suspicion: the American conviction that the U.S.S.R. was intent on expansion and world conquest, and Soviet antagonism to Western imperialism and capitalism, which, it believed, would inevitably seek the destruction of the Soviet system.

Starting as a conflict over a divided Germany, the cold war spread to Asia after the Chinese communist victory in 1949. The future of East and South-East Asia was uncertain after the withdrawal of Japan from the territories it had occupied there. The likelihood of a communist government in the whole of the Korean peninsula brought U.S. involvement in a land war there in 1950, resulting in the partition of that country which persists to this day. In Africa the dramas of the cold war were to be enacted in the former Belgian Congo (later Zaire and subsequently Democratic Republic of the Congo) culminating in the murder of Patrice Lumumba, its first democratically elected prime minister, and then in Angola and in the Horn of Africa in the 1960s and 1970s.

The intensity of the ideological rivalry between East and West, especially in economic terms, was given more poignancy in 1961, when Khrushchev made a speech confidently predicting that within ten years his country would overtake America in total industrial production, and that by 1985, the Soviet Union

61

would have higher income per head of population. "We will bury you," Khrushchev told the West (Skidelsky 1996, p. 1).

More importantly, after an interesting and tense encounter in Vienna, in June 1961, between President Kennedy, the newly elected young American leader representing an exuberant philosophy of the New Frontier, and Chairman Khrushchev, the former went to London and confirmed to British Prime Minister, Harold Macmillan, that the Russian leader's threats were no idle boast. Russia was no longer frightened of American aggression. The Russians had nuclear forces at least as powerful as those of the West. They had a buoyant economy that had achieved an annual rate of growth of about 10 percent between 1950 and 1960 and could soon outmatch capitalist society in the race for material wealth.

In other words, the struggle for world supremacy between two conflicting ideologies was so intense that any leader in the Third World, especially leaders in Africa such as Nkrumah or Nyerere who advocated the ideology of socialism was instantly branded an enemy of the West. John Foster Dulles, the powerful American secretary of state under Eisenhower, had stated that "whoever was not with America was against her." With the perception at that time that America was a nation losing ground militarily, technologically, and ideologically to a worldwide communist offensive, backed by rocketing Soviet military might and a powerful, growing economy and technology, any world leader who espoused policies that even smacked of socialism had to be destroyed at any cost. This was at the height of the cold war, and it was therefore impossible for any Third World country caught in the midst of this rivalry to thrive. There is a saying in Africa: "When two elephants fight, it is the grass that suffers." The realization of a black African Renaissance in one form or another would have been impossible immediately after the post war years under these circumstances.

This is why Thabo Mbeki's idea of an African Renaissance,

which attempts to address the question of Africa's endemic poverty, economic deprivation, and marginalization after the end of the cold war, comes at a critical moment in the continent's history.

3.4. African Conflicts

A recent article on Africa entitled, "Hopeless Africa," expresses the following views about the present condition of the continent, giving Sierra Leone as an example:

> "At the start of the nineteenth century, Freetown was remote and malarial, but also a place of hope. This settlement for destitute Africans from England and former slaves from the Americas had become the main base in west Africa for enforcing the British act that abolished the slave trade. At the start of the twenty-first century, Freetown symbolises failure and despair. …and since Sierra Leone seemed to epitomise so much of the rest of Africa, it began to look as though the world might just give up on the entire African continent." ("Hopeless Africa," *The Economist*, London 13 May 2000, p. 17)

The United Nations Security Council, at America's instigation, responded to such accusations of indifference towards Africa by starting the third millennium with a "month of Africa". American Ambassador to the U.N. Richard Holbrooke paid a lightning visit to Africa in December 1999 accompanied by six other U.N. ambassadors, and invited several African leaders, including Nelson Mandela, Robert Mugabe, Sam Nujoma, Eduardo dos Santos, Yoweri Museveni, Paul Kagame and Laurent Kabila, to attend a special session of the Security Council on Africa. It focused its attention on war, poverty, and HIV/Aids, and the meeting seemed to have gone well because there was agreement to send 8,000 troops to Sierra Leone and 5,500 troops to the Democratic Republic of the Congo as long as the cease-fire in the regions held.

These decisions were, of course, greatly compromised by the renewed outbreak of fighting in Sierra Leone between the Revolutionary United Front and government troops; and also by what was considered by many people in the West and in Africa as the shameful and completely unnecessary fighting between Ugandan and Rwandan troops for the control of the city of Kisangani and the nearby diamond mines. These two countries had been great friends and allies during the earlier years of the Congolese war. It is good news, however, that at the time of writing they have healed their political and economic differences over the Congo, and let us hope that this was a genuine rapprochement that will stand the test of time.

Africa's critics should bear in mind that the DRC and the nine nations that surround it sit on what may be the richest patch of land on this planet. There are, as we shall see, diamonds, oil, uranium, gold, copper, zinc, manganese, cobalt, timber, plentiful water with great hydroelectric potential, fertile land, and exquisite wildlife. That is why it continues to be one of the biggest battlefields in African history, the object of a conflict that has been dubbed "Africa's First World War." Six foreign or outside African states are fighting inside the DRC alone, with at least 35,000 soldiers, men and boys, battling for a bewildering number of reasons. Some armies, such as those from Rwanda and Uganda, for example, are allied with rebel groups who wanted to overthrow the Congo's president Laurent Kabila, and later his son who took over after his father's death. Others, such as those from Zimbabwe, Angola and Namibia, are protecting him. Nine rebel groups in the Congo are fighting to overthrow governments in neighboring countries. Nearly everyone carts off the Congo's riches.

Remember that these conflicts are a series of related wars, fuelled by ethnic conflict, by a scramble for power and riches among people with very little of either, and by leaders with little notion of responsibility for those people. Rooted in the Rwandan genocide of 1994, the fighting has smouldered inconclusively since 1996, when rebels and invading armies expanded their reach to half of Congo's vast expanse; but the war remains largely a stalemate. So far, it is only President Robert Mugabe of Zimbabwe who has owned up, admitting that President Kabila gave his country and Namibia one diamond mine each as payment for their military and political support. This confirms what I was told recently by a former Congolese cabinet minister who had served in the past governments of Lumumba, Mobutu, and Adoula; that the behavior of their African brothers, in so far as wanting to exploit Congo's riches, is no different from that of Western European and American imperialist powers.

I am not trying to suggest that two wrongs make a right, but I would like to point out that the Berlin Conference of 1884, during which the European Scramble for Africa began, was convened primarily to reduce the conflict between the European colonial powers in their quest to partition Africa into spheres of influence. It was during that conference that King Leopold of Belgium, in gratitude for his adroit diplomatic skills, was given the Congo as his personal property, a decision that Britain and France would later regret, as this turned out to be one of the most valuable pieces of real estate on earth!

So the world should not blame only Africans for the present political and economic rivalry and the existing chaos in the Congo. The problem is that both the West and Africa have the same interests. A similar situation applies in Angola, Sierra Leone, Congo (Brazzaville), and Sudan. In the case of Sudan, the discovery of oil in the south and its exploitation by Canada,

65

China, and Malaysia, with Austria, Sweden, and France slated to join in, has vastly complicated the ethnic war in the south of the country. In fact, a BBC commentator has remarked that although the Sudanese civil war has lasted for over seventeen years, the "oil war" has just began. It has greatly strengthened the economic position of the Sudanese government, enabling it to prosecute the war and, given the Sudan People's Liberation Army, providing a reason to continue the war. In a similar context the Burmese opposition leader and Nobel peace laureate Aung San Suu Kyi has made an apt and telling observation with regard to the UK's Premier Oil involvement in Burma. "It makes the government feel that, however repressive they may be, they still have the support of big companies...it gives the military regime the chance to say: 'Look, even companies from Western democracies support us...'" (Mark Thomas/ Channel 4 TV, October 1999).

The war in the Democratic Republic of the Congo, in which at least seven African countries are deeply involved, is a glaring example of conflict within the continent, but one could also mention the on-going war between Ethiopia and Eritrea, the clan war in Somalia, ethnic conflicts in Sierra Leone, Lesotho, Liberia, Republic of Congo, Uganda, Guinea Bissau, Angola, Rwanda, Burundi, and the religious wars in Sudan and Algeria.

With regard to ethnic conflicts in Africa, the West and the United Nations Security Council must not give up and abandon Africa. It must continue to carry out its mandate to help the people of Africa as important members of the human race, regardless of the difficulties and obstacles, just as it has done for the people of Bosnia, Kosovo, and East Timor, and just as it will do for the people of any other country similarly threatened in the future. Otherwise the credibility of the West and the United Nations would be seriously jeopardised.

Actually, it is not only Western skeptics who have voiced severe reservations about the realization of the African Renaissance at this point in Africa's history. Some prominent intellectuals, Professor Wole Soyinka, the Nigerian Nobel laureate playwright, essayist and memoirist among them, have been highly critical. In a 1999 speech Soyinka announced that he was researching the prospects of a "renaissance" by exploring the interplay between cultural and literary awakening and broader political events. He concluded that: "A lament can be purifying.... . But a lament does not emerge from atrocities, for an atrocity is the very silencing of a human voice. Therefore, among the slaughter, there can be no African Renaissance" (*Mail and Guardian*, 3 September 1999, Cape Town).

There are also other African leaders who thought that the idea of the African Renaissance at this stage was merely a distant hope, an empty policy vessel, an abstract ideology whose implementation was still a long way off; although they considered that it could be a millennium equivalent to "African socialism or humanism". Some went as far as suggesting that it was a populist smokescreen intended to cover policies that were not particularly beneficial to ordinary Africans. Lionel Cliffe considered this idea ubiquitous and went on to express his skepticism: "Is it rather a vaguer entity, a mood of tentative optimism to replace the dark pessimism occasioned by economic crises, debt, war and famine in the 1980s and 1990s?" (Lionel Cliffe 1999, unpublished article).

In spite of these expressions of strong skepticism, which describe the African Renaissance more as a future aspiration than as anything immediate, with some critics going so far as likening it to a utopian idea, there is a certain consensus about some of the requirements that must be desired and actively sought, namely, peace, governance and democracy, and economic development. Lionel Cliffe notes that: "The African Renaissance discourse associates itself with calls for more initiatives from within the continent to resolve conflicts...."

There is, therefore, a general international consensus that in spite of the disillusionment and disappointment with Africa, it would be wrong for the world to turn its back on the continent. There should be no lack of concern for the onset of war, ethnic conflict and resultant suffering in Africa, because there are also international economic dimensions to the causes of these wars over which the African countries have no control, e.g. the almost equally deadly bidding war between rival Western mining houses competing for mineral rights and favors from the new order.

3.5. Africa's "Big Men" and "Strong Men"

3.5.1. *Illusion of hope*
An article in *The Economist* laments the fact that the new millennium has brought more disaster than hope to Africa:

> For a brief moment in the mid-1990s, there were signs of improvement. World Bank figures showed a clutch of African countries achieving economic growth rates of more than 6 percent ...multi-party democracy spread across the continent. A new crop of leaders emerged.... . Democracy and liberalization seemed to flourish. There was talk of an "African Renaissance". ("The heart of the matter," *The Economist*, London, 13 May 2000, p. 23)

Then the writer becomes despondent: "It was an illusion. The new leaders became embroiled in wars, some with each other, and the cheerful statistics were the result of good rains and bad accounting."

After giving details of how Africa is fast losing the battle for economic development, with all the lowest places in the world league tables filled by African countries and the gap between them and the rest of the world widening, the writer points out that only 15 percent of Africans today live in an environment considered minimally adequate for sustainable growth and development. He further states that at least 45 percent of Africans live in poverty, while their leaders joyride around the world in custom-designed private jets and squander most of the taxpayers' money in expensive hotels in Europe and America and on unbelievably extravagant shopping sprees. While engaging in these criminal financial activities abroad, back home their people are dying of hunger and disease. Unemployment is the order of the day, and in most cases the physical infrastructure is so completely destroyed that there is no on-going, meaningful economic activity.

The high rate of crime caused by unemployment and corruption has made life in most African cities hell on earth, especially when on top of this is added the absence of such basic amenities as water, electricity, education, and health facilities. The problem with some African leaders is that they will always blame everyone else, including God, for this chaotic state of affairs instead of themselves or their corrupt government. And yet African countries need growth rates of 7 percent or more to begin to turn the corner in not less than twenty years. One distressing fact is that some African countries are growing at the rate of less than 2 percent per annum, and yet they are still busy producing public propaganda material promising their people greater industrialization and economic prosperity in the not-too-distant future. The African masses have now realized that these promises are nothing but pie in the sky.

As *The Economist* points out, this sad and dismal picture has led some people in the West to wonder: Does Africa have some inherent character flaw that keeps it backward and incapable of economic development? *The Economist* goes on to comment:

> There are, however, others who blame the way the world has treated Africa, citing exploitation going

back to the slave trade and European colonial rule. They blame cold war rivalry for propping up greedy dictators in the first 30 years of African independence, and now they trace the continent's failures to debt, exploitative trading relations and too-strict demands for economic reform from the International Monetary Fund and the World Bank ...

Neither theory, by itself, can explain why Africa is the way it is. Those who see the continent as the victim of external forces must accept that parts of Asia, too, were subject to rapacious colonialists and have, within a generation after independence, established viable states and successful economies. Even where they fail, Asian countries do not blame their past imperial masters. ("The Heart of the Matter," *The Economist*, London, 13 May 2000, pp. 23–24.)

3.5.2. *"Big Men"*

It is, however, not only the Westerners or Europeans who are deeply concerned and agonizing about African leadership. Chinua Achebe, the celebrated Nigerian novelist and essayist, began a critical examination of what went wrong with Nigeria as far back as the 1960s, immediately after independence, when the country began to witness one military coup after another. He came to the firm conclusion that the failure of leadership was the root of all evil in Nigeria: "The Nigerian problem is the unwillingness or inability of its leaders to rise to the responsibility, to the challenge of personal example which are the hallmarks of true leadership" (Achebe 1984, p. 1).

Wole Soyinka came to the same conclusion as Chinua Achebe, for which the notorious Nigerian military dictator, Sani Abacha, bayed for his blood. Soyinka believed that those who wished to understand the catastrophe towards which the Nigerian nation was being propelled would do well to study the personalities of Nigeria's miltary despots of the present and of the immediate past. He started with Babangida, for whom "the potency of Nigeria, in short, was an augmentation of his own sense of personal power. It corrupted him thoroughly, and all the more disastrously because he had come to identify Nigeria and her resources with his own person and personal wealth" (Soyinka 1996, pp. 13–14).

What Soyinka has so vividly described epitomizes the character and nature of an African "Big Man" or "Strong Man". Such men surround themselves with a small and powerful group of self-servers who constitute a minority—a dangerous, conspiratorial, and reactionary clique, but a minority just the same. Their tentacles reach far and deep, and their fanaticism is the secular face of religious fundamentalism. These people are not merely cartoons, for anyone who crosses their path will be dead before the cock crows!

Much more recently, the following commentary by an African writer appeared in the *Daily Nation,* 20 June 2000: "Only after we force our present leaders out and start choosing the right leaders will we achieve what South Africa's Thabo Mbeki is calling the African Renaissance. Until then, the struggle continues" (Mutua 2000).

There has been a great deal said about Africa's poverty; but the poverty has been economic and material in nature. I believe that to this we must add a much more serious and debilitating poverty afflicting Africa—poverty of the intellect.

If a leader's mind is not informed through training, education, and experience, he will suffer from a debilitating inferiority complex that he, then, attempts to overcome by the acquisition of power and wealth, with all the accompanying vices such as dictatorship, resorting to violence, intimidating and killing real and imagined opponents. Such leaders find it difficult to reason or argue; they have no tolerance whatsoever towards those who express a contrary point of view, however innocuous.

71

This sort of leader only tolerates sycophants around him, because his thirst for flattery is insatiable. He must be called "Father of the Nation", regardless of whether or not there were several before him. The 20 June 2000, article in the *Daily Nation* puts it well:

> African leaders are notorious for rewarding people who are loyal to them, as a father would, and punishing those who disagree with them. ... Fathers in African societies have to maintain an image of being the best. This, some argue, has made it necessary for our leaders to steal from their own treasuries so that they can have adequate wealth to purchase gifts to reward those who appreciate them, and also to make themselves richer than the rest and maintain their stature of being the best in everything. (Mutua 2000)

That is why the article in *The Economist* is right on target when it says that "independence often meant little more than a change in the colour of the faces of the oppressors." ("The Heart of the Matter", *The Economist,* 13 May 2000, p. 24). Perhaps we might add that the brutality and bestiality of an African dictator far surpasses that of the former colonial masters, judging by the way certain grisly murders of politicians perceived to differ from those in power have taken place in some African countries. Sometimes one wonders about the extent of the depravity of those who carry out such crimes.

A major problem in Africa today is the tribalism right at the top of the leadership. In fact, certain African leaders have become adept at denouncing tribalism with one hand and practising it with the other:

> The new elite proclaimed national unity and denounced tribalism; but they soon found, like the

imperial powers before them, that manipulating tribal affiliation was essential to preserving power. ("The
Heart of the Matter", *The Economist,* 13 May 2000,
p. 24)

Many thinking Africans, having seen how some of their
leaders have led them into great suffering, have come to the
inevitable conclusion that, since we are responsible for creating
this poor leadership, only a new brand of nationalism by more
educated and enlightened Africans can save the continent.

A writer in *The Economist* also gives an accurate account of
the African scene:

> In Africa, a politician has to show that he has escaped
> from ordinary life: that he is a "Big Man", powerful
> and rich, a benefactor far above the people whose
> support he seeks. Many African leaders grew up in
> dire poverty, and like to demonstrate their change of
> circumstances through conspicuous displays of West-
> ern wealth. Few African palaces have anything in
> them made in Africa. ("The Heart of the Matter",
> *The Economist,* 13 May 2000, p. 24)

The accumulation and personalization of power in the
hands of one man has ensured that these African leaders cannot
be dislodged from power through the ballot box or by any
other peaceful means. It is quite true that since the colonial system was, for the most part, a benevolent dictatorship, and
existed only for less than a century, it did not give the new crop
of African leaders, some of whom were not well-educated,
experience with the democratic ideal. The Westminster model
which was bequeathed to most of Africa was alien to us. What
we did immediately after independence was to try all kinds of
political experimentation such as the "one-party state," several

variants of African socialism such as *ujamaa*, or the "no-party movement system" being experimented with in Uganda. Although it is too early to know how the Uganda system will fare, it is now clear that the one-party system was a great disaster for Africa, because it produced the concept of the "Big Man", with all the trappings of dictatorship that this entailed.

The concentration of too much power in the hands of one man proved to be highly immoral. "Power tends to corrupt and absolute power corrupts absolutely", Lord Acton wrote. That is why the greatest problem in Africa today is how to remove these "Big Men" through constitutional reform, which they are fighting tooth and nail.

This, however, is not a phenomenon peculiar only to the African dictator. In Mexico, the Institutional Revolutionary Party was defeated in the elections on 3 July 2000 for the first time in seventy years! Nevertheless, this occurred only after the electoral laws were changed. Unless, therefore, the constitution and electoral laws in Africa are changed, there is no hope of the opposition winning any elections, and it does not matter how many foreign observers are allowed to monitor the elections. These African dictators, the "Big Men", are adept at orchestrating violence, intimidation, and vote-rigging. The recent elections in Zimbabwe are a case in point, but they are no longer the only ones on the continent who are masters of political gerrymandering.

3.5.3. *"Strong Men"*

The second phenomenon that emerged after independence was military government which spawned the concept of the "Strong Man". Emerging throughout the continent, "Strong Men" as rulers were primarily, but not exclusively, the product of the cold war. They were neither schooled in the precepts of democracy nor in the beneficences of socioeconomic development. These men ruled with the barrel of the gun, and their subjects were greatly traumatized. This did not matter as long as the exigencies of the cold war were fulfilled. These men suppressed the demands of their people for democracy and freedom. Dissent by ethnic minorities was swiftly and brutally put down. Under such a system there were no democratic elections. If one "Strong Man" had outlived his usefulness, he was simply replaced by another, either violently or by a mere changing of the guards.

Richard Sandbrook has set out a clear characterization of this kind of African leader (Sandbrook 1986). He wrote that African states are not, in any real sense, capitalist states. Elsewhere, including Japan and the Asian tigers, the state has played a crucial role in facilitating capitalist expansion, but in postcolonial or postindependent Africa one finds a form of personal rule to which Sandbrook applies the term "neopatrimonialism,".i.e. personal rule. It exists and is practised widely, spawning a variety of economic irrationalities. Productive economic activities are impeded by political instability; systemic corruption destroys the smooth functioning of governmental departments and institutions; maladministration of the civil service is widespread. This inevitably sets in motion a downward spiral of political and economic activities that is difficult to halt and to reverse.

In view of the supreme importance of the concept of neopatrimonialism, which can also be described mildly as the cult of personality, sycophancy, or the "Strong Man", it would be instructive to quote from Sandbrook:

> [The Strong Man], usually the president, occupies the center of political life. Front and center stage, he is the centrifugal force around which all else revolves. Not only is he the ceremonial Head of State, the president is also the chief political, military and cultural figure: Head of Government, Commander-in-Chief

75

of the Armed Forces, head of the governing party (where there is no military rule) and Chancellor of all the local universities. His aim is typically to identify his person with the "nation". His physical self is omnipresent: as in Orwell's *1984*, Big Brother's picture is plastered on public walls, billboards and even private homes. His portrait also adorns stamps, coins, paper money and even T-shirts and buttons, often distributed to the party faithful. Schools, hospitals and stadiums are named after him. The mass media, electronic and printed, herald his every word and action, no matter how insignificant. The cult of personality may even extend to an identification of a country's recent history with the wise, heroic and magnanimous deeds and decisions of the leader. (Sandbrook 1986, p. 90)

German sociologist Max Weber seems to have inspired Richard Sandbrook's use of the word neopatrimonialism. In his book (Weber 1947), and also in joint authorship (Weber and Roth 1968), Weber develops the thesis that this type of political leader even organizes the production of officially inspired biographies that treat him as a hero, one who has vanquished the colonialists and the disreputable domestic foes, benignly building the nation and acting as a world statesman. These biographies are generally disseminated through elementary schools, public libraries, and official organs of the ruling political party. The local press is also tightly controlled, and through the invocation of laws relating to state security—such laws can be widely interpreted to cover everything under the sun—nothing remotely critical of the regime, however objective, can be allowed to see the light of day. The brainwashing of the population is thorough and complete. Every news bulletin begins with a photographic display of his portrait—usually an out-of-date one depicting how young he still looks! His every word and movement, however mundane and insignificant, is treated as headline news.

The "Strong Man" demands complete obedience from a close group of sycophants who must constantly demonstrate their belief in his superior wisdom and generosity. These are people who specialize in winning favor from the "Strong Man" by constantly flattering him and other rich and powerful lieutenants around him. As Sandbrook has pointed out (Sandbrook 1986, pp. 90–91) most, if not all, of the strategic positions in the political, bureaucratic, police, and military hierarchies are filled by loyal individuals—i.e. close relatives, friends, and classmates, kinsmen, and tribesmen. These followers expect to benefit from "the spoils of office", reinforcing their personal link to the chief. Should someone cross the path of one of these people who have the power to dispense life and death, the result can be swift and fatal.

It has been necessary to elucidate this point thoroughly, because if we want the African Renaissance to succeed, Africa cannot afford to be led by such people. Thabo Mbeki has spoken of a generation of Africans who: "must resist all tyranny, oppose all attempts to deny liberty, to resort to demagogy ... and reassert the fundamental concept that we are our own liberators from oppression ." (Hadland and Rantao 1999, p. 173).

Thabo Mbeki went on to state that this is an Africa that is already confronting the enormous challenge of uprooting corruption in African life. The insistence on such notions as transparency and accountability addresses, in part, this vexed question. He concluded this aspect of his speech, saying: "On this, as on other questions on which the continent succeeded, however difficult they may have seemed, we are convinced that victory is certain."

77

3.6. The End of Colonial Rule

European colonial rule was, at its root, brutal and oppressive, but it imposed an external restraint on local excesses (albeit perpetrating excesses of its own); and the simple removal of that restraint has in many instances had the immediate effect of seeming to exacerbate the state of government and to increase the insecure condition of the ordinary people. Efforts by the European colonial powers to mitigate this have been dubious, intermittent, or ineffectual. The French have maintained a gendarmerie in Africa with occasional interventions such as their removal of Bokassa or "Operation Turquoise" in Rwanda. British governments have tended to err the other way, for example, in their failure to take action over the atrocities in the Luwero triangle during the time of Obote's second administration in Uganda. The exception to the normal British reserve is the recent intervention in Sierra Leone in support of the elected government there. The British and French record, nevertheless, compares favorably with that of the Belgians or indeed the Portuguese, who abandoned their colonies in such a way that they directly prepared the way for the horrors that were to follow.

The period of European decolonization almost exactly coincided with the cold war between the West and the Communist blocs, led respectively by the Soviet Union and China. Africa became a battleground for this world struggle, with rival regimes and guerrilla movements being sponsored and supplied by the West, by the Soviets or by the Chinese. Intervention by these powers had disastrous effects in the Congo, Angola, Mozambique, Ethiopia, Sudan, Rwanda, Burundi and Somalia—to name but the most extreme examples. Furthermore, the fear of the "communist onslaught" may possibly have rendered a peaceful accommodation of the European settlers at an early stage by the European-African led government with the African nationalists then led by the moderate Abel Muzarewa, the slightly more accommodating and less extreme Joshua Nkomo, and the left of center Ndabaningi Sithole prior to the declaration of Rhodesian UDI in 1965; and certainly delayed transition in South Africa by several decades with the election of the hard-line National Party there in 1948 with the specter of the "Black Danger" being combined with that of the "Red Danger".

The fall of the Berlin Wall and the disintegration of the Soviet bloc unfroze lines of confrontation and contributed to, among other things, the possibility of transition in South Africa. At the same time, it has tended to remove Africa's concerns from the superpower map, since it is no longer an element in the struggle for world mastery or supremacy between West and East. (The key areas of focus are those traversed by the complex three- or four-way dance between the West, Russia, China, and the Islamic world, which extends across the fluid faultline from the Balkans through the Caucasus to Afghanistan and the Asian steppes.) The salience of Africa to the international community and to the United States, the present sole superpower, is as a source of vital raw materials— but here the leading role is being played by transnational corporations rather than by the KGB or the CIA. Within the context of the international community, the old Anglophone/Francophone rivalry has surfaced as a point of division, with occasional virulence but with nothing of the deadly life-or-death nature of the East–West rivalry!

The problem of international debt, largely contracted in the 1970s, has been a crippling burden to Africa; but just as serious, probably more so, is the continued exclusion of Africa from playing a significant role in international trade, except as an exporter of primary resources. An important factor in this is the inability to generate an internal market of sufficient capacity to create the critical mass and economy of scale necessary to compete with the well-developed and powerful trading blocs in the Americas, Europe, China, Japan, and the Far East. Lines of communication and trade are still orientated towards the old colonial powers. Sub-Saharan Africa as a region is in a situation of considerable disadvantage in international markets, and its economy is falling behind that of the key international trading blocs.

3.7. Democracy in Africa

It is perhaps more appropriate to talk about the problems of democracy in Africa instead of the problem of African democracy, for there is no such thing as "African democracy", any more than we have "African electricity" or "African sun, moon or star". Democracy is both an expression and expansion of freedom and has over time become synonymous with human progress. Democracy is the option that the governed prefer but which is often denied them by the governor under one pretext or the other. Taken in its totality and at a more ecumenical level, the natural instinct of man or woman as a governed animal is for democracy. I believe that the basic reason for the persistence and recent phenomenal spread of democracy is the ever-alluring appeal it has to humankind's finer instincts and ideas about the process of governance. Democracy, in concept and in practice, is dynamic. While the principles may be the same and the factors similar, the practice will surely be different, as it must reflect the history and the culture of the people and the practitioners.

Democracy is not a static phenomenon; it has a built-in dynamism that requires development and consolidation. This is made all the more important because democracy releases the total energy of all citizens for development. On the other hand restraint, curtailment, suppression, and oppression associated with authoritarian regimes breed resentment, apathy, and withdrawal syndromes that release negative thoughts and tendencies contrary to the development process.

It is precisely for the above reasons that we must not only lament and discuss the problems now posed by the existence of the "Big Men" and "Strong Men" in Africa, but we must also think of what to do about the phenomenon and how we can ensure that such leaders do not emerge ever again. That is why democracy, like all human interaction and relationship, must not be taken for granted. It must be nurtured and sustained. The establishment, growth, and sustenance of democracy— with its complement of protection of human rights—have never been without struggle, sweat, and blood throughout the history of the human race. Whether in Europe, Asia, North America, Latin America, or Africa, the defenders must be ready to pay the price. Democratic principles will only have their full effect if the democratic state operates in such a manner as to guarantee individual liberties through the observance of separation of powers between the three major branches of any government; the executive, the legislative, and the judiciary. There should also be separation of powers between the state's religious institutions and the political parties. The suppression of national interest by tribal interest, favoritism, clientelism, and nepotism accentuates social and political inequalities and undermines the ethics and practice of democracy. Democracy cannot operate successfully within a tribalistic society. Tribalism often stems from perceived or real frustrations assumed or caused by cultural contempt.

The president of Nigeria, Olusegun Obasanjo, has written the following about the need to inculcate moral principles in Africa's democratic ethos:

> Democratic process must become a way of instituting cultural identity and promoting national unity. It

must not be used to disintegrate as was the case in the past. We must seek a process which unifies law, morality and justice. It must, as a matter of necessity, be an order that conforms and agrees with our culture, with the will and nature of the humanity of our populace. It must not stultify or limit ambitions by practice, convention or constitution. It must give hope and inspiration to all. (Obasanjo and Mabogunje 1992, p. x)

Referring particularly to the Nigerian experience, Obasanjo goes on to write as follows;

It is important that we must not allow our democratic process to be used as a legitimating influence for corruption and tyranny, be it of a group or a person. Genuine democratic process must have embodied in it safeguards against the possibility of its being hijacked by any group. Justice and its pursuit are essential ingredients in the democratic process ... . Democracy need not be too expensive as a form of government. What is gained in unity, freedom, consensus, stability, commitment and development in a truly democratic society easily outweighs the costs of maintaining and sustaining the structures of democracy. Effective democratic process provides checks and balances which limit the abuses of power, corruption, oppression, dictatorial and authoritarian tendencies. (Obasanjo and Mabogunje 1992, p. x)

It is important to note here that Obasanjo is one of the few African leaders to talk about morality and justice in the conduct of political affairs. It is only in Western society that we find leaders—in fact the general populace as well—to be concerned with such seemingly mundane philosophic issues that are nevertheless the age-old central questions of a true democratic society. The shapers of the whole intellectual tradition of the West, particularly of Greek origin, who were disgusted by the violence and corruption of Athenian political life, sought to find such remedies as would render their governments more democratic. One such eminent philosopher, Plato—sickened especially by the execution in 399 B.C.E. of his friend and teacher, Socrates, who had been preoccupied with inquiries into the nature of ethical standards—decided to seek a cure for the ills of society not in politics but in philosophy. After much thought and reflection, Plato arrived at his fundamental and lasting conviction that those ills would never cease until philosophers became rulers and rulers philosophers. This statement has been much misunderstood and misinterpreted, but I believe what he meant was that for a politician to become a good leader, he must be a properly educated person. In other words, he must go through a rigorous step-by-step process of formal education, starting from the kindergarten, through primary and secondary education and all the way up to university level without any short-cuts. Such a person will have undergone thorough instruction and training in nearly all the important disciplines in life, such as religion, virtue, morality and justice. This process of the acquisition of knowledge prepares the human mind to understand the essential elements of good, virtuous, and moral acts. Prior acquisition of such knowledge is a necessary condition for a good politician and ruler.

In Africa, because of the low level of education of the electorate and the general intense desire to obtain political independence from colonial rule as quickly as possible—which seemed quite right and overdue at the time—we allowed some uneducated politicians to slip through the net and later to become national leaders. Such leaders, the majority of whom came from very poor backgrounds, quickly utilized the machinery of state power to enrich themselves at the expense of the ordinary people who had unsuspectingly and enthusiastically voted them into power. These leaders saw the state as their private property and began to milk every institution dry. The natural consequence of this has been the breakdown of socioeconomic and political order. That is why President Obasanjo has suggested the following remedy for Africa.

> Perhaps the first step would be the need to prevent the constant privatization of the state by our power elites. This must be done in addition to a move to separate the business of governance from the business of economic transactions. One of the anchoring bases of this move is the need to embrace, integrate, imbibe and acculturate the spirit of mutual empowerment between the state and the people. (Obasanjo and Mabogunie, ibid, p. x).

The above observation by Obasanjo, who has twice become president of Nigeria, is important because most of Africa's "Big Men" and "Strong Men" have taken it upon themselves to impoverish thoroughly the broad masses of the population as a deliberate strategy, both economic and political, to ensure that no center of organized opposition to their rule can emerge. These leaders abhor any moves in their countries where the democratic system would make the entire society and responsible media politically virile, dynamic, and engaging. For Africa, the fruit of democracy must of necessity include improvement in the living standard of the people and the wholesomeness of society; the intrinsic value of democracy must be completed with real and desirable fruits to hold relevant meaning for the people.

Life generates puzzles of conduct, and I believe that only an enlightened mind can produce a solution. Socrates collided head-on with the intellectual orthodoxy of his day, because he believed that moral values were in some sense fixed and absolute. He argued, implicitly rather than explicitly, that moral concepts such as piety are unchanging standards against which individual actions must be judged. (See Plato, "Early Socratic Dialogues", Penguin, 1987, p. 22.) Socrates'attack on moral relativism was at the heart of Greek philosophical debate at the time. He believed that morality and the problems of personal conduct were closely connected. To him, virtue was knowledge, and this led to such noble characteristics as excellence, efficiency, and goodness. The point of the aphorism is that "if we are to act morally and thus live happily, it is not enough simply to have virtuous intentions or even virtuous habits: there is a certain body of knowledge that must be acquired—knowledge presumably, of the meaning of moral terms such as justice and piety. Only if we know what these are can we be excellent and efficient in moral conduct." (See Plato, ibid., pp. 23–24).

In accordance with the teachings of Socrates, therefore, knowledge is both a necessary and a sufficient condition of a choice that brings happiness. It would be foolish, given present conditions in Africa, to expect a military man who acquired power through the barrel of the gun, or a half-baked civilian political leader, to know that it is proper to relinquish power when either his term of office has constitutionally expired or when the general populace clamors for a change.

It is such a pity that at the beginning of the third millennium, when the world held so much hope for Africa, the continent should be so convulsed in such cataclysmic political upheavals simply because its leaders, or the majority of them, are unable to handle power and the problem of democratic transition. In the conceptualization of democracy in any society, the people must understand that the overall import of any form of good government is whether it can effectively enhance the capability and capacity of the people to manage and control change and to promote national development. That is why the content of democracy is more important than the form of democracy. That is why, as Obasanjo has observed, a purely semantic approach to the definition of the word "democracy" may miss the point as far as Africa is concerned. He went on to comment thus:

> The concept of democracy should be examined from two points of view, that is, as ideology and as politics. Democracy, as ideology, is the philosophy of governance which sets a high premium on the basic freedom or fundamental human rights of the citizen, the rule of law, the right to property, the free flow of information and the right of choice between alternative political positions ... . On the other hand, democracy as politics is concerned with the institutions and processes of governance. These institutions and the procedures of governance that they elicit tend to foster consensus whilst simultaneously promoting and sustaining respect for the ideology of democracy. (See Obasanjo and Mabogunie, op.cit, p. 1.)

As to the last point, we in Africa must stop romanticizing the past and instead establish those institutions, structures, and procedures that will ensure a systematic process of democratic transition and change in the political institutions and processes based on the following fundamental systems and provisions in the constitution: decentralization of political power and authority; periodic and orderly succession through the secret ballot; accountability of the leadership to the governed that is legally enforceable; a truly and completely independent judicial system; unshakeable defence and promotion of human rights; respect for the rule of law and equality before the law;

vigorous promotion of participatory and popular democracy conceptualized as government of the people, by the people, and for the people; a system that promotes freedom of choice, freedom from ignorance and hunger, and one that promotes economic empowerment for the people.

During the demoralizing period of colonial rule, Europeans saw Africans as objects rather than as subjects of governance. Now, after independence, it is tragic that African leaders have also developed a system in which they continue to demonstrate their insincerity, their lack of affection, and even hostility towards those they govern and see them more as objects to be manipulated. The people, for their part, have been made to feel they are not part of government but outsiders always requesting that government do things for them. This has had the effect of perpetuating alienation between the government and the people, and the situation is exacerbated by the influence of kinship loyalties and nepotism. Where political orientation in an African country is based on tribal loyalties, religious bigotry, political partisanship, and nepotism, then leaders will always want to cling to power forever. Without an active and enlightened civil society it will be difficult to remove a leader who wants to cling to power at any cost. The existence of a civil society can thus be seen as vital for the success of democracy in Africa, for democracy is not only about voting but also accountability.

Before concluding we must ask the question: What shall Africans do about the present phenomenon, where its leaders cling to power and refuse to relinquish it? Even though this is in violation of the constitution that they have sworn to uphold and protect in the name of God, they are, in fact, the first to violate the very strictures that they themselves helped to create and to establish. Many of them believe that they are indispensable. Power has become too sweet for most of them. At the time of writing, the problem of a smooth democratic transition of power has become highly problematic in countries such as Zambia, Namibia, Malawi, Gabon, Kenya, Zimbabwe, Togo, and Angola, to mention only a few and excluding those already engaged in ethnic conflicts or interstate warfare. The only shining examples where the transfer of power has been effected smoothly are Tanzania under Nyerere; Senegal under Senghor and Diouf; South Africa under Mandela; Ghana under Rawlings; and Botswana under Khama and Masire. A recent article in the *Daily Nation,* 24 April 2001, about the situation in Zambia is illustrative.

> President Frederick Chiluba is fine-tuning a strategy to extend his rule past the ten year limit but a stunning cabinet revolt shows Zambians are not so willing to make him Africa's new "Big Man"... . The president appears keen to run again, but the Zambian people, through three constitutional review commissions, have adamantly said the two terms must remain enshrined in the constitution.

In an editorial of the same paper, the demand for African leaders to retire gracefully could not have been more eloquently articulated:

> President Frederick Chiluba of Zambia is rapidly becoming a pitiful figure in world politics. Here is a man who has completed his constitutional term in office and he does not want to retire as he should. And here is a man who is keeping a tight lid on his options in the face of growing opposition from members of his own cabinet, including his Vice-President, and he still won't let go. That, by all accounts, is incredible audacity that bodes very ill for the poverty-stricken central African country. (*Daily Nation* edito-

88

rial: "African Leaders Must Agree to Go Home," 24
April, 2001, p. 6)

However, after intense and concerted opposition from the
Zambian people, including President Chiluba's own cabinet
colleagues and members of his party (the Movement for Multi-
Party Democracy) who resigned over the matter and formed a
new opposition party, he relented and gave up the idea of standing for a third term, but only grudgingly. His lukewarm withdrawal was evident in the controversial manner his chosen
successor, Levy Mwanawasa, was elected and eventually
assumed office. There were widespread accusations, by both
the opposition and the international and national election
observers, that the process was anything but free and fair. What
is even more important is that Chiluba ensured that he
remained a powerful chairman of the ruling MMD party, thus
causing the new president to be perceived, by and large, as a
mere puppet or figurehead. It remains to be seen whether
Mwanawasa will be able to be his own man, considering the
recent re-affirmation by Chiluba that after consultations, it was
decided that he remain chairman. He added ominously that the
new ministers were not serious.

This point is important because a new and most dangerous phenomenon, disturbing to supporters of democracy, is
emerging in Africa, in which incumbent presidents try to do
everything possible to manipulate the succession process in
such a way that they remain de facto rulers wielding enormous
power even after they have left office. They often resort to this
sort of political stratagem only if they find that the national and
international opposition to their continuing in power is irre-
sistible. Even in the case of Tanzania, which we have given as
one of the examples in which power was handed over with relative smoothness, Mwalimu Julius Nyerere retained chairmanship of the ruling party, Chama Cha Mapinduzi (CCM), until

his death several years later. He had remained an extremely powerful and influential voice in the choice of his successor, Ali Hasan Mwinyi, and also later in the choice of Benjamin Mkapa. Nyerere, however, was careful to exercise power tactfully but firmly behind the scenes.

This is in sharp contradistinction to what happened in South Africa, where Mandela handed over power to Mbeki completely, without seeking to retain chairmanship of the party. His prestige was such that he did not need to do that. In fact, the political chemistry between him and his successor Mbeki was such that Mandela automatically retained the status of elder statesman, international mediator and peacemaker, with the full support of his successor. He had no desire or need to manipulate the succession process in order to create a position for himself in the post-Mandela government. The only other countries where power was handed over completely without manipulation, but in entirely different circumstances, were Botswana, Senegal, and Zambia under Kaunda.

Another African country with this political "Big Man" syndrome is Zimbabwe. This is tragic, for at the time of independence it had a promising beginning. Another editorial, appearing in the *Sunday Nation* of 29 April 2001, states:

> The once much respected nationalist Robert Mugabe is today a much discredited president who seeks to cling to power by inciting violence against his fellow Zimbabweans. The Mugabe government's attacks on journalists and opposition members are not doing any good to the country's reputation. An African country which was once touted as one of the most promising on the continent is fast degenerating into chaos and violence just because Mugabe, who is in his twilight years, just won't let go. The government's desperation has been heightened by the size-

able gains made by the nascent opposition in the last elections.

The editorial concludes by saying that "the Zimbabwe leader's intransigence and dictatorial tendencies are the hall-marks of a generation that must now give way for true democracy to flourish and catalyse economic and intellectual development."

There could be no clearer exposition of how in a number of African countries a few manipulative cabals foster undemocratic and dictatorial tyranny against their people. The above-quoted editorial continued to say that President Chiluba was one of a growing crop of African leaders who are trying to turn the clock back to the days of life presidencies. There was a time we thought the "Strong Man" phenomenon was history, but this seems not to be the case. The argument of those who oppose bending the constitution to allow an individual to pro-long his tenure goes like this: You have been in power for the past ten to twenty years; what do you propose to accomplish in the extra five years that you could not do in the past ten or twenty? "It is time the Chilubas of Africa realized that they are not the only people who can hold their countries together. We have seen many instances when popular leaders voluntarily relinquished power in favour of younger people. The best examples are former Presidents Julius Nyerere and Nelson Mandela. Did their countries break apart because they were no longer in power?" (*Daily Nation*, 24 April 2001).

All this is excellently put, but the main question still remains: What can the people of Africa do collectively to end this kind of behavior by their leaders and to reverse this dangerous trend? There is one imperative for the African people to continue their efforts to remove such obstacles to democracy that seem inherent in such dictatorial behavior. There is, therefore, the need to establish a new democratic system in Africa based on the realities of our social, economic, and cultural environment with regard for our communal values and basic predilections as a people. Our conceptualization of democracy, borrowing some good and relevant features from the more mature and older democracies in the West that have proved their efficacy and durability, must take due cognisance of our lived reality in Africa; and the structures and institutions that would sustain democratic practice must also reflect the peculiarities of our environment. These institutions and processes of governance that we shall establish in Africa must also foster consensus on the paramount necessity of promoting and sustaining respect for the ideology of democracy. That is why education and the acquisition of knowledge, and hence virtue and political morality in the Platonic tradition, should not be dismissed out of hand.

That is why the ideal of the African Renaissance is to emphasize the importance of civil society and other grass-root support structures in the networking and promotion of the movement and also in the realization that without the establishment of a strong democratic tradition, there can be no African rebirth in economic and technological terms.

In this context, we define civil society in Africa as citizens' organizations outside government that interact and relate on the basis of social values and the culture of the society for the sustenance of good governance and the promotion of economic growth and social development. The existence of civil society can therefore be seen as vital for the success of democracy. It can be a valuable instrument in the sustenance of democracy, especially if organizations such as trade unions are properly mobilized as an integral part of it. Such bodies can promote mass action as a means of rejecting any unwanted nondemocratic behavior. They can encourage large and significant sections of workers to withdraw their services rather than serve an illegitimate and unconstitutional government. Such an action can cripple all activities in the nation and make dictatorial leaders rethink their actions.

What is happening in Africa today is leading many African intellectuals to come to the same conclusion as Plato, that

> no one could take part in political life and retain his integrity under existing conditions; that only philosophical reflection, by implication, perhaps, of the type to which Socrates devoted himself, could enable one to see what was right and just in both public and private life; and that the only cure for the ills of contemporary society was the establishment of philosophical rule: that either philosophers should become rulers, or that existing rulers should become philosophers. (Redhead 1984, pp. 19–20)

It has been said that Plato went a bit too far in his search for an ideal form of state, but still his basic message is that we in Africa need to have a new crop of well-educated and informed leaders as a long-term solution to our present predicament with the prevalence of the "Big Men"/"Strong Men" syndrome. The essential requirement is for leaders who can exercise self-control, leaders whose souls and actions are governed by reason, since reason alone is capable of determining what is truly good for us. If we are incapable of reasoning properly for ourselves, then others must do it for us. If the course of our lives is determined by our irrational impulses, the result can only be misery, the like of which we are witnessing in Africa today.

4

The African Development Problematique

4.1. Africa and the Third World

How and when did the term "Third World" come into being? Wolf-Phillips attributed its first use to Alfred Sauvry who, in 1952, referred in French to the term *tiers monde*, which meant "the Third World" (Wolf-Phillips 1979: Quoted from Simpson 1987, p. 4). Sauvry was, however, using the term to mean a third force, a political force, in a world where the North Atlantic community represented the first force, and the Communist bloc led by the Soviet Union through the Warsaw Pact and China, a second force. It was clearly a distinction based upon military and ideological commitment rather than conditions and levels of economic attainment.

In the latter sense the inclusion of China would have been singularly inappropriate, as it later decided to join the Third World anyway. In fact, this origin appears to have been forgotten, and later, in the early 1960s, the term came to mean countries less economically developed than those of the industrialized nations of North America, Europe, and the Soviet Union; and so the Third World came to incorporate China as well. The situation has been further complicated by the current usage of the terms North and South, which were later popularized by the U.N. during the so-called North–South dialogue. To anyone with any degree of geographical fastidiousness, these are terms that can only be regretted when India and China are allocated to the South, and Australia and New Zealand to the North.

In our view, the real watershed in the development of the term came with the convening of the Bandung Conference on the Indonesian island of Java on 18 April 1955, and later with the founding of the Non-Aligned Movement in Belgrade, Yugoslavia, in 1961. In his opening address to the Asia–Africa Conference, as the Bandung Conference later came to be known, President Sukarno of Indonesia made the following statement, which influenced the movement for many years to come: "We can mobilize the entire spiritual, all the moral, all the political strength of Asia and Africa on the side of peace" (Hadjor 1993, p. 226).

The 1955 Bandung Conference of twenty-nine Afro-Asian countries called for closer economic, cultural and diplomatic ties between the countries of the two continents and marked a major change, a turning point, in the world order—the entry into international politics of a new group of countries that came to be known as the Third World. It is in political terms, and also in the context of international politics in the postwar era, where we find the true meaning of the term "Third World."

The Third World leaders attending the Bandung Conference—Chou En-lai of China, Sukarno of Indonesia, Josip Broz Tito of Yugoslavia, Gamal Abdel Nasser of Egypt, Kwame Nkrumah of Ghana, and Jawaharlal Pandit Nehru of India, to mention only a few—were the very same leaders who founded the Non-Aligned Movement in Belgrade in 1961.

They laid the foundation for the idea of the Third World as a radical critique of the order of world power that had governed international affairs until that time. It was also the ancestor of many later initiatives from the Non-Aligned Conferences that later dominated activities of the United Nations General Assembly, where they had a majority and could influence policy decisions in their favor, although real power remained with the Security Council where the so-called "big five" (U.S.A., U.S.S.R., Britain, France, and China) had the power of veto. (Note that China's seat was occupied by Taiwan for many years, until Beijing reclaimed it in 1978.)

The world of empires, it was said, had produced two devastating world wars in the first half of the twentieth century, and also a string of savageries inflicted upon the subject majority of the world's peoples. Empire was part and parcel of an economic system, capitalism, which had been equally destructive in economic terms, in the swings of boom and slump, and particularly in the Great Depression between the wars. The emancipation of the world's majority, the Third World, offered an opportunity for a new political and economic order based on what Sukarno called the "newly emergent forces." In a world so recently released from the terrible war of 1939–45, and soon thereafter plunged into the cold war, the hopes embodied in the Bandung Conference could not help but be inspired.

At the heart of the new ideology was a series of propositions about the possibility of national economic development in the countries of the Third World. Why were those countries so poor when the Europeans and North Americans were so rich? How far could markets be shaped or superseded to force the pace of national economic growth? What should the role of government in that process be?

Suffice it to say at this juncture that the preoccupations of analysis, explanation, and prescription for government action came to constitute a new branch of economics in the postwar period known as "development economics." In fact, the theorization began much earlier than the 1950s, taking up themes that emerged after the Great Depression in 1929. It seemed then as if the capitalist system had exhausted its potential, and new alternatives were needed for all countries. Economists from countries that exported raw materials in the main—Latin America and Eastern Europe—were particularly concerned about formulating methods by which their countries could escape economic slump.

Until the founding of the United Nations Conference on Trade and Development (UNCTAD) in Geneva in 1964 and the United Nations Industrial Development Organization (UNIDO) in Vienna in 1967, which also led to the formation of the Group of 77 low-income countries as a bloc to press for their trade and industrial development interests respectively, the Third World had been largely concerned with political issues such as decolonization and liberation. Here, we witness a situation in which the semantic history of politics is full of ideas that began life as a radical indictment of the existing social order, but over the years passed neutered into the everyday lexicon.

The Non-Aligned Movement became, in fact, the political and economic linchpin of the Third World. From its inception it took an anticolonial and antiracist stance and adopted the policy of positive neutrality between the two superpowers. It categorically rejected the notion of being entangled in their rivalries and thereby becoming client states of either of them.

Because of their economic and military weakness, the Non-Aligned countries could not influence any major policy decisions of the superpowers during the cold war. In fact, it was the U.N. Security Council that primarily handled important issues of major significance, a state of affairs that persists even today. With the emergence of the U.S.A. as the only remaining superpower, the Security Council has come to be perceived as catering primarily to U.S. interests around the globe. That is why Africa has no option but to play her diplomatic political cards very carefully, in the full realization that the practice of pragmatism does not necessarily involve the abandonment of principle.

In other words, in order for Africa to succeed in its quest to tackle successfully what I describe below as the "African development problematique," we must insist that the U.S.A. and Europe not force us to accept wholesale development theories and ideas already manufactured and packaged in the West without considering their relevance and application to the African scene or local situation. That is another reason to insist that the African Renaissance be home-grown, taking into account the mutuality of interests of our international partners in this economic development process. The failure of postwar theories of economic development emanating from the West in solving the African development question should serve as a warning and a salutary lesson to all of us. This does not mean that we shall not borrow and use other good ideas from well-meaning and well-intentioned peoples from outside Africa. However, this time we shall insist that Africans must make the final decisions as to what suits the continent best.

4.2. Third World in Economic Terms

In order to be able to understand Africa's abject poverty and its technological backwardness, not only within the context of the Third World, but also within the ambit of the world as a whole, and therefore the imperative necessity for its own home-grown economic renaissance, we must understand the meaning of the concept "Third World" in economic terms.

According to the World Bank, one of the leading multilateral financial institutions since Bretton Woods, the world is divided by levels of economic prosperity, primarily by using the most common method of ranking countries according to their economic well-being in absolute terms, namely, the Gross National Product (GNP). There are, in fact, other indicators of a country's level of development, and hence its ranking, such as the level of its industrialization, national, and world integration—a process of modernization and internationalization in which Third World countries play a marginalized role—and other social indicators that measure the fulfilment of basic human needs, freedom, and human rights as measurements of the human development index.

Looking at these other indicators in addition to looking at the GNP is important, because classification using only the concept of average income does not necessarily reflect the development status of a country. Therefore, GNP per capita by itself is not an adequate indicator, but we have to continue using it because the World Bank says so. For instance, Saudi Arabia, Israel, and Singapore, among others, are classified as high-income but developing countries, although for purely geopolitical reasons, Israel does not belong to the Third World.

An alternative measure of average income, however, which would take all these factors into account is Real Gross Domestic Product (GDP) per capita measured in purchasing power parity expressed in U.S. dollars. This has been used in an adjusted form in the human development index, although it requires complex statistical estimation, whereas GNP figures come direct from national income accounts and currency exchange rates.

The above analysis accurately explains the current position of the categorization and definition of the division of the world into First, Second, and Third world in economic terms. In the context of the African Renaissance, however, it is possible to postulate that this has always been so. It is equally reasonable to argue, however, that the contrasts have never been as great as those that now exist and those that had begun to emerge in the eighteenth and nineteenth centuries, with the European Renaissance setting the stage for this upsurge in European development from the fourteenth to the seventeenth centuries, that is, from the medieval to the middle and early modern ages!

That great upsurge in productive capacity with its associated transformation not only of the means of production, but also of the whole organization of societies and their economies, an evolution we call the Agrarian and Industrial Revolution, profoundly distinguished its participant nations from those not directly involved. This distinction came to the eyes of merchants and missionaries who, both wittingly and unwittingly, spun a web of interconnections that tied the Third World countries to the growing industrial nations in Europe and later in North America. As empires grew, especially the British Empire—whose expansion was linked to material financial interests, particularly during the period of the Scramble for Africa—Europe's pillage of the Third World continued unabated. Colonial territories enhanced both the resource base and the potential markets of the industrial economies of Europe. Whether it became colonial or not, the world that was not part of the economic transformation of the eighteenth and nineteenth centuries remained distinct. In terms of technological application and economic organization it was undeveloped and, consequently, poor in material terms. It was variously described as "savage," "primitive," or "backward" by the newly rich world.

Although these descriptions implied less developed in material terms, these countries were highly developed in cultural, religious and political terms. There is ample historical evidence, supported by archaeological discoveries and proven by scientific carbon dating, that there were major civilizations and empires that extended their political power and cultural influence before the expansion of European dominion. Ancient Third World empires and civilizations had existed before 3000 B.C.E, as we saw in Chapter 2.

In order to fully grasp the differences between the First

and Third Worlds, let us revert to the World Bank's classification of countries, using the concept of GNP per capita that we discussed above. It is by clearly understanding these classifications that we shall realize the urgent necessity of an African Renaissance! The World Bank in its World Development Report of 1990 classifies the countries of the world into three main income groups for operational and analytical purposes.

- Low-income economies: countries with GNP per capita income of U.S. $545 or less in 1988, covering thirty-three countries, including China and India which have between them about two-thirds of the world's population.
- Middle-income economies: countries with GNP per capita of more than $545 but less than $6,000 in 1988. Within this group a further division is made to distinguish between lower and upper middle-income economies, fixed for 1988 at $2,000.
- High-income economies: countries with a GNP per capita of more than U.S. $6,000 in 1988. This group ranges from Saudi Arabia ($6,200) at the bottom end of the scale to Switzerland ($27,000) at the top. In this group belong only a few countries, encompassing about 16 percent of the world's population, that is, less than one-third!

Together, low- and middle-income countries have been considered as providing one definition of the Third World. Together these countries constitute 93 percent of the world's total population! The inequality in the share of world income is staggering and the position of the African countries in all this is utterly shameful. The following table gives a dismal picture of the ranking of countries in order of their GNP per capita. What is even more concerning is that among the 28 lowest-income countries in the world, Africa holds the majority with 20 countries, Asia is second with 7 countries, and Latin America third with 1.

Table 2. The Lowest Income Countries (GNP per capita), 1982

1. Chad	15. Somalia
2. Bangladesh	16. Haiti
3. Ethiopia	17. Benin
4. Nepal	18. Central African Rep.
5. Mali	19. China
6. Burma	20. Guinea
7. Zaire	21. Niger
8. Malawi	22. Madagascar
9. Upper Volta	23. Sri Lanka
10. Uganda	24. Togo
11. India	25. Ghana
12. Rwanda	26. Pakistan
13. Burundi	27. Kenya
14. Tanzania	28. Sierra Leone

Source: The World Bank, World Development Report, OUP, New York, 1984, table 1, p. 218

These represent countries at the bottom of the ladder, standing in poverty. Eritrea was added to the list when it became independent from Ethiopia in 1993. Most of these countries were still in the World Bank's list of the lowest per capita income countries in 1998. It is important to note further that in spite of the fact that this categorization was made two decades ago, there has been no significant change in the economic position of these countries. If anything, their plight, in terms of the increase in poverty has actually worsened! Indeed, the World Bank estimates that in current U.S.$ consumption per capita for the countries of Sub-Saharan Africa (excluding South Africa) has declined from $417 to $281 between 1980 and 1999 (source: World Bank Document, African Development Indicators, 2001, Washington D.C.).

During the Algiers Summit of the Non-Aligned Nations in 1973, the conference vigorously called for the establishment of a New International Economic Order, demanding that the economic plight of the Third World nations begin to occupy center stage in international economic relations. It was at this time that some Third World countries formed an association of raw materials producers to obtain more favorable prices for their products. For example, the formation, after the 1973 Arab–Israel October War, of the Organization of Petroleum Exporting Countries (OPEC) and the adoption of the Lima Declaration and Plan of Action at Lima, Peru, in 1974, with a view to increasing the share of Third World countries in the world's industrial production, were cases in point.

It was a time when the United Nations established the so-called North–South Dialogue as a forum where the Third World countries would negotiate with the rest of the world for better terms of trade and higher levels of investment. However, this turned out to be a dialogue with the deaf, the North was not interested in the real development of the South, only in the continued exploitation of the latter's natural resources.

The Third World, then, thought of tackling its own economic development agenda by establishing its own organization, the South–South Secretariat with Julius Nyerere as its chairman. Michael Manley, the former prime minister of Jamaica and other prominent Third World leaders became the moving spirits behind it. Sadly, all these bodies, including the Brandt

Commission ("North–South, A Program for Survival", 1980 *Report of the Independent Commission in International Development Issues*, London) were completely ignored by the industrialized countries, and their voluminous reports and publications have been left to gather dust in the libraries of the world.

As Michael P. Todaro points out:

> While it is unfortunate that numbers such as First, Second, and Third occasionally bear the regrettable connotation of superiority and inferiority when used in reference to different groups of nations, the fact remains that the term "Third World" is widely used among developing nations primarily in an effort to generate and represent a new sense of common identity and a growing unity of purpose. (Todaro 1987, p. xxxvi, footnote 1).

That common identity and unity of purpose is nevertheless rapidly disappearing among Third World countries, as Africa is left stranded in abject poverty. Why does such affluence as we see in other parts of the world coexist with such dire poverty, across several countries but particularly in Africa, at a time of growing world economic interdependence?

To answer the questions, "Why do we speak of an African Renaissance?" (and more importantly) "Why do we need it more now than at any other time in world history?", it has been necessary to understand Africa's position in the world economy and its standing in the context of the Third World, of which it has been, and still is, an integral part in both economic and political terms. Against this background, there should be no doubt whatsoever regarding Africa's determination to embark on a long-term, durable and sustainable economic development agenda, totally different from past efforts, and from which no power on earth should deflect us.

4.3. Dependence on Primary Products

It has been said that the development of an individual depends directly or indirectly on the development of all other individuals. Third World nations, including Africa, are an integral part of the ever-shrinking global economic and political organism. It was hoped that their economic role and influence would increase during the postwar period, but this was not to be, especially in the case of Africa. That is why we believe that a thorough understanding of the unique nature of their problems and aspirations, and the economic well-being of people in the industrialized nations, is an essential component in the education of all people in the low-income nations.

In Africa, nearly all economic development indicators have been in decline during the last two decades. That is, per capita incomes and investments have fallen by at least 25 percent and 50 percent respectively during the last decade; imports are only 6 percent of per capita imports in 1970 ; and exports have fallen by 45 percent since the 1980s. The division of the world into exporters of raw materials and primary products on the one hand, and exporters of manufactured goods on the other—a situation that has led to the perpetual adverse terms of trade for Africa's products—has been particularly disadvantageous for the continent.

Most African economies are oriented towards the production of primary commodities (tea, coffee, cocoa, and other raw materials) as opposed to secondary (manufacturing), and tertiary (service) products. These primary commodities comprise the main exports to high-income nations. For instance, primary products account for over 92 percent of Africa's total export earnings, yet real commodity prices fell by almost 50 percent between 1957 and 1992 in real terms, and the situation is still deteriorating. Thus, between 1980 and 1982, the price of sugar fell by 78 percent, rubber by 37 percent, and

106

copper by 35 percent; and between 1989 and 1992, commodity prices fell by about 20 percent. Tin prices were so low that smelting was no longer profitable, and the real prices of coffee and tea were lower than at any time since 1950. Such declines in commodity terms of trade, the mainstay of Africa's exports, have hurt the continent most severely.

4.4. Escalating External Debt

There is an urgent need to reduce African debt to the West if there is to be an African economic renaissance. Africa is shackled by this debt, just as its people were shackled by the chains of slavery in the past. As the biblical book of Proverbs says, "the borrower is the slave of the lender" (Proverbs 22:7). Africa's external debt has grown from U.S.$10 billion in 1972 to U.S.$183 billion in 1992 and it is still growing. This debt is clearly unpayable and ways must be found to cure the disease of this huge backlog, bearing in mind what a leading advocate of the "Jubilee 2000" campaign for debt relief of Third World countries has said:

> Where part of the debt is due to the corrupt export of capital acquired through misuse of government powers by the President and his immediate entourage, this element will be excluded from the remission and the country concerned will be advised to demand this money back from its corrupt ruler. (Quoted from a conversation with former British Ambassador Bill Peters, co-author with Martin Dent of *The Crisis of Poverty and Debt in the Third World*, Ashgate Publishing Ltd, London 1999)

An important aspect of the unfairness of African debt concerns the issue of compound interest—of paying interest on interest so that the debt escalates exponentially. A $100m loan at 7 percent interest, where the interest is unpaid, becomes a debt of nearly $200m ten years on. The wealthy West must recognize the terrible costs to Africa's children as well as its adults—especially in terms of lost health and education—of extracting these interest payments. However, we must also make sure that we avoid debt in the future and therefore some potential strategies for tackling the debt problem are outlined in Chapter 6.

Africa's deepening economic and social problems are now legendary. The international community's hopes that the long period of production stagnation, of financial distress, and of institutional weakness in Africa would end have been dashed by the fact that the continent is now operating in a world characterized by acute geoeconomic asymmetry, especially in the post-cold war era. We Africans have come to a realization that the world does not owe us a living, that development aid is rapidly becoming a matter of history, and that at the beginning of the third millennium, this source of funding has nearly died out. The continent, wracked by ethnic and religious conflagrations in several countries simultaneously, is also facing the reality that it could well be plunged back into internecine warfare and social conflicts on an endemic scale.

Now is the time when the fundamental principles that guided the foundation of the OAU in 1963 need to be revisited with a view to making them more effective in the context of the African Renaissance. How can the OAU help to uplift Africa from its current Third World condition? First and foremost, we must recognize and acknowledge Africa's development problematique, namely, the presence of acute poverty compounded by the continent's failure to break its economic developmental gridlock.

4.5. African Brain Drain

What must be done to facilitate an African Renaissance in science and technology is more than simply a technocratic issue, that is, a problem of the lack of focus and expenditure in these two areas. One of the main difficulties is that scientists who are trained in the West do not return to Africa, and those who are trained in Africa want to leave. Thabo Mbeki has spoken of this fundamental problem which has bedeviled Africa since attaining independence:

> The difficult period from which our continent is emerging imposed on Africa an enormous brain drain. Many among our best-prepared intellectuals left to seek better lives in countries such as the United States and Europe.... As Africa achieves its rebirth, so will these, who have better possibilities to create something new on the continentof their origin, be encouraged and attracted to return to the challenging and satisfying life of the reconstruction and development of a motherland revisited. (Mbeki 1998, p. 10)

It can be said that Africa's most debilitating poverty is not of a material nature. Rather, it is the poverty of implementable ideas, and the reluctance or inability to convert ideas into a real socioeconomic or technological product. As Albert Tevoedjre has stated, the true dimensions of poverty are existential rather than economic. So indeed, this is largely the case with Africa, which, during the contemporary post-colonial years, continues to behave as if it cannot create its own functional ideas. General Olusegun Obasanjo, in a 1987 lecture to the New York Council on Foreign Relations, said: "We in Africa use borrowed ideas, borrowed experience and funds, and we engage borrowed hands. In short, in our development strategies and programs, not much, if anything, is ours." (*The African Foundation for Research and Development; Rationale and Program Priorities*, Randforum Press, Nairobi, 1994, p. 2) It is with these considerations in mind that we should approach the question of an African economic renewal and survival.

The term "brain drain" is given to the flow of trained and qualified people from one country to another. It was first used to refer to the flow from the Third World to the high-income countries but recently has been applied to the increasing flow of scientists, for instance, from Europe to the U.S.A. The flow from the Third World may be a mechanism making for economic polarization since resources invested in training and education by Third World countries are put to use in high-income countries; the former pay and do not benefit, while the latter benefit but do not pay. The brain drain reflects the fact that in practice a relatively free world market exists in highly skilled labor and an extremely restricted one in unskilled labor. Surgeons and airline pilots can work in virtually whatever country they prefer while most construction workers and farm laborers have to stay at home. This fact, as well as leading to the brain drain, tends to maintain especially high salary differentials within Third World countries.

The brain drain, however, also reflects the fact that a neo-colonial training and the higher education system in the Third World often produces skills better suited for use in the context of high-income countries rather than in activities that promote real economic development. In any case many highly educated people who stay in Third World countries often fail to find jobs that utilize their skills, because of failure of economic policy, to find jobs which use their skills. In this respect the effects of the brain drain may be exaggerated since it is really only part of a larger problem. There is, therefore, the fundamental problem that the educational policies in many Third World countries seem imperfectly tailored to the needs of their economic development or internal manpower requirements. Invariably, the benefits of educational policies followed in so many of these countries do not go to those they are supposedly designed to help, that is, the local folk, but to those countries that supplied the original blueprints of the educational systems, and who have subsequently supplied the experts and the financial aid needed to sustain them. This system has led one expert to comment thus:

> To the advanced countries, and especially the U.S.A. and Europe, the Third World is exploited not only as a source of raw materials but also of those skills needed to service the machine of empire; it is also, and increasingly, exploited as a source of raw data to be synthesized and analyzed in the developed societies and which is critical to the formulation of those policies by which empire is consolidated and expanded. (Buchanan 1975, p. 43).

On the other side of the coin, the brain drain is often part of a family survival strategy and leads to a return flow of remittances from the skilled worker abroad. Thus, it may harm economic development potential but assist short-term survival. In other words, migration as a brain drain has major effects on the economies of the Third World countries from which the migrants come. Migration in this case is often used as a solution to the problems of poverty at home and many migrants send remittances to their families and these reach major proportions in some countries. While migrants suffer discrimination and low wages in the countries to which they migrate, they none the less often succeed in ameliorating their own, their family's and even their country's economic situation. For all the problems of the life of the migrants, the failures of economic development in the Third World mean that the demand to migrate is almost infinite. Inevitably that means that the issue of illegal migration will become an ever more important one in high-income countries, probably with severe consequences for people who are not white. That is why the European Community, at the end of the 1990s, began preparing for a single internal labor market with free movement for workers and introduced legal measures to stem the flow of migration from Third World countries.

Before we can consider, in Chapter 6, the steps that should be taken to alleviate or to resolve the African brain drain, we must not only understand its historical origins and causes; we must also give it a much wider definition. The first and earliest intercontinental migration of wageless labor from Africa to Europe and to the Americas began during the slave trade. Uprooting African people from the continent in such a manner has resulted in the greatest diaspora in the history of the world and, by its severity and an heuristic pervasiveness of half a millennium, has created an almost unbridgeable gap between Africans in their original continental home and ethnic Africans in the diaspora, in terms of a vision, a long-range strategy, and mobilization of resources for Africa's social and economic development.

Ethnic Africans in the diaspora, especially in the Americas, the Caribbean, and in West Asia as well as in Europe, have among them a large number of extremely well-educated and highly trained scientists, engineers, technologists, medical specialists, bankers, marketers, entrepreneurs, economists, and professionals in other disciplines and sectors, who have desperately endeavored to make a lasting contribution to Africa's modernization and economic growth and development but have so far lacked a clear-cut or continuing mechanism to do so. The bi-annually organized African/African-American summits, held in different capitals of Africa over the last seven years, are a signal indication of the strength of this hankering.

The sixth such summit since the series began was held in Abuja, Nigeria, in 2001. Dubbed the "Summit of Hope," it was chaired by its convenor, the late Rev. Leon Sullivan, and hosted by President Olusegun Obasanjo. It united about 10,000 delegates from around the globe, including around thirty presidents or heads of state from African countries, and high-level business, social and government leaders from America, the Caribbean, Asia, and Europe. These leaders worked together to build recognition of African business potential among American and other business leaders. The potential, preservation and development of African business and welfare was the key issue, with other issues such as education, investment and technical assistance from America being among the major topics of discussion. Reverend Sullivan saw these summits as important times for people to unite:

> As a black people, we are one family, and in this world we will rise or we will fall together. It is time for representatives of the United States, the Caribbean, Europe, Asia and Africa to come together once again and address the needs of Africa, so that we may take action to the benefit of all people. (See Africa Today, Voice of the Continent: "Summit of Hope", p. 10, May/June 2001).

Previous summits were held in Abidjan, Cote d' Ivoire in 1991; Libreville, Gabon, in 1993; Dakar, Senegal, in 1995; Harare, Zimbabwe, in 1997; and Accra, Ghana, in 1999. These summits have been working to discuss and implement programs to improve trade between Africa and other nations and result in claims that include:

• The Debt for Development program, which created 200,000 jobs from development projects.

113

- The Debt Relief program, which resulted in $60 billion in debt forgiveness.
- The Best and Brightest Bankers program which trained 350 African bankers.
- The People's Investment Fund for Africa, consisting of loans from American investors at 6 percent annual interest to support 1,000 new businesses in Africa.
- The Teachers for Africa program, which placed 500 teachers in 10 African countries.
- The Schools for Africa program, which initiated the building of over 1,000 schools.
- Digging 20,000 wells and training 1 million farmers in irrigation and farming.
- Hundreds of millions of dollars in new investments in Africa from U.S. companies, most of which had never invested in Africa before.
- Raising the consciousness of the world of the importance of Africa and its economic opportunities.

The Millennium Summit in 1999 was the most successful to date, with more than 4,000 in attendance. Accomplishments include the launching of the People's Investment Fund for Africa (PIFA), which assists small African businesses through grassroots economic development; the Global Sullivan Principles for Corporate Social Responsibility, which emphasizes justice in business globally, and the launching of the Summit War against Aids.

The second type of brain drain relates to a cohesive group of ethnic Africans now living and working all over the world as expatriate specialists, scholars, and professionals—a situation that began soon after World War II and accelerated intensely over the last four decades. This group is part of the conventional brain drain, whereby certain countries and regions have acted as magnets for the ambitious, the very able, and the entrepreneurial experts as new residents or citizens. It is reckoned that there are approximately 100,000 African expatriate scientists, scholars and entrepreneurs now living and working permanently in industrialized countries throughout the world. The same number of foreign expatriates are also working in Africa as technical assistance advisors and experts.

The third type is composed of another group of professionals, not so well defined; those we regard as distressed scientists, scholars, and entrepreneurs, who find themselves in destabilized African countries and regions, where their world is literally falling apart and, therefore, where they can no longer practice their scientific, engineering, and professional skills. National and regional disasters, as well as ethnic or civil wars have become more frequent and widespread from the time of the run-up to political independence—and there seems to be no likelihood of respite in the near future. Often these displaced and professionally disabled specialists have no clear channel for seeking new opportunities within the continent. Furthermore, national requirements for creating employment opportunities for citizens, and the exclusive labor laws of most African countries, necessarily act as roadblocks to engaging distressed scientists, scholars, and other professionals in African countries other than their own—except as refugees or as short-term staff.

Cross-border employment of African noncitizens on the same terms as citizens is rare in Africa. Production and marketing entrepreneurs have difficult legal entrapments to circumvent when they venture to work in a multicountry situation. There are very few Africa-originated merchant banks that consistently operate across borders. There are few legal structures within Africa, other than those promulgated by the United Nations system, that provide an open house for diaspora and expatriate professionals prepared to assist the continent in its long-term social and economic development. Yet, the degree of distress is very real and becoming endemic.

The examples given below illustrate the depth and pervasiveness of the brain drain and professional distress, even though the quality of the statistical data is not consistent and requires up-dating (this again is due to the backwardness of data collection in Africa, a symptom of underdevelopment).

The United Nations Economic Commission for Africa (UNECA) has compiled the data on migration of African skilled professionals since 1975. By 1987, the ECA estimated that approximately 70,000 high-level professionals had migrated from Africa, representing almost 30 percent of the total stock of high-level professionals existing in Africa at that time.

Between 1987 and 1989, about 120,000 Nigerians sought visas to visit Britain, the U.S., and Germany. Of these, 40 percent (or about 38,000) were potential brain-drain professionals. Those most directly affected in Nigeria are universities, hospitals, and engineering establishments. Indeed, nearly 30 percent of emigrants were engineers, and 50 percent were medical specialists.

Although expatriate Africans make up only a small proportion of the total number of immigrants from all over the world entering the United States each year (at present it is estimated that at least 500,000 new migrants enter the country each year legally, and possibly the same number illegally) it is significant that the proportion has climbed up from 2.6 percent at the start of the 1980s to 2.9 percent at the end of that decade. This translates to over 5,000 professional African migrants entering the United States each year.

In 1978, some 180,000 Sudanese were working in the Middle East as expatriates, of which 10 percent were trained university personnel. At the same time, 45 percent of all qualified surveyors had emigrated from the Sudan, 30 percent of all engineers, 20 percent of all university academic staff, and 17 percent of all medical doctors and dentists. The level of migration has increased steeply since then. Over the period 1983–1987, only 600 African professionals returned to the continent on a permanent basis, and that was through externally-funded programs.

From these examples there is no doubt, then, that Africa's most important resource for enduring and sustainable social and economic development—namely, human capital—is steadily receding at an alarming rate, spinning out of reach of Africa's vision for economic development (through distress and expatriation), or that it is not becoming organically integrated into the development process (because this invaluable resource has been left unengaged within the diaspora situation).

The reasons scientists do not return to Africa can be traced primarily to political stability issues: the absence of political stability and the high levels of ethnic tensions that result in a lack of physical security for them and for their families; corruption, especially among politicians and civil servants, making it difficult to carry out effective work, and at the same time undermining university education; low levels of pay and poor service conditions, both in the universities and in government research agencies; poor housing, education and health service provision, which makes life much less comfortable than living in the West both for them and for their families, which is traceable to the issues of political stability and corruption mentioned above. If Africa is seeking a renaissance in the areas of science and technology, it will need to address the issues of cultural confidence, and the political and economic systems that are the key to creating social stability and tackling corruption.

However, it is not only the inhospitable conditions in African countries that result in pressures for Africans trained in the West to stay in the West. A further rapidly growing factor is the desire of the West to keep trained manpower from low-income countries to boost their own economies and to increase their own wealth. In part, this is being driven by the reluctance of the citizens of many Western countries to have sufficient children to maintain the ratio between those who are retired and those who are working. A recent U.N. publication, *Replacement Migration*, states that the European Union of fifteen member countries with a population of more than 375 million will need 219 million immigrants between now and 2025 to maintain the 1995 ratio of one senior citizen against four persons of working age (*Replacement Migration*, UN, 1999, quoted in *Jakarta Post*, 25 August 2001).

This means that Western countries will be making it increasingly easy for Africans to stay in the West, and it may even come to the point where they are offered substantial additional financial inducements to do so. This is unfair to the African countries that gave these professionals their education to degree level, which will generally have cost the state tens of thousands of dollars. It becomes another form of theft by the rich from the poor, rationalized by arguing that it is an individual's free choice to stay in the West or return home.

In summary, the factors responsible for the African braindrain phenomenon can be stated as follows.

- First, the main cause relates to economic factors that have plunged most African countries into a food-insecure, unhealthy, debt-ridden, pervasively corrupt, uncompetitive economic region, where high unemployment and underemployment has become the norm, and where there is little functional linkage between the academic research community, the productive sector, and the entrepreneurial community.
- Second, there are the social and psychological factors that have created a disabling environment for creativity, innovation, and productivity, and where the flow of refugees (including those fleeing from

economic, environmental, and destabilizing circumstances) has become proportionately the
largest in the world.

- Third, we have in Africa the chronic and endemic
geopolitical and security factors of ethnicity, war-
lordism, civil war, excessive and inefficient bureau-
cracy, patronage, and irreconcilable political
differences that have led to the incapacity of many
specialists to pursue their professional calling within their own country.

- Finally, Africa is prone to great natural disasters,
including prolonged drought, periodic famine,
pestilence, and major epidemics, which have often
prevailed upon segments of the professional and
entrepreneurial to emigrate.

4.6. National Political Integration

We have spoken a great deal about the problems of Africa's political leadership and how the situation in some countries is looking
extremely hopeless, at least for the foreseeable future. But when
all is said and done, questions remain: Is there nothing Africa can
do to change the situation? Is it really so trapped in its own hopeless political and economic situation that it can do nothing but
wait for God's benevolence to put things right in His own time?
It would be instructive to consider Africa's prospects, including
the immense difficulties that it has to overcome. Viewed from a
wider historical context, it would be an enormous achievement if
Africa attained political stability in the next forty years or so and
"took-off" economically, for the reasons set out below.

Apart from the economic analysis given above, the heart of
Africa's "development problematique," it seems to me, is the
problem of building stable and viable political units (countries,

nations) against the background of centuries of ethnic diversity and local competition for resources. In Africa, today's artificial states were only created some 120 years ago, and Africans have only had access to widespread "modern" forms of education for approximately thirty to forty years. Consider how long it took Britain to create a stable nation-state, from the time of William the Conqueror (1066 Battle of Hastings), to the Magna Carta (1215) to the end of the War of the Roses between the Yorkists and the Lancastrians (1485), to giving Parliament any semblance of sovereignty (civil war 1641–45), to the Act of Union of England and Scotland (1707)—nearly 650 years. Moreover, it is not Britain alone. Consider how long it took Germany (finally unified under Bismarck in the 1850s) or Italy (unified also in the second half of the nineteenth century). Why should Africa be expected to create stable and mature nation-states in decades when it took the West centuries?

In relational terms, national integration in Kenya, for example, will require a shift in the pattern of people's relationships. Until relatively recently, people were expected to relate almost exclusively to relatives and members of their ethnic group. Those of other ethnic groups were either foreigners or enemies. All this is now changing rapidly because of urbanization, which brings people of different ethnic groups into close proximity to each other. Also, the impact of national radio and newspapers, the use of national languages (English, French, Swahili), and the transfer of professional staff across ethnic boundaries are all contributing to changing people's cultural perceptions and understanding.

In this context, the purpose of a constitution can be understood as a means to formalize the relationship between individuals and groups to each other in their polity. A constitution is really no more than a set of rules that carves up political power among different members of society, which sets out the composition and procedures of political institutions and their relationship to each other, and which sets limits on the exercise of all political power in the interests of the common good.

Typically, it is often pointed out that the French colonial legacy concentrated on the building of state, while that of the British concentrated on building the nation. In both instances, however, the attempt was last-minute, shortly before granting independence, and incomplete. Meanwhile the polities that had been destroyed, subjugated, or carved up in the colonial process were in no condition to revert to being successor states after independence—even if they had been allowed to be so. One thinks of the case of Ashanti in Ghana, Buganda in Uganda, and Zululand in South Africa, all of which were potential flashpoints as *foci* of political allegiance, but were balanced by a strong assertion of the national ideal. There is a relationship-building process that must take place at the national level. In Africa relationships are very strong at the familial and communal level, but less strong at the national and/or civil levels; when crises or conflicts of interest occur, the underlying communal faultlines tend to appear. Here the insights of Arend Lijphart are important: There is a need for institutions that cross-cut, without necessarily weakening, communal affiliations. (See, for example, Lijphart 1977, pp. 10–12.)

In *this* generation, however, the primary loyalty is still to other members of the ethnic group. This is because other members of the ethnic group are still the major providers of welfare, emergency help, and emotional support. In addition, central government resource allocations in terms of regional investment, access to education and jobs, and access to the army are often considered to be "unfair" by ethnicities which are not members of the president's ethnic group. This perceived unfairness contributes to continuing ethnic consciousness. Those from other ethnic groups are still "outsiders". Parents pass these attitudes and values on to their children. In the next generation, these traditional attitudes and values will be weakened a step further. How many generations will it take to reach the stage where primary loyalty is to the nation rather than to the ethnic group? How is it possible to keep the positive values of ethnicity (financial support and welfare) and the attendant cultural values that go with ethnicity (such as personhood) and to lose the negative consequences in terms of suspicion of "outsiders", ethnically defined competition for resources, and so on?

Looking at Africa's future from another extreme viewpoint, if we were to give up and become completely lethargic about our own technological backwardness and adopt the path of slow development that Europe experienced from the ninth to the nineteenth centuries, the achievement of effective political integration and democratic government in Africa might take from 100 to 150 years (which would be extremely fast by Western historical standards). The question, then, becomes, how can we maximize political stability and participation in this "political development period"—without expecting democratic governments to work perfectly on a Western model in this period of Africa's political history? This viewpoint is not to be taken lightly, but it is no excuse for Africans to fail to address the problems of their corrupt and dictatorial leaders urgently.

In addition to the problems of achieving rapid political integration in states with a political history of ethnic diversity and conflict, there are other reasons for the high level of conflict within African states. One of these is the colonial legacy of boundaries, and on this point there seem to have been few solutions. Wherever one draws boundaries in Africa, it is certain, in one place or another, to have to divide ethnic groups. Where would one draw the boundary, for example, between Kenya and Tanzania to avoid splitting the Maasai? The only real solution would be to have the whole of Africa as one country, just as the whole of India is one country, but communications in Africa are not sophisticated enough to make that a viable option as yet. In other words, we must work hard to materialize Gaddafi's idea of an African Union, as long as we are determined realistically to pay the price in terms of development of viable communications and economic integration. The problems of national political jealousies must also be addressed. What Gaddafi has been pushing for is not new. Nkrumah had tried in vain to persuade African leaders to unite. Let us hope Gaddafi will succeed where Nkrumah failed—at least he has much greater financial resources than Nkrumah had.

Another important point is the reality of income disparity. The fact that such devastating poverty exists in Africa inevitably means that there is a struggle for control of resources. Unfortunately, in African politics there is a "winner takes all" situation. If you or your group gain power, you enjoy a high lifestyle, that includes the best health facilities, the best education for your children and shopping trips to Europe at will. If you or your group are out of power, you are condemned to poverty, have difficulty in obtaining a job, feel uncertainty about your future, have problems securing your children's education, difficulty in obtaining medical attention when a family member is ill, and so on. No wonder there is such a struggle for power among elites of different ethnic groups! If everyone were equally poor, it would not generate such conflict.

Then, there is the impact of the global economy on African incomes. One of the reasons for such great discrepancies between the income of the elite and the rest of society lies in the way donor/creditor agencies and multinational companies give such high rewards to their staff relative to local salaries. There is no easy solution to this problem either, however. Would it be fair to European and African U.N. employees, doing exactly the same job, to work at different salary levels? Surely not. However, if you pay the African colleague a salary equivalent to the European colleague's salary, then you create a huge imbalance between the African person's salary and that of their colleagues, neighbors, and friends in their home country. This, then, increases the political fighting to gain access to those positions through the political process.

The United Nations tried to solve this problem by dividing its staff into two categories, namely internationally recruited staff and local staff. The former are the more highly paid professional international civil servants who are not allowed, except in special circumstances, to work in their own countries. (I must point out, however, that this rule did not apply to U.S. citizens.) The local staff were those recruited in a country where a U.N. office is located. These people tended to be secretaries, office messengers, and security and maintenance personnel. This system has been much abused because of the jealousies it generated, and it therefore fell under the weight of its own inconsistency.

Although we have already discussed another crucial aspect of the African development problematique, namely, the importance of agriculture in Africa's quest for a renaissance, it is necessary for us, as a purely precautionary measure, also to acknowledge the difficulties as well as the potential of agricultural conditions in Africa. This will enable us to establish realistic expectations about the future. For instance, I have stressed the fact that huge parts of Africa, such as much of DRC and Southern Sudan, are virtually untouched in terms of their agricultural and economic potential.

There are also considerations when comparing Africa with Asia. The problems of water control in much of Africa are more difficult than in many parts of Asia. For example, Asia has much greater ground level irrigation potential, as the main grain growing areas are much flatter, and the water table is higher. Also, the disease factors both for human beings and for animals and plants are greater in Africa than in Asia. Finally, the variability of agricultural conditions is much greater than in Asia, and hence the level of applied research required to achieve a given growth in farm yields is much greater.

4.7. Population Growth

Another area of concern which I have not analyzed in detail is population growth. Much of Africa still has growth rates in excess of 3 percent a year, compared with typically 1.5 cent in Asia, which means that in Africa the population is doubling every 20 years rather than in just under 50 years as in Asia. This then requires extremely high levels of investment in infrastructure and public services, such as education and health, just to stand still. (The UK would have the greatest difficulty in doubling the number of its schools and hospitals every 20 years, even with its high income levels). One reason for the high levels of population growth in rural areas is the absence of any system of welfare for the elderly. If African adults have few children, they are likely to find life difficult when they reach old age. If one or more of those children die before they reach adulthood, which is quite likely in Africa, the old person will be left with virtually nobody to support them in that vulnerable period of their lives.

Secondly, there are other traditional and cultural reasons why large families are important in African thinking. In the past, when availability of land was not a constraint, a large number of children was potentially a source of wealth. Today, however, as a consequence of high population growth people are being pushed "down the ecological gradient" into areas of poor soils and marginal rainfall. Technology has a vital role to play to make farming viable under these marginal conditions, through new crop varieties, small-scale irrigation projects and use of "ratooning" of some crops (where the roots of the plant are left after harvest so it can grow again).

A key part of the solution to the high population growth is to increase the education available to girls, as education of girls is highly correlated with a decline in women's fertility rates. This emphasizes the benefits to all members of the family (both nuclear and extended) of a smaller number of better nutritioned and better educated children. It improves the status, welfare and economic opportunities of the family as a group, and hence increases their self-determination. It is not an issue of individual rights but of a progressive "African Family Policy".

The following table shows the effect of population growth on the availability of arable land in six African countries, with an average fall of 23 percent in hectares per capita for the rural population over just 15 years between 1985 and 2000.

Table 3. Arable Land per capita in African countries

Country	Hectare per capita		Hectare per capita for rural population	
	1985	2000	1985	2000
Kenya	0.73	0.42	0.86	0.66
Malawi	0.73	0.45	0.84	0.60
Tanzania	2.30	1.44	2.59	1.68
Cameroon	3.34	2.09	5.23	4.76
Nigeria	0.71	0.48	1.01	0.88
Senegal	1.62	1.04	2.41	1.76

Source: U. Lele and S. Stone, 1989. *Population pressure, the Environment, and Agricultural Intensification: Variations on the Boserup Hypothesis*, MADIA working paper, World Bank, Washington D.C.

4.8. The Scourge of Disease

4.8.1. The HIV/Aids controversy

When discussing in this chapter great and important issues which affect the future course of the African continent—issues which we have referred to as the African development problematique—HIV/Aids is arguably one of the most, if not the most, important of all of them at this juncture in our history. Therefore, the way we in Africa perceive and treat this subject will influence the success or failure of the idea of the African Renaissance.

It is no secret that the subject of HIV/Aids and the precise link between them has generated heated debate in Africa. I cannot write on the subject of Aids, as an African, without mentioning something about it, in particular the criticisms against Thabo Mbeki, the president of South Africa, emanating from the West and Africa's reaction to them. Admittedly, when the scientists were arguing among themselves and also with the politicians, the ordinary person in the street could only watch helplessly. And yet we must admit, quite candidly, that the African Renaissance movement will be greatly affected if we in Africa do not take particular care to understand what causes Aids and how to combat it.

In December 1997, when I was campaigning for a parliamentary seat in Kenya, I was asked by a predominantly rural African audience what I thought about the controversy that was raging at that time as to the real cause of Aids. I did not have access to a wide spectrum of credible and objective scientific information on the disease, so I decided to answer by using as an example a road accident in which many people had died. If we see dead people all around us and the injured writhing in pain, do we not take action immediately and take the injured to hospital instead of arguing about what caused the accident? Of course, thorough and exhaustive investigations as to the precise cause of the accident must be carried out later in order to avoid a repetition, but first and foremost the immediate saving of life is much more important.

Everybody in Africa agrees that the impact of the global Aids epidemic has been catastrophic and continues to be so every day. It is now a question of doing something about both treatment and prevention. When one considers how many people have died of Aids, particularly in Africa, it is hard to absorb the full reality. A most disturbing article revealed the extent of the tragedy in Africa:

So far, the global Aids epidemic is thought to have killed 19 million people. That is almost twice as many as died in the First World War. It has infected another 34 million people. When they die, as most will in the next few years, Aids will have killed nearly as many as in the Second World War. And the epidemic shows no sign of abating. U.N. Aids, the umbrella group that co-ordinates the anti-Aids effort of various U.N. agencies, reckons that 5 million people a year are being infected with the human immunodeficiency virus (HIV) that causes Aids. If these people were dying from bullets and bombs, they would never be out of the headlines. ("The Battle with Aids", *The Economist*, 20 July 2000).

The OAU Summit on Aids, malaria, tuberculosis and other related infectious diseases, which took place in Abuja, Nigeria in April 2001, released even more grim statistics indicating that Africa is the world's most devastated continent: "According to the U.N., more than 17 million Africans have died of Aids since 1984, while 25 million are living with the virus. Since at least 36 million people are infected with HIV in the whole world, almost twice as many Africans are dying of the scourge as the rest of the world." (*Daily Nation* editorial, 26 April 2001, p. 6). This is mainly because Africa suffers from the double handicap of being both poor and without access to cheap drugs to keep Aids victims alive longer. The statistical estimates given by the U.N. Aids agency indicate that Africa, with only 10 percent of the world's population, harbors 70 percent of the world's HIV cases. And in 16 countries on the continent, more than one adult in 10 is HIV positive.

The 1998 Geneva conference on HIV/Aids claimed to be "bridging the gap between the treatment of the disease in the rich and poor worlds and yet it did no such thing," (*The Econ-*

omist, 20 July 2000). "What needed to be shouted from the rooftops was that, contrary to some popular views, Aids is not primarily a disease of gay Western men or of intravenous drug injectors; it is a disease of ordinary people leading ordinary lives, except that most of them happen to live in a continent, Africa, that the rich countries of the world find it easy to ignore", continues *The Economist*.

When Mbeki talks of the need for Western scientists to take into account poverty in Africa as a vital and important point in the fight against Aids, they should not dismiss his point lightly. The article in *The Economist* says the following on this issue:

> Certainly, Africa has some special features. Africans are beset by many diseases, each of which serves to weaken people and to make them susceptible to others. And poverty aggravates the problem, as do incessant wars. If Africa were as rich and peaceful as Europe or America, Aids might by now be as rare there as elsewhere. But it is not, ultimately, a lack of money that causes Aids. It is a virus. And stopping, or slowing, that virus is not impossible.(*The Economist*, 20 July 2000).

This is of course true. The point we are making in Africa is that poverty, in particular among the rural population and urban-city slum dwellers, exacerbates the problem of treatment, which will for a long time remain unintelligible to Western scientists and pharmaceutical or drug companies.

4.8.2. *The Macro Economic Impact of HIV/Aids*

In so far as the serious impact of Aids on the socioeconomic development of Africa is concerned, we are all agreed. With a third of all adults in many parts of Africa now infected with HIV, and over a third of children born HIV-positive in many places, some believe that the scale of the catastrophe threatens the foundations of any economic growth strategy. It is reported that there are whole villages and regions in African countries such as Uganda that have become completely depopulated as a consequence of Aids. That is why mere numbers do not constitute the whole issue, although according to U.N. estimates, 25 million of the 34 million infected in the world live in Africa.

People talk of waging war on diseases, but in the case of Aids, the rhetoric could be inverted, for the effects of the disease on human populations are similar to those of war. Most infectious diseases tend to kill infants, young people, and the elderly. Aids, like war, kills those in the prime of life, and thus the human disaster for its victims and their families creates a social and economic disaster for the countries affected. With few exceptions, those countries are in Africa, a continent with dire enough economic and social problems already. Indeed, in one way Aids is worse than war, because when armies fight, it is predominantly young men who are killed; but Aids kills young women too, and the result is social dislocation on a grand scale. A war would seem almost merciful by comparison.

The macroeconomic impact of Aids in society is not only serious but catastrophic. In view of the fact that

> Husbands often infect their wives, and mothers can infect their unborn children. Aids destroys whole families. The poor are most affected and least able to cope. Breadwinners fall ill and stop earning. Spouses stop work to look after them. Children drop out of school to find jobs. Medical bills gobble up savings. With less money for food, even the uninfected grow weak. Many Aids orphans, ostracized by their communities, turn to prostitution to survive. (See *The Economist*, 12 March 2001 and the article already mentioned above.)

4.8.3. *Control and Treatment of HIV/Aids*
It has been said that the spread of HIV has been caused by the

breakdown of African traditional social order under pressure of urbanization and modernization. The constraints on sexual behavior of the past have been removed, and few constraints derived from religious morality or from knowledge derived from education, have taken their place. This view is quite correct, and poverty should be added, for in the rural areas it is one of the major compounding factors. The lack of employment opportunities for young primary and secondary school leavers in the rural countryside is a major problem in postindependent Africa. Because of poverty, parents cannot afford to continue paying school fees for their children beyond primary or secondary school. With no gainful occupation, many girls engage in prostitution for a pittance in order to help their poor families. Likewise, owing to the breakdown in university education through lack of proper funding, young women do not have proper financial support and some will be drawn into prostitution by the sheer necessity of survival.

Who is demanding the services of these poor girls? It is mainly salaried civil servants and teachers, professionals and businessmen, members of Parliament and government ministers. Some members of the clergy, especially the unmarried ones, do not have clean hands either. When life becomes a little easier, these girls move to urban areas where the demand for their services is greater and the pay better than in the rural areas.

How about the men in rural areas? Abject poverty causes them to turn to alcoholism in large numbers. The availability of cheap illicit brews, such as "changaa" and "busaa" in Kenya provide them with an escape route from their misery through intoxication. These men will engage in petty thieving to obtain the money to buy this cheap alcohol, not only for themselves but also for young girls. Under these circumstances, the fight against HIV/Aids will remain an uphill task.

An important factor in the rapid spread of Aids in Africa is so-called "disassortative mating," that is, individuals in a group mating from another group rather than from among themselves (as in assortative mating). Disassortative mating, for example, between young girls and older men, greatly increases the rate at which the virus spreads from small high-risk groups, such as prostitutes and their clients, male homosexuals and injecting drug users, to low-risk groups. It is believed that in an area where Aids is already highly prevalent, older men form a high-risk group because they are far more likely to have picked up the virus than younger ones. This, it has been suggested, helps to explain why the rate of infection is higher in young African women than it is in young African men. This observation also implicates the sexual behavior of professional and "upwardly mobile" men, an extremely high-risk group because of their flamboyant lifestyle and a general breakdown in the concept of marriage and family life. In many cases, young women are coerced or bribed into relationships with older men. This risk would diminish, particularly in Africa, if girls were better educated—not least because they would then find it easier to earn a living.

As far as control and treatment are concerned, here again we should be guided by Dr. Roy Anderson, a noted epidemiologist from Oxford University, who has argued that:

> Stopping an epidemic requires one thing: that the average number of people infected by somebody who already has the disease be less than one. And for a sexually transmitted disease, this average has three components: the "transmissibility" of the disease, the average rate that an infected person acquires new and uninfected partners, and the average length of time for which somebody is infectious. (Speech at the Durban conference on Aids, 2000)

Talking about sex is taboo in many African cultures; young people cannot discuss sex with their parents. While Africans

132

have hidden their sexual feelings and behavior, Western society has gone to the other extreme, such that Africans recoil at the immorality of public sexual display so rampant in the West. In order to tackle this problem effectively, we in Africa must strike a balance. Research has shown that in countries such as Uganda, this sexual taboo has often been overcome, without going overboard, in discussions about how to prevent the spread of Aids. The first and most universally recommended method of control is the use of condoms, though it is better also to persuade people through education and advertising to limit their promiscuous relationships. This is difficult, but not impossible; Uganda and Senegal are being internationally applauded for having achieved some spectacular success, though it can be difficult to persuade people to use condoms:

> Partly, this is a question of discounting the future. For decades African lives have been shorter, on average, than those in the rest of the world. With Aids, they are getting shorter still. A Botswanan who faces the prospect of death before his 30th birthday is more likely to be reckless than an American who can look forward to well over twice that lifespan; a short life might as well be a merry one. (*The Economist*, 20 July 2000)

There are, even in the West, those opposed to this Western solution of promoting condoms. Rather, they believe that there are two key policies to consider: first, promoting the rule that there should be no sex outside marriage; and second, relying heavily on educating all teenagers of the dangers of any sex outside marriage. This approach fits with both Christian and Islamic teaching and is a more powerful deterrent, because it is an appeal to conscience and self-preservation, as well as being highly pragmatic. If educational efforts are concentrated mainly on children who have not yet started having sex, the dividends are likely to be high, because this group are still largely unaffected.

It is true that the Western approach of relying solely on the use of condoms is too accepting of loose sexual morality, and at worst is a death sentence in a society where it is both difficult to teach people the right use of condoms, difficult to ensure condoms are universally available and affordable, and impossible to ensure that they are used effectively. There is also a growing body of opinion that says even condoms are not 100 percent effective in stopping the transmission of Aids.

One other major issue in Africa is the question of who wears the condom. Until recently, there was no choice because only male condoms were available, and women in many parts of Africa are in a weak negotiating position when it comes to insisting that a man put one on. The best way out of this is to alter the balance of power, through improved education, particularly for girls. In other words, one way to help stop the spread of Aids is to empower women so that they can say "no." While we all know how difficult this has been in many traditionally exploitative patriarchal African societies, educated women have a much better chance of saying no than women who are not. Men, too, would benefit from better education in the dangers and risks attached to Aids, so this must be added as an important plank of an effective anti-Aids strategy.

It has been pointed out, however, that a stop-gap situation has recently emerged and has proved popular in Africa, particularly among groups such as the Nairobi prostitutes: the female condom. An even less intrusive—and to a man invisible—form of protection would be a vaginal microbicide that kills the virus before it can cross the vagina wall.

However, sex is not the only way that HIV is transmitted; infected mothers can pass the virus to their children during childbirth or through breastfeeding. Here, too, transmissibility can be reduced dramatically. In order to ensure that women in Africa give birth to healthy babies, it would be necessary for all pregnant women to be tested for HIV and then given AZT or nevirapine if they are shown to be infected. It has been suggested that a short course of these anti-retroviral drugs reduces the chance that an HIV-positive pregnant mother will infect her baby during childbirth, although it is not known if breast milk can be kept virus-free by this means.

There is absolutely no doubt about the horrendous scale on which Aids is killing African children. More than 5 million children are reckoned to have been infected in this way in Africa, and almost 4 million of them are already dead, not to speak of the orphans, which number about 12 million in Africa.

The third method of controlling the spread of HIV/Aids is to treat other sexually transmitted diseases using antibiotics, thus making it more difficult for HIV to enter the body. This way of preventing the transmission of HIV is, nevertheless, found to be unreliable because of the lengthy period of infection that someone can have with HIV/Aids.

The most difficult and controversial point of all concerns the search to find a vaccine or a drug that can completely cure Aids. At the moment, there is no cure, particularly for the more virulent strains of Aids in Africa. Although certain drugs can be effective in slowing the lethal effects of Aids if taken early enough, the anti-retroviral drugs and nevirapine that have been highly recommended for use in Africa are extremely expensive for poor Africans to afford, although they are relatively cheap for those on Western incomes. Only a tiny minority who are very rich and highly privileged can afford them in Africa.

Some of us in Africa who are deeply concerned by the plight of our people are, however, encouraged by a growing campaign in the UK as well as in Africa to ensure that the anti-retroviral drugs, which can delay the onset of Aids by up to ten years, are available at a price African governments and people can afford. The final solution to this problem will be for some of the more technologically advanced countries in Africa, like

South Africa, to take the lead in manufacturing those drugs themselves, instead of importing cheaper generic drugs from other low-income countries. Otherwise these Western drug companies will never stop exploiting Africans.

Access to cheap generic anti-Aids drugs had become a burning issue in Africa since 19 April 2001, when thirty-nine global pharmaceutical firms dropped a lawsuit in South Africa against a government move to produce cheap generic drugs. The decline of lawsuits followed tremendous international pressure and also the personal intervention of Kofi Annan. As a result, African leaders were encouraged to adopt a common position and spoke with one voice, demanding that generic drugs be accessible to poor Africans at the lowest price, or even free, as with tuberculosis.

By contrast with anti-retroviral drugs, vaccines are one-shot treatments, and so are not subject to patient compliance with complex drug regimes. (Noncompliance is the main cause of the emergence of resistant strains, since the erratic consumption of a particular drug allows populations of resistant viruses to evolve and to multiply.) It is, therefore, quite clear that the treatment of Aids in Africa will require effective vaccines, yet we are told that these are years away.

When the Aids crisis exploded on the global health scene in the 1980s, Brazil was seen as one of its main casualties. Within a decade, however, their government had stopped the disease in its tracks, through an Aids program that has been described as "a model for developing countries around the world and a beacon of hope for Aids activists in industrialized nations." ("Brazil pushes Aids Fight Beyond Borders," *The People*, 30 April 2000, p. 10).

At the heart of Brazil's success is a policy of providing anti-Aids drugs free of cost. Having decided to start manufacturing anti-Aids drugs rather than pay high industry prices, Brazil has led a fight to ensure that all developing countries, including

South Africa, are guaranteed access to cheap anti-Aids drugs. But Brazil's stance has pitted it against drug companies and the United States, which spurred the World Trade Organization to establish a dispute panel to look at Brazil's patent law. The U.S. government and drug companies say they do not object to Brazil's Aids program, but to its patent laws. Without patents, it is argued, the major pharmaceutical companies in the West would have no incentive to research new medicines.

As part of its successful approach to the disease, Brazil's Evandro Chagas Hospital began treating people with a triple cocktail—the combination of anti-retroviral drugs that has given Aids victims around the world a second shot at life. Instead of paying U.S.$15,000 a year, patients receive them free. It is estimated that about 95,000 people have been treated under this program which, combined with aggressive prevention efforts, has kept the HIV infection as low as 0.6 percent of the population in Brazil, nullifying dire western forecasts. This compares with an estimated 36 percent infection rate in Botswana, so far the world's highest rate, and about 20 percent in South Africa.

Brazil spends $300 million a year to offer free treatment and drugs to Aids sufferers, but says the program more than pays for itself by reducing hospitalizations, cutting transmission rates, and enabling people to remain in the workforce, with consequent positive effects for the economy.

4.8.4. Malaria and Other Diseases
Two OAU Summits in Abuja, Nigeria, in 2000 and 2001 have already added malaria and other Aids-related diseases such as tuberculosis to the African development problematique. Malaria is one of the great scourge diseases of the world, and Africans are its prime victims. According to the World Health Organization, malaria kills an estimated one million people every year, 700,000 of them children. Every year, the disease takes the lives of 3,000

children under five years of age. The U.N. Children's Fund (UNICEF) has estimated that one child will die every thirty seconds as a result of the disease. This also means that Africa's Gross Domestic Product would be higher today if malaria had been eliminated thirty-five years ago. The UNICEF report goes on to say: "In the continent, malaria continues to slow down the GDP by over one percent every year. Countries where malaria is endemic are among the world's most impoverished". (*The East African Standard*, 30 April 2001)

A malaria-stricken family spends an average of over a quarter of its income on malaria treatment, paying prevention costs and suffering loss of income. The greatest challenge in malaria control is that the cheapest antimalaria drug, chloroquine, is rapidly losing its effectiveness in many endemic countries. In some parts of the world, the disease is already resistant to the four leading front-line drugs. While nine out of every ten malaria deaths occur in sub-Saharan Africa, 40 percent of the world's population lives in areas with a high malaria risk. Each year approximately 24 million pregnancies in Africa are threatened by malaria; and this malady contributed 15 percent of all maternal anemia and about 35 percent of all preventable instances of low birth weight, the single greatest risk factor for death during the first months of life. Surviving children living in endemic areas may also face impaired development, and malaria is also a major cause of school absenteeism. Studies in countries such as Kenya and Malawi have indicated that the rates of placental malaria, severe anemia, and low birth weight can be reduced if women in their first and second pregnancies receive Preventive Intermittent Treatment (PIT) as part of antenatal care.

However, sleeping under insecticide-treated mosquito nets remains the most effective solution to the reduction of malaria infection, apart from the fact that governments urgently need to adopt and implement policies on anti-malarial drugs, just as they are doing in the case of HIV/Aids.

A Colombian scientist, Dr. Manuel Patarroyo, believes that a new antimalarial vaccine developed by his team could eventually save a million lives a year globally. This new vaccine works by interrupting the life cycle of the malaria parasite as it tries to invade the red blood cells of its victim ("The Life Cycle of the Malaria Parasite: How the New Vaccine Fights Malaria," *The People*, 20 April 2001 p. 11).

In Africa the large numbers of people affected by malaria have overwhelmed the national health services of many governments, sustaining poverty and weakening societies. And at the family level, the cost of prevention and treatment consumes scarce household resources, and the disease continues to have a negative impact on the health of children. In many cases malaria is both preventable and treatable, if only people can be taught relatively inexpensive prevention measures such as draining stagnant water, clearing away bush around homesteads, and using inexpensive bed nets in perennial mosquito zones.

It is hoped that African governments will treat the malaria upsurge and the prevention and treatment campaigns much more seriously. There is no point in African leaders squandering their country's scarce resources in expensive trips to attend meetings in which they sign declarations that mean absolutely nothing in terms of implementation. Other diseases that currently ravage Africa include tuberculosis, haemorrhagic fevers, and trypanosomiasis.

Many enlightened Africans are now saying: "We Africans have been one of the greatest survivors of the human race. We survived slavery, we survived colonialism, imperialism and neocolonialism, which were responsible for the great exploitation of the continent. We have, so far, survived the ravages of the major diseases of this century, but we now have genocidal ethnic conflicts all over the continent and the HIV/Aids pandemic. The question is: Will the African people be able to survive this time around, especially in view of this last scourge?" Never before has a large section of the human race been threatened by extinction!

4.8.5. Economic and Political Issues

It is one thing to point out the problems facing Africa in particular with regard to the HIV/Aids pandemic, but we must also suggest to those well-meaning and good people in the rich world, mainly in the West, what they can do to help Africa, for some of them have tried to help us to help ourselves. Africa should not, therefore, give the world the impression that we are incessantly complaining. After all, some of our countries have been independent for more than forty years. That is at least sufficient time to get our act together. The example of South Korea would be good to emulate. Nearly thirty years ago, the country was still extremely backward. The Korean War devastated the country, and yet now it is a highly industrialized nation. We in Africa could achieve similarly spectacular progress if we did the right things, but it is a big "*if*"!

What is even more important is that in spite of the behavior of the major pharmaceutical companies in the West towards Africa, there is evidence that attitudes are at last begining to change. Early in 2000, the American government upgraded the threat of Aids from one that merely affects people's health to one that affects the security of nations. In addition, the president of the World Bank, James Wolfensohn, declared at the same time that there was "no limit" to the amount the bank was prepared to give for Aids, and it announced that U.S.$500 million was now available. At the same time it was reported that five large drug companies agreed with UNAIDS not only that something must be done, but that they might help. They have done nothing so far. One such company, Merck, had announced that it would set aside U.S.$50 million to help, adding that, together with the Bill Gates Foundation, it was going to deliver a comprehensive anti-Aids package for Botswana, one of the worst affected countries of all.

At least from the World Bank and other bilateral sources, some African governments have been receiving money to try to mitigate the impact of Aids on their populations. *The Economist* of 20 July 2000 has written:

> such initiatives are welcome, even if they are a drop in the ocean (the World Bank estimates that Africa alone may need to spend U.S. $2.3 billion a year on the disease). But it is rarely possible for outsiders to solve other peoples' problems. Aids in poor countries will not go away so long as their leaders do not give a lead in fighting against it. And Africa's rulers, with one or two shining exceptions, have not yet done so. Some have simply ignored the problem.

This is precisely the point, and it could not have been better stated; that is why I posed the question earlier, What are African leaders, through their governments, doing to tackle the Aids problem?

The saddest thing in Africa is that most of these leaders think that public political propaganda can be a substitute for realistic action. Merely shouting at the top of their voices to carefully selected audiences and cautioning them of the dangers of HIV/Aids pandemic will not do the trick, however. In doing this they believe that they have demonstrated to the country that they care and are concerned about the spread of the disease. They also believe that this will demonstrate to the potential bilateral and multilateral financial institutions their supposed commitment, and thereby attract more financial resources from those quarters. This is indeed sad because the story is not so simple, and closer examination of what really happens on the ground is heart-rending.

First and foremost, there is the problem of the breakdown of health systems in most African countries. The ministries of health, which alone should be professionally equipped to deal with Aids and should therefore also deal with all outside financial institutions offering money for this particular program, are not mandated to do so. Moreover, the systems of health and administrative and financial control in some of these ministries have all but broken down. In most countries the health sector is in a complete shambles. In view of the fact that doctors are not properly and adequately remunerated—in fact they feel neglected—they decide to set up private practices and businesses in addition to their work in government institutions. So when patients go to a government hospital, they are usually expected to pay for the prescriptions, and in advance of receiving any treatment.

Invariably the medication so prescribed is only available at the private pharmaceutical centers owned by a few rich and influential people in the government, or their friends and relatives of those in government, and in conjunction with these doctors. This means that the entire health system is converted into a private business organization so that even if medication is donated from outside the country to be utilized by the patients free of charge, these donations often find their way into privately-owned clinics. Consequently, health ministries in most African countries are usually short of medication, and patients who cannot afford to pay for their own treatment in government hospitals die. That is why privately-owned hospitals in most African countries are often the only remaining safe and viable institutions that can offer proper treatment to whoever can afford it.

The second problem follows directly from the first one above in that the ministry of health usually finds itself starved of funds. Apart from the fact that funds are often diverted to other, doubtful causes, even after parliamentary budgetary approval, hospitals in the urban and rural areas usually have insufficient funds with which to operate. Health clinics in rural areas are usually in pitiful condition, completely neglected by the government, so that the ordinary poor people in the rural areas only survive by the grace of God. As it is in the rural areas that 80 percent of the population still live, they are the ones who suffer most from HIV/Aids, as I have indicated above.

In the particular case of the Aids problem, some African governments are only too aware of the short-comings in their health ministries: that is why they have removed themselves from the responsibility of handling this problem, placing it into a government department or ministry that is not even remotely capable of handling the issue in a professional manner. So, the aid money will go astray, given to the wrong department and handled by the wrong people. It is, therefore, pathetic to see politicians and public servants busily addressing people on the dangers of Aids and what they are supposed to do to avoid contracting the disease. It is even more pathetic to see that their message does not sink in, for the people know that little is being done at a practical level to find a cure or to avoid the spread of the disease to match the political rhetoric. The people know that the fundamental problems that African governments must solve first requires thorough reorganization of the health ministries, proper funding and trained, knowledgeable staff. Although it is all very well for politicians, religious leaders and public servants to educate the public about the dangers of the disease, the main responsibility should be given to doctos and scientists to find a cure and advise on avoiding the spread of the disease. The ministry of health must be empowered for this purpose.

Finally, a word of caution for those who donate or lend money to fight against the disease. They must beware of falling into the trap of believing political pronouncements as evidence of commitment to curb the spread of Aids. They should scrutinize the government's economic policies to deal with the problem of rural poverty, as well as its health policy.

5

African Renaissance: Seeds of Hope

5.1. The Desire for African Renaissance

It cannot be denied that in Africa, particularly in the rainbow nation of the Republic of South Africa, we are beginning to witness the hunger and thirst of the African people, surpassing that of any other time in our history, for a new beginning. We believe that the African Renaissance will inspire the growth of men of genius that can guide its socio-economic rebirth and renewal—men and women who will devote their time to the search for the truth, wherever this might lead. As Thabo Mbeki has said: "Those who have eyes to see, let them see. The African Renaissance is upon us. As we peer through the looking glass darkly, this may not be obvious. But it is upon us." (Mbeki 1998, p. 10).

Nelson Mandela gave further impetus to these ideas in a speech to the assembly of Heads of States and Government of the Non-Aligned Movement in Durban, South Africa in September 1998, where he spoke of Africa's yearning for an African Renaissance.

There are three main foundations on which we base our hopes for an African Renaissance: (i) the right timing—in the context of post-cold war global politics, now is the right time for a renaissance; (ii) strong leadership—Thabo Mbeki has emerged as an inspirational advocate of renaissance; and (iii) resources—Africa's mineral wealth, natural resources and agricultural potential can sustain the economic development we so desperately need. We will examine each of these factors in turn, but first we must consider what some critics of the African Renaissance are saying.

5.2. Answering Skeptics

Critics of an African Renaissance have pointed to the prevalence of African dictatorship, and to wars and ethnically determined internal conflicts, which Africans have proved incapable of solving, How can any clear thinking person even dream of, let alone talk of, an African Renaissance, or an economic renewal? It is, of course, precisely for these reasons that we need an African Renaissance. Italy, and later the rest of Europe, achieved much of its greatest cultural development during its renaissance, when violence and war dominated the minds of men. Europe and its culture had suffered the effects of violence, poverty, and the bubonic plague which decimated the population. Now in Africa we have the scourge of HIV/Aids and malaria, in addition to ethnic conflicts.

The more charitable critics of a renaissance in Africa wonder whether, like all ideas dreamed of by so many, it can only be attained by a few. Which is to say that with such a heterogeneously governed continent, in terms of the understanding and behavior of African leaders, perhaps the idea of embracing

146

the whole continent in such a renaissance may be too ambitious. Can some sort of selectivity be applied? After all, Kofi Anan, the United Nations Secretary General, has expressed his deep frustration with the African situation, lamenting the practice of what he termed "military adventurism" by African states. The mere mention of the word Africa, he went on, immediately conjures up in the minds of many people images of a continent in chaos, full of troubles, and, one might add, hopeless. Being an African, Anan must know whereof he speaks, especially considering that the high position he holds as the world's number one international diplomatic and political civil servant.

In so far as the First World characterized the Third World as primitive, savage, and backward, thereby implying that these countries were not developed in terms of culture, religion, and political systems, it was due to both the ignorance and arrogance that is typical of Western writers and intellectuals regarding issues affecting the Third World in general, and Africa in particular. As Mbeki has aptly pointed out, Africa is still perceived in the eyes of the Western world as the home of an unending spiral of anarchy and chaos, at whose unknown end is a dark pit of a complete and unfathomable human disaster. They think that Africa remains as of old, torn by interminable ethnic and other kinds of conflict, unable to solve its problems, condemned to the netherworld.

In fact, many commentators from outside the continent have already begun criticizing the concept of an African Renaissance in precisely these terms. Luke Baker, a white correspondent writing from Johannesburg on 19 October 1998 on "African Renaissance, a continent's rallying cry," thought of it purely as a catch-phrase of the continent that remained ill-defined, despite being bandied about by many, including former South African president, Nelson Mandela. He said that the concept has been taking shape only slowly, despite a gestation period that began in 1994, when the African National Congress (ANC) won South Africa's historic all-race elections, which brought Nelson Mandela to power. Baker concludes that, "to achieve renaissance for Africa will take more than a couple of days of conference brainstorming", not least because, "where politics are concerned Africa is awash in a sea of troubles" (*Daily Nation*, 20 October 1998, Nairobi, p. 6).

This sort of criticism of any initiative launched in Africa by Africans is valuable only when it is constructive and well informed. We in Africa are not so naïve as to imagine that merely by waving a magic wand, the African Renaissance will have come and gone in a matter of months, thus solving instantly all of Africa's endemic and deep-rooted problems. In fact, the criticism lacked intellectual appreciation of the sweeping historical significance of such a gigantic movement. In Europe, the Renaissance covered a period of several hundred years. I am not saying that Africa should also take that long, but certainly we are aware that we are unlikely to achieve the development scenario we want for Africa in less than forty to fifty years. No one is more aware of this than Mbeki himself, who had the following to say:

> Our message to those who come from outside of Africa is that the moment has come when you should suspend your disbelief. Africa is readying itself for growth and development, fuelled by her own efforts and the profitable and safe injection of international private capital. Let us do what we have to do together to achieve the sustained development of Africa (Mbeki 1998, p. 11).

In spite of the above criticisms of anything emanating from the Third World, attitudes have changed considerably in recent years. Both the nature of the imperial powers and the

148

political status of the Third World have changed; the world of today is not that of 1400, or 1750, or 1885, or indeed of 1945, and the terminology has likewise changed. What remains are the differences—differences in the levels of affluence and poverty, development and underdevelopment, between the many independent sovereign nations that now constitute the international community. There are still several worlds and, as noted above, the differences turn largely upon the comparative levels of wealth and poverty. Development is about transforming both economies and societies in ways that diminish this difference without diminishing cultural distinctives.

5.3. The Right Timing—End of the Cold War

The dramatic shaking of the global kaleidoscope that found its *raison d'être* in the cold war, by the collapse of the old Soviet empire and the socialist system as the linchpin of its ideological force of state dirigism and central planning, has constituted a profound political mutation in the world. This has come to mean that the deeply ingrained bloc politics of international affairs has given way to a more pragmatic approach to the conduct of the affairs of nations, in which practical self-interest has superseded mere political theatricals.

A new world order has therefore emerged that requires global mediation and centers for multilateral cooperation whose main objectives would be to contribute to the solution of the relatively new area of ethnic conflicts within nations, as well as conflicts between nations, and promotion of African economic growth, development, and welfare. (See Appendix B: African Institute for Training and Research on Peace)

The collapse of communism in 1989, symbolized by the dismantling of the Berlin Wall, prompted many people in the Western world to greet the event as a triumph of liberalism over collectivism. The battle between these two superpowers, the intense ideological struggle of the second half of the twentieth century, was the underlying justification for the cold war in which the African countries found themselves sandwiched between the protagonists, in spite of their avowed policy of positive neutrality.

As a result of these accelerated historical developments, "the optimists looked forward to the reconstruction of the post-cold war world on Western lines and their incorporation into a Western-led international order." They thought that "a world integrated by trade and democracy would not only soar to unmitigated heights of prosperity but would also realize the nineteenth-century liberal dream of universal peace" (Skidelsky 1996, p. xi).

This ethnocentric view of the world may not necessarily be shared by the African Renaissance Institute, but this is not the place to belabor the point, except to mention that Africans will also devise their own views about the New World Order and how they think they can play their part in ways that are mutually beneficial to everyone.

We in Africa emerged from the cataclysmic changes that the end of the cold war brought about, leaving us even worse off than would otherwise have been the case. In terms of political leadership, we were suddenly left with an inheritance that most African countries are still struggling, with much difficulty, to shake off. The bipolar hegemony of the cold war had produced certain African rulers of countries whose economies, legal systems, and political and social life they had decimated and disfigured by decades of oppression, corruption, ineptitude, and mismanagement. Some of these dictators have departed from the scene in one way or another, but those who came to power after them are still finding their feet, while those who still cling tenaciously to power have found it difficult to change their age-old totalitarian tendencies and to embrace the new political order of multiparty democratic politics. Their underlying mind-set is that of neopatrimonialism.

In other words, at the beginning of the 1990s, history accelerated in such a way as to make the world more than usually contradictory and confusing. One month, nothing but the end of the cold war seemed of any importance; the following month, it seemed that only the eruption of ethnic conflict had any relevance. There was greater peace in some areas, but appalling and worsening violence in others. In some countries there was greater formal democracy, but that did not always mean greater real freedom.

We have witnessed situations in Africa that have developed into an explosion of ethnically determined conflicts, sucking in neighboring African countries. However, as argued throughout this book, the fact that the continent may be engulfed in various kinds of wars does not necessarily mean that the African Renaissance cannot take place; nor does it follow that we in Africa should repeat the mistakes made by war-torn European countries. After all, the European Renaissance occurred during the Middle Ages, long before the Industrial Revolution and modern scientific and techological advances took hold; the hoped-for African Renaissance will be taking place in the twenty-first century.

The prospects, therefore, for the success of an African Renaissance, at this particular time in world history, in the third millennium, are bright, as long as we can address the problem of political leadership in Africa, that is the question of democracy and governance, a subject to which I will revert below. We must be more vigilant than ever and redouble our efforts to ensure that peace reigns among us. Our objective must be to strengthen democracy, good governance, and peace on the continent as an important prerequisite to the success of the African Renaissance. Thabo Mbeki has eloquently addressed this issue in many of his speeches over the last two years.

The collapse of socialism in the Soviet Union and Eastern Europe, effectively ending the cold war, has provided Africa with a unique opportunity to pursue its own agenda for socio-economic transformation and industrialization through trade and investment with the rest of the world, without inviting military interference in its internal domestic affairs from any quarter.

The two superpowers, the U.S.A. and the U.S.S.R., declared the end of the cold war in 1989; Germany was reunified in 1990; and the U.S.S.R. itself broke up into its constituent republics in 1991. Despite this apparent victory for the capitalist side in the cold war, several "proxy" disputes continue as protracted civil or ethnic wars, wreaking havoc on development prospects in countries such as Angola and the former Yugoslavia. It is important to note that if Africa could convince the U.S.A., as the only remaining superpower, and, then, the European Union, as a major economic giant of the New World Order, to support the concept of an African Renaissance and to embrace the continent as their future partner in international economic relations, there would be greater hope for our future.

Many have voiced admiration for the economic success of Japan in the postwar period, and later for the so-called Asian tigers, but we should realize that in the case of the former, its economic success began with the U.S. spending during the Korean War of 1950–53, which was reinforced by the privileged Japanese access to the American market from 1956 onwards, and was given a further boost by the Vietnam war in the mid-1960s.

Having grown up in the shadow of the United States, the most successful East Asian countries by the 1980s included South Korea, Taiwan, Hong Kong, Singapore, Malaysia, Indonesia, the Philippines, and the coastal areas of China. China has now become a dynamic economic area in its own right, a source of inspiration but also of fear to the stagnating West.

While Africa does not want to become a mirror image of Western capitalism, it has the enviable possibility of winning the West in its quest for an African Renaissance. The end of the cold war provides that opportunity. Although we may not completely subscribe to the view that "the failure of communism and all other forms of collectivism [have] vindicated capitalism and political democracy, and ... removed any systematic obstacles to their universal application" (Skidelsky 1996, p. ix), as highly respected Western professors such as John Kenneth Galbraith and Robert Skidelsky confidently claim, we in Africa can and must use our own diplomacy to chart an economic development paradigm that is pragmatically suited to our own social and political conditions.

In other words, we do not have to agree entirely with Professor Skidelsky's view of "the end of Communism, the rolling back of the frontiers of the state, and the globalization of economic intercourse, as the most hopeful turn of the historical screw since 1914" (Skidelsky 1996, p. xiii). Professor Galbraith is perhaps more astute when he said that in the post-1989 world we should no longer be concerned with the search for an alternative economic system, but should concentrate on making more effective and equitable the economic system we have (Galbraith 1992).

The end of the cold war began to manifest itself with a speech that Mikhail Gorbachev, then General Secretary of the Communist Party of the Soviet Union, gave at the U.N. in 1988, when he said, "Our ideal is a world community of states with political systems and foreign policies based on law" (Skidelsky 1996, p. 15). This "ideal" spelt political doom for all whose political systems were based on dictatorship, whether they were of the Eastern, Western, Northern or the Southern type. The communist countries that were formerly under the Russian empire underwent revolutionary upheavals from which many new independent states were born overnight. The speed with which this occurred caught the world unawares, with Africa, as usual, being the least prepared continent.

Not only were the African countries least prepared, but it has taken their "Big Men" and "Strong Men" some time to absorb what happened in the world community and to adjust their political philosophies and international relations accordingly. In fact, whatever little signs of democratic change took place in a few countries proved to be a sham. It is now growing impossible to effect smooth and democratic changes of government in Africa, because most of Africa's "Big Men"and "Strong Men" intend to rule until God calls them home, or until other "Strong Men" emerge on the scene.

We must not forget, however, that there have been shining examples of power changing hands in Africa, and the one most worthy of emulation occurred in South Africa in June 1999. There were also smooth transitions in Tanzania, Botswana, Ghana, Nigeria, and Senegal. Would that the list were longer. Nevertheless, to Africa's critics we can say that although there is war, corruption, and dictatorship in Africa, all is not lost. As we have seen, the European Renaissance was born in an age of violence and anarchy. So, as I and some of our political leaders believe, we in Africa must forge ahead regardless of the difficulties, mindful of the fact that nothing good in this life comes easily.

5.4. Strong Leadership

Even though Azikiwe spoke of "Renascent Africa" in 1938, no one paid any attention, because it was during the Great Depression and the beginning of the Second World War. Similarly, Nkrumah spoke of "Black Renaissance" in the late 1950s and early 1960s, but he spoke at the height of the cold war and the African liberation struggle against colonialism and imperialism. Since the complete liberation of Africa has been achieved, especially after the attainment of democratic and nonracial rule in South Africa in 1994, it has been South Africa's President Thabo Mbeki who has traveled widely, internationally and in Africa, to popularize the idea of the African Renaissance. To him, it has become an article of faith and a dream that encompasses the whole continent of Africa.

For the first time in the history of Africa, Mbeki has attempted to articulate the necessary conditions to facilitate germination and flowering of an African Renaissance in economic terms. Luke Baker wrote in Nairobi's *Daily Nation* that the concept of an African Renaissance is Mbeki's brainchild, and it is true in that no other African leader has so passionately embraced the idea and tried to articulate and popularize it with the intention of revolutionizing thought on a new African economic development paradigm. Also, Mbeki does not think of its application in only one country but throughout the African continent.

If an African Renaissance is to be successful, we must not just engage in euphoric rhetoric, but put into action pragmatic measures on a long-term basis that will enable us to achieve practical results. Africa is already fortunate in having both Mbeki and Mandela to champion and spearhead this movement. South Africa, as the most powerful country in Africa economically and militarily, can speak on behalf of the continent. Any great idea or movement requires a reputable and important godfather to push it, popularize it and place it on the national and international economic political agenda.

In the early 1960s, at the time when most African countries attained their political independence, the notion of African socialism flourished, and most prominent nationalist leaders throughout the continent espoused some variant of it. The leading advocates of this ideology were Kwame Nkrumah, who put forward his own variant of African socialism in the

155

form of what he termed "philosophical consciencism"; Julius Nyerere, whose version of African socialism was the most developed, as elucidated in the Arusha Declaration on African Socialism; Kenneth Kaunda, who attempted to evolve a more coherent worldview through the humanist philosophy that endeavored to bring together strands of capitalist, populist, and socialist views into one eclectic framework; and finally, Modibo Keita, to name only the most prominent among them.

These leaders are mentioned merely to indicate that at every point in the history of a people, a leader or a group of leaders emerge who, by the force of their own personality and providentially endowed vision, take it upon themselves to guide the rest. They have the gift of inspirational and courageous leadership. There is no attempt to analyze their contribution to thought in this instance, but merely to draw attention to the impetus behind the African Renaissance, namely, that every great movement requires great leaders.

For centuries prior to the great upheaval of the Second World War, it was the countries of Europe and those established by European immigrants that monopolized the starring roles on the historical stage, i.e., according to Western texts other countries appeared in small supporting roles as causes of European rivalry or as areas of European conquest. Since 1945, however, the most significant change in the nature of world history has been the emergence onto center stage of the countries that Europe once eclipsed, which are now beginning to assume important and often determining roles.

In the latter half of the twentieth century, most major social and political upheavals have taken place in what has been variously known as the East, the Middle East, the South, the "Colonial World" and the Third World. The independence of India, the revolution in China, war in Korea, revolution in Cuba, war in Vietnam, the question of Palestine, the end of apartheid in South Africa, and war in the Gulf are some of the events that have dominated postwar international relations, apart, of course, from the cold war itself. From the African standpoint, and even from the standpoint of the Third World as a whole, the end of apartheid in South Africa and the emergence of that country in 1994 as a nonracial, united, democratic state was in itself an event of major historic significance.

That Nelson Mandela, the man who spent twenty-seven years in prison and who became the focus of an extraordinary worldwide campaign of solidarity against apartheid and a unique symbol of resistance and liberation in Africa, survived to lead his nation was an event of even greater historic proportions. It is in this context that the leaders of South Africa have become so important when any one of them is inspired by the vision to lead Africa into the ranks of the technologically developed nations. The rest of the world, and Africa in particular, should not begrudge the leaders of South Africa the decision to blaze the trail of the African Renaissance, just as Nkrumah, Nyerere, and Kaunda did in the case of African socialism and humanism.

It is the continent of Africa as a whole that has captured Mbeki's heart and imagination like Nkrumah before him. In this he has the unflinching support of a leader of an almost equally powerful African country, President Olusegun Obasanjo of Nigeria, Yoweri Museveni of Uganda, Joachim Chisano of Mozambique, as well as Prime Minister Melez Zenawi of Ethiopia, to mention only four. The former secretary general of the geopolitical body in Africa, the Organization of African Unity, Dr. Salim Ahmed Salim, has thrown his weight behind the idea of the African Renaissance, as has the executive secretary of the Economic Commission for Africa, Amoako.

In his address at the launching of the African Renaissance Institute (ARI) at the Presidential Guest House in Pretoria, South Africa, on 11 October 1999, President Mbeki referred to a shared vision of African unity and solidarity, of African eco-

nomic development and renewal, and the need now for returning this vision to the peoples of Africa so as to initiate a popular
movement for the African Renaissance (see Appendix A). This
movement would, in his view, embrace all political organizations and governments throughout the continent, as well as
the continent's intelligentsia, professionals, traditional leaders,
business people, trade unions, women, youth, cultural workers, and media specialists, and "bring them into the popular
struggle for Africa's rebirth."

President Mbeki believes that the conditions for Africa's
rebirth and renewal now exist, so that the continent can be
transformed with the change "from a dream dreamt by vision-
aries to a practical program of action for revolutionaries."
Three political conditions now favor an African Renaissance:
First, completion of the liquidation of the colonial system in all
of Africa, as exemplified by the recent liberation of South
Africa; second, bankruptcy of neocolonialism, which is today
widely recognized by the peoples of Africa, including the middle strata; and, third, the reduced jostling among the hitherto
major powers for spheres of influence in Africa, as a result of
the end of the cold war, and the accelerating process of
globalization.

In this context, President Mbeki believes that the continent shares a common destiny, having created and hosted leading centers of learning, the arts, and technology in ancient
times; but having, in more recent times, experienced various
epochs of trauma, "each one of which has pushed her peoples
deeper into poverty and backwardness" (Quoted from
Mbeki's unpublished speech given in Pretoria at the inaugura-
tion of the ARI, 11 October 1999). Slavery robbed the continent of its healthiest and most productive inhabitants;
imperialism and colonialism led to the rape of Africa's natural
resources, and the destruction of traditional agriculture and
domestic food security. Neocolonialism led to the perpetua-

tion of a global economy in which Africa was a subservient participant; the emergence of new national elites who joined the dominant global forces to exploit the continent, thriving on the looting of national wealth and the entrenchment of corruption; and the growth of an impossible international debt burden that is unlikely to be repaid in the foreseeable future.

President Mbeki's view, which Olusegun Obasanjo of the newly democratic Nigeria and the ARI Council of Elders supported wholeheartedly, is that the task of the ARI derives from the experience of these epochs of social and economic trauma.

The intellectual and political commitment to the idea of an African Renaissance received encouragement and a tremendous boost in a speech that Mbeki delivered in Cape Town on 8 May 1996 to the South African Parliament on the occasion of the adoption of South Africa's 1996 Constitution. Speaking at that time in his capacity as deputy president, that is before becoming president, and also on behalf of the African National Congress (the presidency of which he subsequently assumed in December 1997), Mbeki's speech was entitled, "I am an African" (Hadland and Rantao 1999, pp. 153–158). Here he expounded for the first time the concept of an African Renaissance—a concept that was intended to give concrete expression and philosophical, sociopolitical direction to the idea of a rainbow nation, and one that envisaged the unleashing of energy and creativity in South Africa, as well as a new vitality for the whole continent.

What is novel and encouraging about Mbeki's idea of an African Renaissance is that, like Kwame Nkrumah almost four decades before him, he sees it as an unequivocal reinforcement of South Africa's commitment with regard to the establishment of genuine and stable democracies throughout the continent. In this speech, Mbeki emerges as a leader who passionately believes in the rule of law and in human rights. He believes in the dignity of the individual and thoroughly abhors the idea that one person can have superiority of force over another, whereby the stronger appropriates to themselves the prerogative even to annul the precept that God created all men and women in His image, making them equal and endowing them with certain inalienable rights, including life, liberty, and the pursuit of happiness.

In a further political image of the African Renaissance, Mbeki envisages an Africa where the governed are free from fear—the fear of oppression of one national group by another, the fear of the disempowerment of one social echelon by another, the fear of tyranny, and most importantly the fear of the use of state power to deny anyone their fundamental human rights.

Mbeki makes it abundantly clear that there can be no African economic renewal or rebirth in a situation where a rapacious oligarchy brooks no obstacle in its quest for self-enrichment, seeking to benefit from the vulnerability of children, of the disabled, and of the elderly—an oligarchy that believes in the conscious and systematic oppression of other human beings. It is axiomatic that human existence itself demands that freedom of the individual must be a necessary condition for that human existence.

In April 1997, exactly a year after his "I am an African" speech to the South African Parliament in Cape Town, Mbeki gave another significant speech to the Corporate Council summit at Chantilly, Virginia, in the U.S.A. on the subject "Attracting capital to Africa." It is in this speech that he articulated his economic philosophy for an African Renaissance. He painted a vivid picture of a new Africa where genuine and stable democracies would be established, and where systems of governance will flourish because they derive their authority and legitimacy from the will of the people.

Significantly, Mbeki was not intending to extol only African virtues and successes; his purpose was to recognize and condemn its failures, pointing out that the new political order he envisaged must owe its existence to the African experience of many decades that taught us, as Africans, that one-party states and military governments will not work, that the way forward must be informed by what is, after all, common to all African traditions, that "the people must govern". It is rare in African politics for a leader to candidly admit our mistakes. That is why the continent has produced so many dictators and mediocre leaders but so few statesmen. With his detailed and highly significant vision of a future Africa, Thabo Mbeki set the stage for African thinkers and intellectuals to translate these ideas into a pragmatic development program.

5.5. Natural Resources

Africa, with 11.5 million square miles, is the world's second largest continent, exceeded in area only by Asia. Its population at around 650 million, although growing at a high rate, is still much smaller than that of Asia and China.

Africa's physical geography is very different from any other continent, and its mineral resources are varied and plentiful, especially at the southern end of the continent. As an essential component of its industrial development, the West has relied on many of these minerals for centuries. Moreover, some are vital for today's high-tech sector. The most significant, relative to total world production, are gold, diamonds (industrial grade and gemstones), and cobalt; followed by platinum, chrome, manganese, phosphates, uranium, copper, bauxite, and iron ore. Fossil fuels (oil, coal, and gas) are also significant, and it is likely that further extensive reserves will still be surveyed and exploited in several countries, including Sudan, DRC, Angola, Togo, Chad, Central African Republic, Rwanda, and Burundi. That is why Africa is referred to as a "virgin" continent, because most of its wealth still lies beneath the surface of the soil and has hardly been explored at all.

In terms of agricultural production, there are still large areas of Africa that are virtually untouched in terms of harnessing their agricultural and economic potential, especially through irrigation. There are obvious examples: the Sudd regional basin in the Southern Sudan, with massive opportunities represented by the Nile waters (White Nile) flowing through the area; and central DRC, with the potential of the rain forests. In this connection too, although Africa lacks irrigable plains in most regions as compared with Asia, in many areas Africa has the advantage of volcanic soils that contain many fertile levels.

Another area in which Africa has the greatest potential, as compared with other regions of the world is hydroelectricity. There is potential for many varied large and small hydroelectric schemes, especially in the more mountainous parts of the continent: for example, dams and hydroelectric power generation from the waters of the Blue Nile in the Ethiopian highlands before they run down into Sudan, smaller schemes in the hills of Western Rwanda, and in the Rwenzori mountains in Western Uganda. In the DRC, however, many larger-scale projects could be established. For many years, there has been much talk about the Inga Dam on the Congo River. It has been estimated that the hydroelectric potential of this dam could be enormous and could have far-reaching implications for African economic development. In fact, this is a project that should be at the heart of the African Renaissance program.

As for plant varieties and farming systems, Africa has an extraordinary variety of food crops. According to Stefan Padulosi, head of the Under-utilized Food Crops section of the International Plant Genetics Institute in Rome, although we know of 1000 edible food crops in India and 1100 in North America, Ghana, alone, has 2500! This is only one small country in Africa; just imagine what the whole continent may hold. These are not only potentially vital for short-term food security, but will provide a crucial resource for genetic engineering applications in the long-term (*New Scientist*, 2 September 2000, p. 43). In addition, there are a large number of plants with medicinal qualities as yet not properly studied and with unrealized potential.

Tourism and ecotourism are other areas that still have substantial earning capacity from visitors from Northern Hemisphere and from Asian countries that have become affluent in the last twenty years. This is not, however, the place to expand on this subject in great detail.

We shall go on to look at the type of policies Africa should adopt, in the context of the world's dwindling resources, to achieve economic growth and development spurred by the Renaissance motivation. Africa undoubtedly possesses potential in its land, rivers, water and mineral resources that can contribute to both an agricultural and an industrial revolution.

6

Renaissance as Reality: Policies for Success

6.1. Development Strategies

We have seen from World Bank statistics that almost the whole continent of Africa falls in the low-income category. So the hope of Africa depends on its ability to raise the standard of living of its people through economic growth. In order to do so, Africa must choose an economic strategy suited to its particular situation and needs. Although there is no model that can be universally applied to the great variety of subjective and objective conditions existing in different African countries, the economic development experience—both successes and failures—may perhaps yield a number of concrete variables that countries could use to formulate their own economic strategies.

In this chapter we are concerned with the meaning of the words "economic growth" in the African context, and the sort of appropriate policies that an African Renaissance can and should adopt to ensure its success. We will consider policies concerning science and technology, natural resources, agriculture, livestock and fisheries, and, since peace is a prerequisite for the success of all other policies, mechanisms for conflict resolution and prevention will also be addressed. Finally, we will discuss political and regional strategies.

6.2. Advancing Science and Technology

6.2.1. A New Economic Growth Paradigm
The only way that Africa can break away from reliance on primary commodity exports is to adopt a policy of science and technology-led development. Technological developments of this nature, accompanied by major transformations in the organization of production, have taken place throughout the world apart from Africa. Knowledge-intensive rather than materials-intensive industries are setting the pace, with traditional raw materials being substituted on an increasing scale by synthetics, and even the production of raw materials being based to a greater extent on knowledge-intensive techniques.

This does not imply that countries should ignore the production of raw materials when they have a competitive advantage, but it does mean that governments and the business community will have to pay careful attention to selecting new technologies appropriate to maximizing productivity and increasing the local value-added components of all exports. This can only happen, however, within an economic integration context where markets are large and economies of scale, which will facilitate restructuring at a higher level of efficiency and productivity, are certain to be realized and exploited.

In other words, the Renaissance should enable Africa, as a contribution to the solution of its development problematique, to reduce its historical dependence on the industrialized

166

Western world that has done nothing but further compound its economic disadvantage. This will require the adoption of innovative and knowledge-intensive approaches at all levels of the production process by harnessing science and technology in the service of economic growth.

There is no doubt that Africa needs to adopt a new paradigm for long-term and sustainable growth. That economic growth paradigm can only last and become a motive power for the advancement of the African if it is both compelling and intimately touches the African mind and soul. Consequently, to facilitate the flow of technological innovations that might flow from problem-solving research and development in the natural sciences, any economic growth paradigm must be tempered by an equally creative social dispensation leading to social innovation, so as to enable the African to pursue his or her development in a multidimensional manner. Such a socio-cultural transformation is critical to the long-term vigor of African economic development; and the latter will certainly be strengthened by the readmission of science as a principal component of African culture.

Capacity building in science-led development—in terms of human capital development, institutional strengthening, and functional enhancement—has become a new imperative for the economic growth of countries of the Southern Hemisphere, and particularly so in Africa, where institutional and human capacity are still comparatively small and fragile. Building the capacity to select, to adapt, and to apply known technologies from abroad, as well as the capacity to develop new and relevant technologies and processes, has become a key element in Southern strategies to acquire a competitive chance to play in the international marketplace and to build a viable domestic foundation in economic and social development.

6.2.2. Role of ARI

To a large extent, the success of Africa's economic renewal and development, both in the medium and long term, will hinge on two factors, namely: utilization and integration of science and technology in the economic growth process, and attention to the question of governance and peace on the continent. As to the former, we have recommended that the African Renaissance Institute work closely with the African Foundation for Research and Development (AFRAND) (see Appendix C). The rationale for the establishing of AFRAND was to provide an enduring resource base for sustaining development-oriented research and development (R & D) in Africa. It is vital that ARI ensures that AFRAND operates as an effective, independent, Africa-wide scientific and technological research and development organization, dedicated to delivering in a timely manner the tasks for which it has been established. For an African Renaissance to succeed, the results of R & D in Africa must be transformed into the continent's obligatory technological products and services. These must be demand driven.

As a further support and practical amplification of the idea of establishing mechanisms for creating an interface between science and industry, the South Commission, which had been working under the chairmanship of Julius Nyerere, in its final report (*The Challenge to the South*, The South Center, 1990: Geneva, Switzerland, foreword by J.K. Nyerere) made useful and specific recommendations with regard to science-driven development. The report recommended the need for African scientists, backed by advanced research facilities, to enable African countries to develop technologies suited to their needs and factor endowments. It is only in this way that Africa will be able to transform its production system through the utilization of knowledge-intensive techniques of production. In other words, a shift is required in the pattern of production and exports from raw materials to processed ones, and, within the latter, to products with high R & D intensity, in order to counteract the adverse consequences of decline in the prices of Africa's commodities and primary products, including oil and minerals.

The Committee of Ten of the African Development Bank (ADB), in its final report (28 March 1989) to the board of governors on specific priority areas in which the ADB needed to concentrate the financial resources of its lending program in order to avert Africa's economic decline and power economic growth, mentioned science and technology as one key area for development:

> As we approach the closing years of this century, and usher in the twenty-first century, the pace of scientific discoveries and technological innovations continues to accelerate. Africa has no choice but to join this progress; otherwise, the technological gap between its fellow members in the rapidly changing order of ranking of the developing countries, will widen to an embarrassing degree. (*The African Foundation for Research and Development: A Strategic Framework for Implementation*, p. 14: Randforum Press, Nairobi, 1994)

The committee further recommended that the African Development Bank take the leadership role in the task of creating a science and technology environment for social and economic development: by ensuring that issues of appropriateness and specificity of technologies are considered in its lending policies; by promoting programs and project activities that will stimulate the expansion of the Africa-specific knowledge base in those problem areas crucial to national and regional growth; by expanding and improving the human and institutional infrastructure for scientific discoveries and their application in developing problem-solving technologies; and by encouraging a continuing interaction between this infrastructure and the geopolitical community in Africa.

The most important and primary role of the African Renaissance Institute now and in the coming years is to gather a critical mass of first-class African scientists and to give them large enough grants on a continuing basis, as well as sufficient infrastructure, to enable them to undertake meaningful problem-solving R & D applied to industrial production that will lead to really important results of economic dimensions. This will make it possible for African research to feed directly into the growth process through technological application and utilization, thereby ensuring the incorporation of sound and relevant science and technology to national economic development.

The African Renaissance Institute will ensure linkage of basic and applied research, so that research results are immediately and directly translated into new technologies, new processes, new solutions to socioeconomic problems, and full utilization of the scientific and technological infrastructure of the national and regional systems to reach these goals. This strategic approach will embrace the circulation of knowledge used to conduct feasibility or marketing studies and to manage varied services such as transportation and distribution, including mastery of the criteria for evaluating and selecting from among numerous technological alternatives—the kinds of specialized knowledge needed to engineer designs or construct plants and the skills required to market these innovative products and services demanded by the market, both domestic and external.

This is a growth model in which governmental decision-makers, engineers, scientific researchers, technological designers and developers, as well as entrepreneurs involved in deciding what is to be produced, and marketers who are responsible for eventual sales of the product, must all be constantly in touch with each other in a process of continual consultation. Companies must have access to, and have influence on, university research workers and technicians. Conversely, government planners must be able to influence the election of strategic technologies manufacturers will use. No group should be in an ivory tower by itself.

The model's underlying image is best expressed as a triangle, a geometric figure with three interconnected vertices. One vertex represents scientific researchers, technologists, designers and developers; the second, financiers and entrepreneurs, including those responsible for production and marketing; and the third, governmental policy, geopolitical and geoeconomic leadership and similar decision-makers. Each vertex must be linked by a flow of information with the other two; unless circulating information links all elements of the triangle, there can be no sound incorporation of science and technology into national economic growth.

The science-led paradigm should move Africa into the global scene as an industrial producer and marketer. To facilitate such a move, Africa must take three strategic steps: first to mobilize its existing scientific and technical manpower worldwide; second, to harness all its entrepreneurial skills and to reorientate them towards demand-driven production and marketing, and, third, to develop a strong partnership between the government and the private sector as a necessary step towards empowerment.

In emphasizing the need that Africa fully embrace and implement a science-led development, Professor Thomas R. Odhiambo has pointed out that this can only happen

> when planned steps are taken to, first, create a culture of excellence and relevance in R & D and, second, foster an environment and program for capacity building in research and effective application of these

171

R & D results into demand-driven and market-oriented technologies. (*The African Foundation for Research and Development: Rationale and Program Priorities*, Randforum Press, Nairobi, 1994, p. 3).

The president of the International Planned Parenthood Federation, Mrs. Arabai Wadia, stated it well on accepting the Third World Prize for her organization in 1987:

Those countries which became independent in Asia and Africa after the Second World War are still in the process of entering the mainstream of modern scientific age... Their empowerment has to come now through science and technology, but so utilized, as to enhance their human as well as material capital, whilst retaining their own distinctive ethos. (Ibid., p. 1)

6.2.3. Developing Human Resources

The stark reality of the strategic framework for African science and technology is its impoverished state in terms of its institutional and educational capacity. There are few centers of excellence in Africa demonstrating a virile work ethic and an effective program of development-oriented R & D. As a result of the brain drain, most of the continent's brilliant scientists and scholars live outside the continent; and the frayed and fragile university system is failing badly in the task of raising a new generation of talented and dedicated R & D specialists. The continent's unnatural dependence on foreign financial support for its R & D work, has led to a trend in agenda-setting alien to the best long-term interests of the African people.

Let us now look at what can be done to stem the brain drain. The migration of scientists, engineers, doctors, economists, and other highly trained professionals from African countries to other states in the world, particularly to Britain and France as the former colonial powers and to other European countries and the U.S.A. and Canada, has reached enormous proportions. Indeed, it has become a major crisis, threatening the very viability and sustainability of the social and economic development of the continent, particularly in a world dominated by science, whose economic growth is driven largely by technology.

Even though expatriate specialists can, to some extent and for a limited period of time, substitute for this brain drain, they certainly cannot contend, in the long run, with those vital issues of creating a competitive edge to the continent's overall productive and marketing enterprise. When, therefore, we examine the question of the brain drain from Africa, we must look at it in the context of education and human resource development, a program that the ARI has given top priority. Most economists are agreed that it is a nation's human resources, not its financial capital or its material resources, that ultimately determine the character and pace of its economic and social development. For example, according to the late Professor Harbison of Princeton University:

> Human resources constitute the ultimate basis of wealth of nations. Capital and natural resources are passive factors of production; human beings are the active agents who accumulate capital, exploit natural resources, build social, economic and political organizations, and carry forward national development. Clearly, a country which is unable to develop the skills and knowledge of its people and to utilize them effectively in the national economy will be unable to develop anything else. (Todaro 1987, p. 325; Harbison 1973, p. 3)

173

No country in the world has proven the above statement to be more correct than Singapore, South Korea, and Japan. Peter Large has written the following about Singapore:

> Singapore holds the richest asset for success in the post-industrial world—the asset of having nothing: no long-standing heavy industry to deaden its itch for change; no rich raw material resources, like North Sea Oil, to provide a treacherous cushion. Singapore's only exports that spring from its natural resources are goldfish and orchids...Therefore, it depends starkly for the 1990s and beyond on what the Singapore establishment calls the "brain industries"—on how its 2.5 million people, crammed on an island smaller than the Isle of Man, succeed in selling their skills and services to the rest of their region and then to the world. (See *Asia's New Industrial World*, Methuen, London, 1985, p. 39)

So, what can Africa do in precise terms, within the framework of the ARI, and in cooperation with African governments and the international bilateral and multilateral financial institutions and governments, to turn the tide of the devastating phenomenon of the brain drain? What the continent must put in place—and there is no institution better placed as a coordinating mechanism than ARI—is a set of policies and mechanisms that can ensure the achievement of at least three goals:

- Establishing and nurturing of a geopolitical climate and legal framework that will enhance the incentive of those resident in Africa to continue to work and live on the continent, while at the same time attracting those now living abroad to contribute to its social development and economic growth.

174

- Establishing an institutional channel for those wishing to contribute to economic development and growth, to be readily and deliberately encouraged to do so, without necessarily insisting that they renounce their adopted citizenship or residence in order to do so.
- Establishing of a database containing continuously up-dated profiles of African high-level professionals and entrepreneurs living outside Africa, those living as refugees within the continent, as well as key entities of the productive sector—whether they be enterprises, institutions, or programs—that require the services of such distressed and expatriate scholars from Africa (DESSA), so as to enable them to reach their individual targets in the context of Africa's science-led development paradigm.

Between 1976 and 1982, when I was chief of Economic Cooperation Among Developing Countries in the United Nations Industrial Development Organization (UNIDO) in Vienna, I set up a program in conjunction with the United Nations Development Program (UNDP) in New York that aimed to alleviate and/or reverse the brain drain from the Third World, and especially from Africa. The program was known as the Transfer of Knowledge and Technology of Expatriate Nationals (TOKTEN) from high-income countries to the poorest countries. The UNDP assisted this program through its section that was responsible for Technical Cooperation Among Developing countries (TCDC).

I believe that ARI and UNDP, could jointly undertake or resuscitate this program in order to help reverse the brain drain from Africa. This would be a momentous event in Africa's long search for a constellation of instruments that will jump-start the continent's economic development in a sustainable and productive manner. Through its Council of Elders, the ARI could help create and nurture a geopolitical and geoeconomic environment that would enable entrepreneurship and technological innovation to flourish and promote the emergence of an Africa-based and home-grown scientific community as well as a concomitant realization that a science-led development paradigm is a key element in fuelling Africa's long-range economic development. Africa's human capital worldwide, and its interactive linkages with the entrepreneurial and end-user demands on the continent on the one hand, and the R & D innovation capacities on the other, are pivotal to this new science-led economic growth paradigm.

The ARI should therefore put in place a long-term program for the mobilization of Africa's cross-sectoral brainpower resources for productive engagement in Africa's social and economic development. The specially-sought brain drain human capital embraces R & D specialists, engineers, technologists, designers, entrepreneurs, financial and banking experts, industrialists, marketers, business and enterprise managers, policy specialists, economists, planners, social and community workers, institutional managers and administrators, venture capitalists, and other key professionals. Such sustained mobilization and concomitant utilization should be undertaken, coordinated, and regularly evaluated under the auspices of the ARI, always in close cooperation with (i) the policy and administrative organs of African governments; (ii) selected academic research institutions on the continent that can productively utilize the high-level personnel mobilized under the brain drain referral scheme; (iii) enterprises in the productive and service sectors in Africa that can profitably utilize such recovered entrepreneurs and professionals; (iv) selected institutions and enterprises within the diaspora zones that are willing to work in partnership with ARI for internship, or under cooperative exchange programs, or within a joint venture arrangement ; and (v) international organizations already involved directly with parts of the brain-drain reversal initiative, such as the African Capacity Building Foundation (ACBF), the UNDP, the UNHCR, the UNECA, the International Organization for Migration (IOM), and the International Federation of Red Cross and Red Crescent Societies.

This multifaceted approach will require that ARI concludes cooperation agreements with all relevant institutions and enterprises and a memorandum of agreement with each of the African states, allowing for cross-border movement, permitting the establishment of safe havens, and enabling recruitment and utilization of these talents in a transparent manner for short, once only, or periodic tenures.

ARI has prepared three projects that are the key instruments for meeting the needs of mobilizing and utilizing African talents and skills, in the context of the brain-drain phenomenon, for Africa's long-range and durable economic development. These projects will be presented to and discussed with the relevant multilateral and bilateral financial institutions for possible collaborative assistance.

As one of its main priority areas, ARI has elected human resource development, because Africa lacks a critical mass of innovative scientists and technologists who are motivated to create new opportunities for productive engagement. It has a dearth of first-rate entrepreneurs with managerial skills capable of mobilizing their nation's human and material resources into productive enterprises, for, above all, African states desperately need the kind of leadership, at the head-of-state level, that recognizes and drives forward science and technology as the key element for society's transformation.

6.2.4. Case Study: of India

Perhaps one of the greatest Third World leaders, who, though not a scientist himself, did more than any of his contemporaries to promote and to inculcate the culture of science in his country was Jawaharlal Pandit Nehru, prime minister of India from independence in 1947 to his death in 1964. Science had a profound influence on expanding Nehru's intellectual horizon and on his vision of history. He saw science primarily as an instrument to combat poverty and economic subjection and to free the mind from superstition, irrational fear, and the attitude of helplessness.

One of his great contributions to Indian history was to utilize science and technology for economic development and the quest for self-reliance. While he devoted all his energy to the rapid industrialization of his country, to making every effort to set up new plants and factories, he was not entirely happy that this should be done with foreign assistance, by foreign consultants, and with foreign technology. He believed, quite rightly, that operating a particular plant set up with foreign assistance did not make the country an industrially advanced nation any more than using a car or flying an airplane purchased from abroad makes one capable of designing and manufacturing them.

Nehru believed passionately that only when a country has acquired the ability to design, fabricate and erect its own plants without foreign assistance would it become truly advanced and industrialized; and to achieve this objective, much greater development of science and technology was still necessary: "We have to produce not only machines that are to be used, we want men who will design machines and improve them. There must be creativeness." (*Nehru and Science*, Nehru Center, Bombay, 1975)

In one of his most important speeches as Prime Minister, Nehru stated the following:

> Science has developed at an ever-increasing pace since the beginning of the century so that the gap between

the advanced and backward countries has widened more. It is only by adopting the most vigorous measures and by putting forward our utmost effort into the development of science that we can bridge the gap. It is an inherent obligation of a great country like India, with its traditions of scholarship and original thinking and its great cultural heritage, to participate fully in the march of science, which is probably mankind's greatest enterprise today. (*Nehru and Science*, 1975, Nehru Center, Bombay, p. 22).

It is our firm hope and belief that an African Renaissance will bring forth an African Nehru in this regard. Africa has produced leaders of outstanding international stature and caliber, and names such as Nelson Mandela, Julius Nyerere and Kwame Nkrumah come easily to mind. Africa badly needs a political statesman who will take it upon himself or herself to champion the cause of science and technology as a necessary condition for Africa's economic recovery, in the same way that Thabo Mbeki has given leadership and impetus to the wider cause of the African Renaissance.

Of course, one does not have to be a scientist to champion the cause of science; Nehru was not a scientist, but his studies and interests encompassed a wide field: economics, sociology, history, technology, science, politics, and international relations. It stands to his credit that he was the first national leader of independent India to assert the capacity of science to promote the advancement of life for everyone. It was he who granted official recognition of the importance of science in the economy of the country and took positive steps to find and promote centers of scientific research. He promoted the study of nuclear science, not only to impart a touch of modernity to the nation as a whole, but to tap an inexhaustible source of cheap and abundant energy, that would on its own connote rapid national progress.

179

6.2.5. Science-led Development Initiatives

Although science is the cultural element that affects us most deeply, to some extent even against our wishes; yet, during Africa's dark age over the last 500 years, it was drummed into the minds of Africans that science was alien to their heritage, and that they might well find it impossible to realign their thought processes into acceptance of the scientific method or even to engage in theoretical thinking. Such musings are contrary to the considerable experiential knowledge that Africa has accumulated in crop production, the manufacture of textiles and ceramics, the study of astronomy from ancient times, and other areas of human scientific endeavor over the millennia. Consequently, Africa must get on with the reintegration of science and technology into everyday life and business.

It is encouraging, however, that Articles 51–53, establishing the African Economic Community, signed at Abuja, Nigeria, in June 1991, addressed in a strong, all-embracing relevant manner, the importance of Africa's science-led development. According to Article 51, member states shall:

> strengthen scientific and technological capabilities in order to bring about the socioeconomic transformation required to improve the quality of life of their population, particularly that of the rural populations; and that, in doing so, they shall reduce their dependence and promote their individual and collective technological self-reliance; while at the same time strengthen existing scientific research institutions and, where they do not exist, establish new institutions.

Article 52 requires that member states "shall take all necessary measures to prepare and implement joint scientific research and technological development programs." Article 49, on industrial development, requests member states to "facilitate the establishment of the African multinational enterprises and encourage and give financial and technical support to African entrepreneurs." (Article 49f). The main problem is that such resolutions passed in the OAU fora have had no practical meaning because no sooner are they passed than they are forgotten and left to gather dust in the archives and libraries of the world.

The Lagos Plan of Action, which was meant to enable African countries to achieve self-reliance primarily through industrialization, and to establish an African Common Market by the year 2000, was adopted in Lagos, Nigeria, in April 1980 by the heads of state of the OAU, but was later discarded in 1985. By again adopting the Abuja Treaty eleven years later on exactly the same issues, the OAU had done nothing new except to move the goalposts established at Lagos.

We believe the African Renaissance will make a difference this time. Africans and their leaders will have to be taught to be more serious about the implementation of resolutions which they are so fond of passing during their annual gatherings. The age of state protocols, banquets, the playing of national anthems and the rolling out of red carpets, should now be over, or greatly de-emphasized. If we want the world to take us seriously, we must first of all take ourselves seriously. The habit of the annual OAU summits of investing huge sums of money on protocol and the purchase of expensive Mercedes Benz cars for two or three-day use by heads of state and their entourage would be justified if these meetings achieved something concrete and tangible for Africa. It would be interesting to evaluate the practical and concrete achievements of the OAU summits since its inception in 1963, in relation to the huge costs and expenditures incurred. The fact that the Lagos Plan of Action was abandoned midway, before its implementation, should provide an object lesson for the possible fate of the Abuja Treaty also.

As indicated in the discussion above, the adoption of an

economic growth paradigm that places science and technology at the center of an African Renaissance is the only way of ensuring that in the next few decades we shall witness significant achievements in the economic and social regeneration of Africa. The poverty of our people, which has reduced us to beggars in the international financial centers of the Western world, will begin to disappear.

We must not allow the world to think that Africans want to depend on charitable handouts forever—that is, if there is anything at all to be handed out. We cannot, after all, ourselves be the major cause of capital flight from our countries and then go around the world, cup in hand, begging for aid and asking for debt forgiveness. We give Western politicians the opportunity and excuse to engage in constructing massive and harebrained schemes ostensibly aimed at bailing out Africa from its economic predicament. All this is done in spite of our wealth!

Science is, among its other attributes, an economic force that, together with land, labor, capital, and managerial capacity, significantly contributes to the economic growth and social development of nations. It is precisely because science is given high priority in countries of the North that they have been able to lead in industry and social welfare and to enjoy an optimistic vision for the future. The deepening economic disparity between countries of the South and those of the North is now acknowledged to be caused by the lack of a culture of science-inspired creativity and technological innovation linked to the entrepreneurial enterprise. The African continent is hit harder by this crisis than any other low-income region for a number of historical, geopolitical, geoeconomic, and international trade reasons. The crisis has become a monumental challenge to the survival and long-term economic development of the African people within a global context.

The above statements about the importance of science and technology in the African growth paradigm needs to be underpinned by further practical suggestions on what could be done to make it happen. Africa still has advantages, because scientists will go wherever there are unique opportunities. Since the continent has a high degree of biodiversity, unique natural resources like the tropical rain forests, and also a range of diseases not found elsewhere in the world, Western scientists would find it a fertile ground for their work.

However, scientists usually need first-class research facilities, and yet at the moment there is serious, in fact chronic, underinvestment in physical facilities such as laboratories, equipment, and materials required for scientific research in the universities and research institutes. It is not, however, just the shortage of equipment, but also the absence of the kinds of back-up facilities required to maintain high-tech equipment in good working order. This sort of infrastructure support is just as important as the equipment itself.

Another problem that Africa faces and needs to address urgently is the severe underinvestment in training scientists. Related to this is the fact that when a few African scientists return to their countries after training in the West, many of them go into senior government positions and stop doing leading-edge scientific work.

This is where Africa's partners in the international financial community could really make a significant impact with technical and financial help. For instance, they could make a long-term commitment to training, and providing technical support, for science and technology development. This will require political support from Western leaders at the highest levels. Chapter 7 points out the importance of the Millennium African Recovery Plan (MAP) to the African leaders, which they are currently discussing with leaders of the G8 as well as with the heads of the World Bank and the International Monetary Fund. Science and technology is one of the priority subjects. African political leaders have realized, not only within the

183

context of the African Renaissance movement, but also in endorsing a resolution of the Non-Aligned Movement Summit in Durban, South Africa, in September 1998, that they must give a high priority in their national budgets to science and technology development. In view of the importance of this statement as a major policy instrument of the Non-Aligned Movement, we quote part of it here:

> while the per capita income of the 24 richest countries is about 60 times that of the 50 poorest countries, the science and technology expenditures of the former are 250 times greater than that of the latter. The OECD countries account for 85 percent of total world R & D expenditure on science and technology. The narrowing of this gap must, therefore, be a major objective of the countries of the South and an issue of the highest priority in any agenda of the South. (See *Elements for An Agenda of the South*, Report of the Ad Hoc Panel of Economists of the Non-Aligned Movement—NAM—presented to the Twelfth NAM Summit, Durban, South Africa, September, 1998. Published by the South Center, Chemin du Champ-d'Anier 17, 1211 Geneva, Switzerland, April 1999, p. 37).

This is easier said than done. African countries must take practical action, through their domestic budgets, to allocate a substantial portion of funds to promote R & D in particular. They should also negotiate with the European Union to set up a "framework project" for science development in Africa which could bring about substantial and sustained investment in facilities and in the training of African scientists. African countries must bear in mind that scientific and technological capability, including the all-important human resource capacity, grows in many ways, through national actions, through South–South cooperation, and above all through a variety of interactions between Africa and the West. International trade, foreign direct investment, facilities for education, advanced studies, work experience, links between centers of research and learning, arrangements for the purchase and sale of innovations and intellectual property, are among the multiple channels through which scientific and technological advances are developed and disseminated across national boundaries.

It is, therefore, most important for the African countries to realize that science and technology cannot be developed in Africa or by Africans in isolation, given the global interdependence in modern scientific progress. Technical progress seems to rely on a great deal of networking amongst high-level scientists, crossing all national and international boundaries. Any attempt, therefore, to tackle Africa's technical and technological problems through science must stress the importance of effective communication channels with scientists in Asia, Latin America, and Western countries.

6.3. Utilizing Natural Resources

6.3.1. Mineral Resources

In the history of economic renewal and development, the role of a country's natural resources cannot be overemphasized. Agriculture and minerals are the mainstay of most African economies and also the foundation for their future economic development. Since Africa has valuable mineral resources, it is vital that effective policies be adopted with regard to the means of ore production and beneficiation. Science and technology can play a crucial role here in enabling African mineral products to be exported in a more highly processed form with a high value-added content.

A large proportion of Africa's mineral exports is in the form of raw materials, such as iron ore, which we then re-import as processed iron and steel at many times the price of our exports. Why should this be so? In fact it need not be if we could only adopt an economic growth paradigm that is science- and technology-led and combine it with a policy of strategic man-power development in key industrial sectors. In fact, Africa's thrust towards industrialization could be spearheaded by the establishment of core industries, based on the continent's access to the requisite raw materials and factor inputs.

The vulnerability of a state dependent on minerals is nowhere better illustrated than in Sierra Leone, where, after forty years of operation, iron-ore mining ceased abruptly in 1975, leaving thousands of people unemployed and, in the words of the former President Siaka Stevens, "with not a token of development in the whole of the mining areas." (See a *Report of a Joint UNIDO, UNCTAD, FAO Inter-Regional Report On Economic Cooperation Between Sierra Leone and Liberia*, Geneva, 1971). Even the railways that had served the iron-ore mines were ripped up. Worse still, mining develop-ment had had a negative effect on the formerly rich agricultural sector, not least because diamonds in Sierra Leone are found in alluvial deposits, and thousands of people try their luck legally and illegally. Once a net exporter of its staple diet, rice, the country now has to import virtually everything. The mineral failure not surprisingly led to a major economic crisis, and the only way out seems to be more of the same—underground mining of a kimberlite diamond pipe. In fact, the civil war in Sierra Leone is closely linked to the struggle for the control of its diamonds. This is, however, not a subject for discussion here.

6.3.2 Hydroelectric Power
Let us now consider one source of energy that could be of crucial importantance, if fully exploited, in advancing Africa along the

path of industrial development, namely, hydroelectric power.

In Ghana, Kwame Nkrumah conceived and relentlessly pushed for the construction of the Akosombo Dam in the teeth of Western opposition at the height of the cold war. The World Bank argued that it was a costly white elephant and was therefore a waste of funds. Later it transpired that hostility to the project stemmed from the fact that the West did not like Nkrumah's political philosophy of nonalignment and Pan-Africanism, and also that Nkrumah made it quite clear that he considered the dam to be the basis of Ghana's push towards industrial take-off to self-sustained growth. In fact, even American companies, one of which won the tender to build the dam, vouchsafed for the project's economic viability.

Note that the dams at Kariba, Owen Falls and Cabora Bassa, proposed by the white colonial regimes, did not encounter the same kind of hostility. That is why we must hope that the idea of an African Renaissance will not be blindly opposed by the West simply because it is an African idea being implemented by Africans.

As yet there are only two rivers, the Nile and South Africa's Orange River, that have been the subject of fully coordinated development plans. The importance of the Nile in the whole framework of an African Renaissance cannot be overemphasized, for harnessing the waters of the Nile has vast economic, social, political, and even military implications for many countries through which its waters flow and whose livelihood it supports. Although a lot has been achieved through dams and pump irrigation schemes, much remains to be done before the Nile's resources are fully utilized by the countries that should benefit.

There is, therefore, a great and urgent need for Nile river basin planning to be undertaken, with international initiatives to avoid future conflict that could arise if one or two countries perceive their vital interests to be threatened. The situation might be made even more dangerous if countries that are more advanced technologically are better able to utilize the Nile resources, while those less advanced feel at a disadvantage, with all the socioeconomic and political tensions such a situation implies. Here, through early-warning, cooperation, and coordination, the African Renaissance Institute can play a pivotal mediating role. For example, it has been said that, had the Nile's Gezira irrigation scheme succeeded, with the fertility of the soil covered by the scheme, Sudan could easily have become the bread-basket of the whole of Africa and the Middle East. Perhaps the ARI could be the vehicle to sensitize the world community to support and revive the project. The Sudan government and the United Nations Food and Agriculture Organization have made extensive studies of this project, as have the Egyptian and British governments.

6.3.3. Global Perspectives

The need for global support for an African Renaissance could not have been made more eloquently than in Lester R. Brown's article, "The Acceleration of History." Brown writes that the world economy has been growing at an exceedingly fast rate, from an output of $4 trillion in 1950 to $20 trillion in 1995, and that has meant an intolerably huge squeeze on the world's available resources. What is more, the newly industrializing countries of East Asia have learnt to utilize the past experience of the Western countries that developed before them, especially in the area of science and technology, to achieve high rates of economic growth that averaged about 8 percent per annum for a long period of time. From 1991 to 1995, the Chinese economy is believed to have grown by a staggering 57 percent, raising the per capita income of 1.2 billion people by more than half! (See the International Monetary Fund's publication entitled; *World Economic Outlook*, May 1995.) As Brown says:

The pace of change in our world is speeding up,

188

accelerating to the point where it threatens to over-whelm the management capacity of political leaders. This acceleration of history comes not only from advancing technology, but also from unprecedented world population growth, even faster economic growth, and the increasingly frequent collisions between expanding human demands and the limits of the earth's natural systems. (Brown 1996, p. 3).

He goes on to postulate that as world population has dou-bled since the mid-twentieth century, and the global economy quintupled in size, the demand for natural resources has grown at a phenomenal rate. Since 1950, the need for grain has near-ly tripled. Consumption of seafood has increased more than four times. Water use has tripled. Demand for the principal rangeland products, beef and mutton, has also tripled since 1950. Firewood demand has tripled, lumber demand more than doubled, and paper consumption has increased sixfold. The burning of fossil fuels has increased nearly fourfold, and carbon emissions have risen accordingly.

In other words, the demand for firewood, lumber, and paper is overwhelming the sustainable yield of forests in many countries. With the earth's capacity to fix atmospheric carbon dioxide (CO_2) more or less unchanged, the rise in fossil fuel use and carbon emissions has upset the natural balance, push-ing CO_2 levels higher each year. As this happens, average tem-peratures are also rising, altering the earth's climate. No one knows what the long-term consequences will be, but it has been suggested that the history of the next few decades will be defined by food, specifically by rising prices of both land-based and oceanic food products, by a spreading politics of food scarcity, and by an increasing intense struggle to achieve a sus-tainable balance between food and people (Brown 1996, ibid).

The problem of environmental degradation will continue

189

to be crucial in the realization of an African Renaissance. Moreover, the sheer weight of authoritative scientific evidence now commands attention of governments and the public alike. Moreover, with globalization has come new recognition of our shared responsibility for stronger institutions to regulate the global commons. Global warming, the loss of biodiversity, and other problems related to the global commons are slowly being recognized as problems that the community of nations must take on collectively and that, if left unattended, will worsen as the planet becomes more crowded and development increases resource utilization. This constitutes a major shift in development perspective, even though the implications of environmental change continue to be hotly contested.

For instance, Andrew Goudie, has written about this problem in the following terms:

Current forecasts indicate that in the year 2100 carbon dioxide concentrations will reach 600 parts per million (ppm)—two to three times the level in 1750. Average temperatures could rise by some 2 degrees Celsius from now. This projection continues to be disputed, however, because the variability of climate over the eons, driven by little-understood natural mechanisms, is well documented. Still in the realm of scientific conjecture are the severity of weather fluctuations in a warming world, the global distribution of the effects of warming on agriculture and living conditions, and the extent of adaptation to warming. Although higher carbon dioxide concentration might enhance plant growth and will certainly increase the efficiency of water use, changes in tissue chemistry will render plants less palatable, and heat and water stress on vegetation will offset some of the gains from increased carbon dioxide. (Goudie 1977;

see also Vitousek 1997, p. 496)

Although these are complex scientific issues, Africans must also understand them because global climate change will affect us all. Although an international scientific consensus has yet to emerge, and that is probably why the Bush administration which came to power in 2001 refused to sign the Kyoto Treaty, we Africans must watch the debate very carefully and press America to join the rest of humankind and sign. Warnings of impending global food shortages and environmental catastrophes have frequently been voiced, but thus far, these have not materialized, perhaps because technological ingenuity will enable humankind to sustain economic growth indefinitely. Nevertheless, the magnitude of demographic change that will be telescoped into the next two decades and the certainty that the world will become warmer, lose biodiversity, and push against the limits of the resource envelope are deeply worrisome.

The spiraling human demands for resources, it is alleged, are beginning to outgrow the capacity of the earth's natural systems. As this happens, the global economy is damaging the foundation on which it rests. Evidence of the damage to the earth's ecological infrastructure takes the form of collapsing fisheries, falling water tables, shrinking forests, eroding soils, dying lakes, crop-withering heat waves, and disappearing species. Evolution has prepared us to compete with other species, to survive, and to multiply; but it has not equipped us well either to understand or to deal with the threat we pose to ourselves with the uncontrolled growth in our numbers. We are at a loss to grasp the meaning of adding 90 million people annually, year after year, until we are faced with firewood shortages, water scarcity, and rising seafood prices. We have not yet learned how to stabilize our demands within the sustainable boundaries of the earth's ecosystems. This doomsday scenario for our present world concludes by pointing out that the slow down in the grain harvest in the face of increasing demand has been occasioned by three factors: a gradual decline in grainland area since 1981; little or no growth in irrigation water supplies since 1990; and a decline in world fertilizer use since 1989.

The views expressed above were published by the Worldwatch Institute in its "State of the World" publication in 1996 (Brown 1996, pp. 3–16) on progress towards a sustainable society. Summarizing some of Lester Brown's pertinent arguments regarding the world economic situation simply highlights how he completely ignores Africa. In fact, he writes as though Africa never existed. This is not to deny the fact that some of the problems he enumerates actually exist in Africa. They may, of course, but not in such a highly exaggerated form. We have found advice on African affairs from non-Africans more often than not lacks the proper balance and perspective. This is simply because the writers lack a deep understanding of the African ethos. When, for instance, Brown writes about world agriculture, food production, both land and sea-based, and environmental degradation, he does not accurately reflect the African situation, either from ignorance or lack of interest.

A main area of concern for an African Renaissance is the type of policy options in development terms that can be used to achieve economic renewal and recovery, bearing in mind that up to now the theories of economic development advanced primarily by non-African writers, intellectuals and economists have failed to address the "African development problematique" which is explored in Chapter 4. In fact, the World Bank announced early in February 1999 that because improvements in technology in the West and the increased use of synthetics, the prices of raw materials and commodities from Africa have fallen by over 50 percent in real terms! This situation is likely to be permanent, the World Bank adds. Unfortunately, prices for manufactured products and capital input on Africa's imports for its modernization or economic development programs continue to increase year in and year out. If Africa's earnings from its raw material and commodity exports are its only source of foreign exchange for the import of industrial inputs, then an African Renaissance will continue to be in grave jeopardy. The situation needs to be addressed urgently.

6.4. Increasing Agricultural Production

6.4.1. Agriculture and Development

The African economy is characterized by its large sector of low-productivity labor, opportunities for land-use intensification, and the possibility of addressing both input and output market imperfections—all of which create the potential for increases in production in one sector, with knock-on effects for the growth of other sectors. Agriculture forms the largest sector of most African economies, relative to the other nonagricultural sectors, and it is known that the faster agriculture grows, the faster its relative size declines. The essence of agricultural growth and its causal relationship to the structural transformation and aggregate growth of an economy is quite evident, from both theoretical and empirical historical evidence.

The growth of agriculture laid the firm foundation for industrialization in most high-income countries in the world, which in turn led to broader economic development. Agriculture has proved to have a great potential for accelerated economic growth. This suggestion arises from the historically proven concept that technologies capable of increasing agricultural production can also defeat the growth-restricting effect of a rising population, even where the land area is fixed, which is not quite the case with Africa.

This, however, implies a relationship rooted in Engel's law,

193

whereby the proportion of total expenditure on food declines with rising income, even while total food consumption and the proportion of expenditure on important subclasses of food increases. The underlying assumption here is that agriculture is a large component of most economies in their early stages of development. To achieve structural transformation in such economies, it is necessary to increase agricultural income and expenditure and rapidly increase labor productivity in agriculture, which will further accelerate structural change in the employment distribution of the labor force. Production can also be boosted by introducing methods of highly input-intensive farming, coupled with innovative technologies and injections of capital and equipment. As a result, both farming income and farmer demand for industrial products increase.

This growth in domestic markets also enables industrialists to develop export markets. At the same time, the export of unprocessed and processed agricultural products has helped many countries that have adopted such a strategy to earn foreign exchange. This foreign exchange is used to purchase the machinery and equipment required for industrial development, and industry receives further capital through transfers from agriculture through a number of taxation measures.

This economic strategy of first stimulating agricultural growth and then using the resources of agriculture to aid in industrial development is in striking contrast to methods often employed by low-income countries. The pattern has been to squeeze agriculture for all it was worth, without upgrading production technologies and investing in scientific-technological R & D. The outcome of such an approach is invariably an imbalance in economic development. Despite the fact that such policies may succeed in expanding industrial production and then gradually moving from import-substitution industries to manufacturing industries for export, and finally to capital-intensive heavy industry, a number of problems usually emerge as a result of stagnation in the agricultural sector, for which solutions must still be found.

For instance, if such a policy succeeds in producing initially rapid development of industry and commerce, there will be a growing shortage of food products to meet the increased demand for food from the industrial labor force. Rising food prices then lead to rising wage levels, which chokes off industrial growth. The shortage of foreign exchange makes it difficult to meet the growing demand for food imports. These are the problems facing some of the newly industrialized countries in Asia and Latin America, and they cannot be resolved without a clear understanding of the role of agriculture in industrialization.

The policy implications of the above analysis are that we now know that the disciplined and structured organization of human ingenuity and accumulated scientific knowledge accelerate technological change applied to agriculture beyond the rate of population growth. Productivity is further increased by the specialization made possible by reduced transaction costs and expanding trade. Increased trade and rising incomes make it possible to change the composition of output and thereby to boost productivity still further. These forces in combination move agricultural growth toward the upper reaches.

Technological change that increases output per unit of input in Africa's massive agricultural sector could boost national income substantially, and thereby hasten economic transformation and the shift to the potentially faster-growing industrial and service sectors. Conversely, if technological change begins in the smaller nonagricultural sector, it will have to proceed at a much higher rate than in the agricultural sector to achieve the same effect on national income. Moreover, in view of the great diversity of the nonagricultural sector, it may be more difficult to achieve accelerated technological change across the entire sector than it would be in agriculture. Africa must therefore adopt a policy of "building up industry through agriculture", and using industry to develop agriculture in order to attain a balanced development of both.

Agriculture can make three major contributions to a country's economic development. First, it can satisfy increased demand for agricultural products created by the rapid growth of both the economy and the population. This can serve to stabilize food prices and keep wages low. Second, it can provide the labor that the industrial sector needs to proceed with economic development. It is axiomatic that as agriculture becomes more developed through improved seed varieties, increased fertilizer use and farm mechanization, it releases a significant proportion of its labor force to be redeployed in other sectors, particularly the industrial and mining sectors. Third, it can provide a portion of capital needed for industrialization, through production of an agricultural surplus that can be exported to earn the foreign exchange required for purchase of the necessary capital equipment and industrial raw materials.

The development of agriculture can be accelerated by a realistic land reform program that would have the effect of greatly increasing access to land for rural households and of reducing farmland rents by a significant percentage, releasing public land for farming, and transferring land to the "tiller." However, landowners losing land through compulsory purchase orders must receive reasonable and adequate compensation for their losses. By adopting this procedure any possible resistance to such a policy can be reduced to a minimum, and land can be smoothly transferred into the hands of those who can best use it. Once farmers are able to enjoy the full fruits of their labors, their motivation to increase production will rise considerably.

The above discussion has focused on agriculture as the leading economic sector serving as an engine of growth, and this means that science and technology should focus on that sector as the biggest industry in Africa. As in India, the priority must be to apply science and technology to increasing agricultural production and processing. This also means that there must be an increased focus on improved crop varieties, animal husbandry, disease control in crops and animals, and weed control. It should be noted the experience in India which we have cited above, was made possible because the donors played a key role in providing the educated specialists necessary for the green revolution to take place. America offered large numbers of scholarships in the agricultural sciences to Indians and Pakistanis throughout the 1950s and 1960s. Returning to their respective countries, these scientists planned the research facilities to provide necessary support for the green revolution when it came in the 1960s and 1970s.

On this important question of increasing agricultural productivity, we in Africa will have to work closely with the donor/creditor community, especially from the West, in order to realize our objectives, for we need them to play a critical role in supporting and facilitating an African Renaissance. We must, however, be careful to ensure that we tell the West exactly what we want from them and how. We would not like the imposition of ideas that are unacceptable to us and that could distract us from our declared African objectives. Since we have noted above that our focus will be on science and technology as an instrument for improving agriculture, this suggests that training African personnel is a key role the West should play.

A study by Wye College in the UK has argued that perhaps the most important role for Western countries is to help in the training and support of high caliber scientists from Africa to increase land and labor productivity in agriculture and to reduce unit costs of production. This involves training in management as well as in science to sustain institutional capacity, to produce a detailed policy framework, and to ensure adequate production management and marketing expertize.

The heart of this training program must lie in the provision of scholarships for postgraduate study, with special scholarships for women and further opportunities for education through distance learning. In addition to the periods of formal education, a key role for Western academic institutions is to ensure adequate professional follow-up support for an extensive period after formal training has been completed. This enables scientists, often working in relatively remote regions in Africa to maintain close links with colleagues in Western universities and scientific institutions, to keep abreast of the latest scientific developments, and to feel a part of a wider network of professionals. While Western governments must make funding available to their own universities, they should clearly earmark funding for these training and support programs and for implementing an African Renaissance. (Wye College, University of London, African Development Unit, Department of Agricultural Economics, *The Revival of African Agriculture: Training and Sustaining Skilled Manpower*, a report to Citytrust, October 1986). Other important roles for donors are the improving of urban and rural infrastructure to assist with input and output marketing, establishing modern telecommunications systems, irrigation systems, both large and small, and helping to alleviate international debt.

6.4.2. Food and Nutritional Security

It should be evident from the above discussion that, with the adoption of appropriate policies, the achievement of an African Renaissance and economic renewal would not be out of our reach. The food and nutritional crisis in Africa need not continue. Through an African Renaissance, we must, as a matter of urgency, develop a realistic strategic agenda to achieve basic food and nutritional security in Africa as soon as possible.

In fact, the colonial legacy for Africa, in terms of agriculture, has made the situation even worse, because it left the continent dependent on the export of a few cash crops, such as coffee, tea, cocoa and tobacco, which are really nonessential to the domestic population from a nutritional and dietary perspective. They are merely beverages, produced by many similarly low-income countries, that suffer from having only a slowly increasing demand on the world market. They do not form a sound basis for nutritional security.

The current statistics on Africa show that 60–70 percent of sub-Saharan Africans are malnourished; close to 200 million of them are facing starvation. As we enter the third millennium, one out of every two Africans will be eating imported food. Not too long ago a Zambian farmer needed to produce one bag of maize to buy three cotton shirts. Today, he can hardly buy one shirt with the same bag of maize. This is the sad commentary on the state of affairs in modern-day Africa.

Agricultural production, which increased at an annual average growth rate of 2.9 percent (still low by normal standards and in the light of a rate of population increase of over 3 percent per annum) in the sixties, immediately after most African countries gained independence, has dropped to a negative growth rate of minus 2.4 percent in the 1990s. Hence Africa, which was a net exporter of food in the 1960s, is now a net importer. More and more people go to bed hungry every day. Surely, then, it is not a wonder that socioeconomic insecurity and political instability are the order of the day?

Africans must not continue exhibiting televised misery and starvation to the Western World in the hope that they will gain sympathy and pity. The donor is tired. African hunger is an African problem; it can and will only be solved by an African solution. The reality is that food security is not just a production and supply issue. It relates to income as well as to the purchasing power of the people. About 200 million people in sub-Saharan Africa do not have enough income for a minimum calorie diet that would prevent serious health risks. About 370 million people do not have enough income for the diet that is required for an active life. The largest number of these people are located in arid zones. Therefore the reality is that the hungry African has the common characteristics of poverty. The poor cannot produce enough to pay for marketed food; the food and nutritional security problem in Africa cannot be addressed in isolation from the issue of poverty.

The African people eat cereals and root crops, and depend on fish and livestock. Advances in science and technology have been extremely influential in developing high-producing varieties and genotypes of many of these commodities. That is the success of the green revolution in South Asia. Performance in Africa has, however, been variable. Southern Africa has done extremely well in maize production, but this is not true of West and Central Africa, which have tended to do better in root and tuber crops.

The performance of livestock as a food source has always been rather poor. In the last five years of the 1990s meat, milk and egg production has not grown at the targeted rate of 4 percent per annum. Africa now imports more of these animal products, at a price that the average African person cannot afford.

The total production of inland and marine fish has increased by some 29 percent since 1985. The total production is now estimated at 4.6 million metric tons, with about 40 percent ascribed to our inland waters such as Lake Victoria. Regional analysis of these statistics indicates that West, North, and East Africa have done reasonably well. However, this is not the case with Central and South Africa. It is apparent that agricultural development in Africa has really not done as well as other regions of the world. African agriculture is a minuscule 0.6 percent of total world production.

There is also an associated problem. The consumption of traditional crops such as millet, sorghum, peas, roots, and tubers has been in steady decline. This is part of the legacy of the colonial era. Research indicates that traditional crops have high nutritional value. Millet, for example, is quite close to wheat in its protein and carbohydrate content. It is easily storable and transportable and can be milled and packed. The same is true of soya beans and cow-ghee. These traditional foods are easily produced in Africa, and they resist harsh conditions such as drought. African people have been discouraged from producing them, brainwashed into growing instead foreign-demanded crops less essential for human survival. This is part of the reason why in Uganda bananas replaced finger millet as food crop; bananas were perennial, requiring less labor for planting, cultivating and harvesting, and hence labor could be released to grow foreign-demanded cash crops such as coffee and tea.

It takes three units of edible weight of matoke to provide the energy in calories given by only one unit of millet. The protein comparison is even more dramatic. It takes eight units of edible weight of matoke to provide the same protein as that of one unit of millet. Mass starvation in Africa will be averted when the economy is reoriented in such a way that traditional food production is given the emphasis it deserves.

Inappropriate action on national and international policies has been a further constraint on delivering food and nutritional security. African leaders have met several times and agreed on resolutions touching on issues of food security, such as the Lagos Plan of Action in 1980 and the International Conference on Nutrition in 1993. Most of the strategies needed to move Africa from chronic food crisis to accelerated food production are in all these resolutions. The problem is one of commitment; the prescriptions are never implemented or utilized. When there is no commitment to address these issues, even if adequate research and development is achieved, hunger will continue to persist. African governments should start listening and acting on the advice of their own institutions and experts.

This time we are determined, more than ever before, that an African Renaissance will make a difference. Within the next five years, Africa must establish appropriate agroindustrial development policies to attain a minimum growth target of 6 percent per annum in food and agricultural production. The industrial sector should also grow at a minimum rate of 8–10 percent per annum because this is the sector that traditionally is not only the largest labor absorber, and therefore the largest provider of new employment, but also the sector that is usually responsive to economies of scale. The growth multiplier is usually bigger in the industrial than the agricultural sector. With Africa's population still growing at close to 3 percent per annum, it means that within the next three decades African food needs will triple. Per capita arable land will also fall dramatically. Unless an African Renaissance succeeds, Africa will surely die.

We would like, however, to add a word of caution here about African agriculture. It is difficult to come up with a single set of policy prescriptions for agriculture, although we may have seemed to do that above, due to the extraordinary variation in land quality, rainfall, irrigation potential, population diversity, and availability of alternative employment opportunities in other sectors. Moreover, there are few "quick fixes" for raising agricultural production in Africa, except where market liberalization and "getting prices right" still offer potential for each crop in each region.

The key to achieving growth in African agriculture must lie in raising factor (land, labor) productivity, and this involves taking at least three appropriate policy steps. First, we must build adaptive research capacity. Developing the necessary trained manpower, as noted above in the case of science and technology, is a painfully slow business. In Africa today there is still a chronic shortage of trained agricultural scientists, and still an absence of long-term commitment by the donors to fill this deficit. Second, this adaptive research is the key to developing "packages" of improved inputs and farm management practices, including the use of chemical fertilizers that dramatically increase yields. These "packages" should be specific for each crop in each region. Third, this research is also the key to export crop performance, so that Africa ends its international market share loss to Latin American and Asian countries, by lowering unit production costs and identifying new markets.

With respect to fertilizers specifically, it is probably worth adding that sub-Saharan Africa has by far the lowest application in the world per hectare of arable land. For example, in 1999 the total fertilizer use in sub-Saharan Africa was only 1.3 million metric tonnes, as compared with India's 18.4 million metric tonnes (source: the website of the Food and Agriculture Organization of the United Nations at http://apps.fao.org). There is, therefore, a great need to increase the use of chemical fertilizers in conjunction with a variety of policies that promote soil conservation and farm management techniques. The other key issues are fertilizer pricing, subsidies and distribution policies, where short-term gains in levels of use, and hence in levels of production per hectare, are possible.

In the final analysis, the importance of agriculture in economic development derives from the sort of growth linkages that will accrue from it to the other sectors of the economy. As smaller farmers earn more money for their agricultural products, they spend it on the kinds of goods that have high labor content. For example these goods include products such as milk, eggs, and vegetables and also industrial products such as radios, bicycles, soap, and cooking oils that can be manufactured locally in many parts of Africa. This, then, creates an increase in employment in the manufacturing sector and therefore leads to a further increase in the demand for food. If this increase in the demand for food is not to increase food prices and to choke off the virtuous circle of increased employment, it is vital that improved crop varieties become available, and there is increased use of fertilizers and improved systems of water control for farming. In contrast, when very large-scale farmers have some increase in their income, they will spend that additional income largely on imported goods, like Mercedes Benz cars, imported clothing, and luxury goods for their houses, foreign travel, and so on.

6.4.3. Fisheries

With regard to fishery production, Lester Brown has sounded the following warning:

> By 1989, all oceanic fisheries were being fished at or beyond capacity. ...As long as there were more fish in the sea than anyone could hope to catch, managing fisheries was a simple matter of deciding how much to invest in trawlers to satisfy any given level of seafood demand. Now that the demand for seafood exceeds the sustainable yield of fisheries, those managing this resource must determine what the sustainable yield of a fishery is, negotiate the distribution of that catch among the competing interests, and then enforce adherence to the quotas established. Where fisheries are shared among countries, as is often the case, the process becomes infinitely more complex. (Brown 1996, p. 5).

The above quotation shows a dramatic comparison between Africa and Europe in so far as food production is concerned. The complex process mentioned above refers to cod "wars" between Norwegian and Icelandic ships, and other fishing conflicts, such as those between Canada and Spain over turbot off Canada's eastern coast, between China and the Marshall Islands in Micronesia, between Argentina and Taiwan over Falkland Island fisheries, and between Indonesia and the Philippines in the Celebes. Greenpeace describes "tuna wars in the north-east Atlantic, crab wars in the North Pacific, squid wars in the south-west Atlantic, salmon wars in the North Pacific, and pollock wars in the Sea of Okhotsk." Although these disputes only rarely make world news, they are now almost a daily occurrence. Historians may record more fishery conflicts in these parts of the world during one year in the 1990s than during the entire nineteenth century. (Brown 1996, p. 5).

This last point speaks volumes for Africa. We have not yet reached a situation where African nations have gone to war over exploitation and utilization of their sea-based resources. Perhaps this is because we are still in the situation where Europe and North America were in the nineteenth century. Perhaps not, but what is certain is that in Africa we still have abundant sea-based natural resources, but the technology available for their exploitation is still so primitive and limited in application that their areas of operational activities are still very much circumscribed—unless, of course, African waters are invaded by the huge Russian and Japanese trawlers that operated off the east coast of Mozambique to exploit its offshore fisheries in the 1970s and 1980s.

6.4.4. ARI's Agriculture Policies

The above example has been given in order to demonstrate that in Africa there is still plenty of economic space and possibilities for recovery and renewal, in spite of population growth, environmental degradation, and myriad other problems that have bedeviled the development of Western civilization. We must, of course, be careful in Africa not to repeat the same mistakes the industrialized countries have committed. Nonetheless, our own economic development must proceed, and we believe that rational and judicious application of the advances in science and technology to exploit resources such as our abundant fisheries in our seas, lakes, and rivers can be, and should be, vigorously pursued as a matter of policy.

In this regard, the ARI must have clear policies on technology and investment that can exploit these resources. In Africa we can still look at technology as a means of creating new wealth and as an instrument allowing its owners to exercise social control in various forms. We have not yet reached the stage where technology relates directly to patterns of alienation characteristic of affluent societies.

We would like to suggest, that the ARI should adopt, as a matter of policy, a development strategy that will address the following specific issues:

- Review and compile relevant policies that are needed at national, regional, and Africa-wide levels. These policies need to address general agricultural development and the promotion of sectors that support agriculture such as agroindustries.
- Identification of environmental conservation strategies that will continue to preserve our natural resource base.
- Changes in the African food consumption patterns, with due emphasis on traditional food crops.
- Addressing other related issues, such as marketing and food storage, capacity building in agriculture, and demographic issues.

6.5. Preventing and Resolving Conflicts

Conflicts have always existed in human societies. What changes over time are the sources of conflicts, the forms that conflicts take according to available arms technologies, and the types of parties involved in conflict, such as tribes, ethnic groups, racial minorities, and states. Finally, conflict behavior changes too. It depends on the culture, the political system, and the socioeco-

nomic system of society. In the post-cold war era we have witnessed the amazing mushrooming and proliferation of ethnically determined conflicts around the world, in particular in
the Third World, with Africa leading the field.

The ethnic conflicts in the former Yugoslavia (i.e., in
Bosnia-Hercegovina, Croatia, Kosovo-Macedonia) and Africa
are clear indications that internal tensions that were sub-
merged and/or suppressed during the East–West superpower
rivalry, have now been brought to the surface and, in the
course of these tensions, whole ethnic and religious communities are trying to assert their own identities. Already, more than
sixty wars identified by the end of 1994 have been violent
interethnic conflicts, and few of them interstate wars.

The end of the cold war in 1989 also ushered in a new
international political and economic system known as
globalization. After the fall of the Berlin Wall it replaced the
cold war as the defining international system with its own
structure of power. This new system has led to widening hori-
zons, greater international interdependence, and increased
awareness of happenings beyond the confines of the community and the nation. It has, therefore, spurred a parallel tendency
towards localization, which in this particular context means
crystallization of local or ethnic identities that is, in part, a reaction to globalism.

Localization represents a demand for greater political, fiscal, and administrative autonomy in a post-cold war geopolitical environment in which the pull of centrifugal forces on the
state has grown much stronger. The assertion of identity and
the demand for autonomy are tied to an upsurge of participatory politics that has given many people a voice and provided foci
for organization. In other words, it requires effective decentralization that must respond to the specific attributes of the country and local communities not only in political terms but in
economic, fiscal, and administrative terms as well. In fact, the

recent emergence of economic regions in many countries constituting linked industrial clusters that have exploited powerful agglomeration economies to enter a virtuous circle of development are clear manifestations of the new doctrine of localization also. California's Silicon Valley and Italy's North-eastern Emilia Romagna region are the most famous examples, but they are being joined by many others in India and China (Cooke and Morgan 1998, Porter 1998, Scott 1976).

Professor Joseph Stiglitz of Stanford University and formerly chief economist and senior vice-president of the World Bank, and Shahid Yusuf, research manager in the Development Economics Research Group of the World Bank, have defined this important phenomenon of localization in the following terms:

> Localization was already in the horizon in the late 1980s. Since then, it has moved towards the foreground. Localization is not exclusively a result of a change in the international political climate; in many countries it stems from acute dissatisfaction with the central government's ability to maintain law and order and to fulfil its promise to raise income, increase the number of jobs, and provide public services. Ethnic divisions, widening regional income disparities, and deepening inequalities between skilled and unskilled workers have at times fanned the discontent, while the rise of national political activity has opened avenues for articulating demands for local autonomy. (Meier et al. 2001, p. 237)

The proliferation of new states over the past decade has provided strong evidence of centrifugal forces. The cases of former Yugoslavia and Soviet Union and states in central Europe are clear examples. Both the increasingly violent protests in parts of

Indonesia in late 1999 as well as the votes in Scotland and Wales for devolution point to a declining faith in the capacity of central governments to deliver high-quality public services, to promote sustainable economic growth, and distribute the benefits of such growth equitably. Furthermore, improvements in communications technologies have made it easier for local activists to create and, more importantly, organize dissent. Though it is an individual country's political decision, the devolution of power to local or subnational entities is now widespread.

The greatest problem and pity in Africa is that the majority of African leaders are still so enamored with power that they not only stick to the enormous political power that they currently enjoy but want to accumulate even more of it. Too much power not only acts as an aphrodisiac, but it provides those leaders in Africa who wield it with a blank check with which to steal from the coffers of the state with impunity. This is really the scourge of Africa, and management of globalization and localization will be a central challenge for all countries—industrial and developing alike—during the coming decades. For many African countries this is compounded by the fact that central governments or states have never faced such comprehensive demands to cede power and resources, even though in many instances local politicians and civil servants may not have the administrative experience to match their aspirations. Furthermore, even the most embryonic institutional framework has yet to materialize to reconcile the competing demands of disparate elements in society; so strong is the sentiment for local autonomy that discontented regions are seeking to secede in ever greater numbers.

It has been calculated that "since 1990 on average 3.1 new nations were born each year, compared to the previous thirty years where on average the number of new nations grew by only 2.2 per annum." (Enriquez 1999, pp. 30–50). Our contention here is that we Africans must try to understand how the interplay of these local political dynamics and global forces is transforming the development landscape, raising new questions for the development agenda and altering the scope and effectiveness of policy alternatives. In some countries, China, Germany, and Italy for example, prosperous provinces or regions are increasingly reluctant to finance transfers to poorer regions of the country. In Africa, we have Nigeria and Sudan, as both countries contend with problems of sharing of oil revenues between regions in their south and north. That is why managing of ethnic conflicts in Africa in the coming decades will have a great effect on the success of the Renaissance movement as we will spell out below.

While during the European Renaissance there were many wars of this nature, we believe that Africa must do everything possible not only to reduce these wars in its midst, but to eradicate them completely if an African Renaissance is to have a good chance of succeeding. In view of the above reasons, there have been widespread discussions in Africa as to whether the already-existing international mechanisms for conflict prevention, resolution, and management are adequate to handle the task. At the moment we have the following mechanisms and procedures in mind: The Organization of African Unity's Mechanism for Conflict Prevention, Management, and Resolution (otherwise known as the Central Organ), established by the Assembly of Heads of State and Government of the OAU in Cairo, Egypt, in June 1993; and the United Nations Security Council.

Apart from these two international bodies, there are numerous *ad hoc* mediating missions by individual African Heads of State in certain conflict situations that have so far failed to yield any fruitful results. There were also efforts by Julius Nyerere to mediate the Burundi crisis between 1995 and his death in 1999, but the talks between the conflicting parties did not yield any fruit despite the economic sanctions that the

210

East African Community's member states imposed on the country. These sanctions were removed in January 1999 following recommendations of the U.N. Security Council.

In view of the failures of the above institutions to bring peace to Africa thus far, should we not return to the drawing board and thoroughly examine the need to establish a more private and independent mechanism for this purpose? A meeting held in Addis Ababa, Ethiopia, in January 1999, and hosted by the Central Organ, and also a meeting at the All-Africa Conference on African Principles of Conflict Resolution and Reconciliation held in November 1999 at the United Nations Economic Commission for Africa's headquarters, recommended the establishment of the African Institute for Training and Research on Peace (AITROP). (See Appendix B)

The need to establish AITROP is further reinforced by the fact that there is practically no training place for the next generation of Africans to whom the current internationally renowned African mediators and peacemakers can bequeath their knowledge and experience. Lack of capacity-building is why Africa has lagged behind in practically every sphere of development; capacity building of this nature should not be the exclusive preserve of the Western world. Africa has already proved that it can also produce its own peacemakers of the same caliber as Henry Kissinger and Jimmy Carter. What is even more important, the area of peacemaking and preventive diplomacy is a new field of activity in international relations and will require further study and research from an African perspective, without interference from any quarter.

It would be immensely helpful if the international community could support African mediators in playing leading roles in conflict prevention, management, and resolution, and in peacemaking, peace-keeping, and peace-building in Africa. Dr. Salim Ahmed Salim, former secretary general of the OAU, has said often enough that Africans should determine the conditions under which it is helpful to have the international community engage in conflict-resolution efforts. What we envisage is the involvement and utilization of African elder statesmen, within the context of the newly-established Council of Elders of the ARI, working as Nyerere did and as Mandela later continued to do, in Burundi.

A typical example where there has been some confusion of role between Western and African initiatives is in the horn of Africa, as Lionel Cliffe has mentioned: "Ethiopia has in fact sought to exploit confusion between whether specific initiatives have been by the OAU or the U.S." The OAU, under the chairmanship of its former president, Abdelaziz Bouteflika of Algeria during that conflict, managed to persuade Ethiopia and Eritrea to sign a cease-fire agreement ending the war. But immediately after that, further talks were shifted to Washington D.C. under Antony Lake, the former national security adviser to the Clinton administration, who had previously failed to negotiate a cease-fire between the two countries.

The same situation applies to Sierra Leone, where a rebel army under the Revolutionary United Front (RUF) leader, Foday Sankoh, began a war out of frustration that the export of the country's diamonds led to no apparent benefit to the people. In fact, the RUF published a booklet that gave its reasons for initiating the war, citing foreign exploitation of diamonds in particular, and other mineral resources in general, as the major contributory factor. Diamonds constitute more than 60 percent of Sierra Leone's foreign exchange earnings, and high-level corruption by successive governments had led to the military overthrow of one government after another.

So the U.N. Security Council passed a resolution imposing a global embargo on diamond exports from that country in the belief that a thriving gems-for-guns trade has been the primary factor responsible for fuelling the war. The resolution banned all rough diamonds from Sierra Leone until the government could set up a proper certification system for the gems, and regain access to diamond mining areas under the control of the rebel Revolutionary United Front (RUF).

Here again we have a classic case where conflict resolution instigators were only partially right. They were only blaming one side in the conflict, forgetting that the Sierra Leone civil war raged for five years before the RUF gained control of the diamond fields, and this happened only as a result of the signing of the Lome Peace Accord which gave responsibility for minerals to RUF leader Foday Sankoh in the government of national unity of which he was effectively also the Vice President. In fact, the government of Sierra Leone had control of these diamond fields, and had even employed Executive Outcomes, the South African mercenary company which recruits mercenaries and sends them as paid fighters into Africa's ethnic wars. They fought in Angola for many years. Incidentally, Executive Outcomes has now been registered in Britain in order to avoid getting into problems with the new South African government.

Only a politically negotiated, comprehensive peace settlement—recognizing the interests of Sierra Leone's poor, their government, and those foreign companies that have invested their capital in these mines—will end the war permanently. The trial, imprisonment, or execution of Foday Sankoh, as some people have recklessly been demanding, will not solve a problem that has deep roots beyond the RUF. The civil war is only a symptom of the disease in Sierra Leone; the world has to deal with the disease itself, namely, the issue of governance and massive corruption, which is not peculiar to Sierra Leone alone in Africa.

Resolving and preventing conflicts in Africa is therefore of crucial importance and needs further examination. The issue of peace and governance is both intrastate and interstate, and it is not possible to separate the two entirely. We can start with those societies in an acute state of conflict, both negatively—to limit the harm arising out of that situation—and positively, to build models of what is possible ("plausibility structures" as Peter Berger terms it), and to disseminate values to inform these and other situations.

This process can be conducted in the public arena as consensus is built up on issues of common concern; but it can also be promoted behind the scenes, especially in situations where the rhetoric and reality of the conflict precludes clear listening and mutual acceptance, or the recognition of common values is hampered by the adversarial nature of debate. These common values should be of a transcendent nature, that is, they should be able to transcend particular ethnic, cultural, ideological, religious and indeed party-political divisions.

The issue of peace and governance is not something to be tacked on to the material assistance of the people, but is an integral prerequisite for economic growth and social development. Conflict resolution has not been fully taken into account in the West, where, if is it considered seriously at all, it tends to take the form either of military intervention or, alternatively, of sanctions with externally imposed conditionality. This is not to deny the place of military intervention or sanctions, but, as instruments to promote peace and governance, they tend to take up a disproportionate share in the already meager resources allocated to peace and governance. Further, even the most benignly intended military intervention, or the imposition of external sanctions, will be profoundly ambiguous in nature; and this ambiguity is heightened if the action is taken in isolation from a more broadly constructed package.

A virtuous cycle of confidence building needs to be set in train, whereby the good relations achieved at one stage provide a secure platform for the achievement of good relations at another. This can set up—in a social context—the dynamic cycle that operates on an individual level: Acceptance leads to sustenance which produces status and results in achievement. In a social and political context this means that the parties involved need to accept the credentials of the others as equal and valid negotiating partners as the first step in the process. This, then, should result in proximity in a safe and secure location, where the issues are explored on an open basis, freed from the pressure of the ongoing struggle for power. The outcome of this is that the parties are given status on an equal and multilateral basis with the common purpose of implementing these shared deliberations. Thus the implementation is not the vindication of a particular party's position, but the resolve and resolution of a new culture of negotiation that all can equally celebrate.

In the process, there are internal as well as external factors. Internally, there is the nurturing of crosscutting affiliations, especially through encouraging the development of mediating structures (i.e., the range of institutions across the nation that can operate as bridges between individuals and groups). This needs to be opened up by a vision shared across the different groups of the centrality of relationships as the bedrock of a free and dynamic society. The emphasis on individual rights is important in ensuring that all have a stake in society and are able to enjoy the benefits of its overall well-being; but an exclusive emphasis on individual rights without putting it in the context of the need to nurture the richness and diversity of relationships and their development can intensify divisions rather than build a stable but dynamic consensus. Externally, the process can be facilitated by both governmental and intergovernmental agencies as well as informal bodies acting on a disinterested basis.

Facilitation of peace and good governance can take place on at least three levels. First, high-level facilitation that moves towards formal mediation. Of necessity, this operates confidentially while in process, but it is also high profile, and therefore still under public and media gaze. This may also be preceded or accompanied by secret preparation of the modalities between the protagonists. Second, the road to such modalities must be opened by intermediate-level facilitation which operates on a low-profile basis. Confidential rather than secret, this is an informal process to which the protagonists do not make overt commitment and is deniable by them at any point. Nevertheless, it is important in helping to develop ideas and to create space for both the first level as well as the third level, namely the development of intercommunal consensus. This should take place nationwide or within a particular region and should take place publicly.

A considerable amount of work has been done in various contexts at the last level, and there is also a body of emerging accounts at the first level. Although level two has been much less practiced or understood, it is a vital link in the chain of facilitation at the various levels. It is much more flexible than the others, but by its very nature is invisible in its process and intangible in its effects; and yet it is capable of drawing on the experience of the third level and of creating the conditions for the first to succeed, without the high-risk nature of the first (for should it come to nothing, or become public knowledge, it is not itself a negotiation; and it therefore does not bear the political freight of the negotiation process itself). It is also freer to explore the overarching value framework that is necessary for any soundly-based process of negotiations to succeed.

Since the end of the cold war in 1989, Africa's greatest problem, apart from malaria and HIV/Aids, has been one of leadership; poor governance is now the root cause of ethnic or tribal wars across the continent. However, the international creditor community, including multilateral financial institutions such as the World Bank, has taken a dangerous one-sided position, preoccupied with identifying and funding HIV/Aids programs in Africa, to the exclusion of programs aimed at ending Africa's ethnic conflicts. Even malaria programs do not feature prominently in the financial aid policies of these organizations, and yet a combination of malaria and ethnic wars has killed and continues to kill more people in Africa than the HIV/Aids pandemic, as has been confirmed by the World Health Organization. ARI recognizes all three to be severe threats to Africa, and it would be wrong for the international community to impose aid conditions that ignore this fundamental objective fact. All three should be tackled together, because whatever money African countries borrow for any of these programs generally swells their indebtedness to these organizations.

6.6. Designing New Political and Economic Strategies

6.6.1. Regional Economic Integration
As indicated above, unless African governments, business entrepreneurs, and manufacturers adopt a science-led development paradigm, feeding technological developments from intensively improved R & D directly into demand-driven industrial processes, the continent will continue to face a bleak future. An economic growth scenario that utilizes knowledge-intensive technologies in addition to labor-intensive technologies should be, and must be, firmly adopted. In fact, employment of the latter production technique should only take place or be preferred in a situation where the law of comparative advantage in factor inputs would enhance competitiveness. Moreover, African countries must enlarge their own domestic markets through economic integration.

In view of the importance of economic integration for the success of an African Renaissance, it is important to examine the subject in some detail. The main preoccupation of African states since the attainment of independence in the early 1960s has been the pursuit of economic integration as a means of achieving economic growth and thereby improving the quality of life for the masses of their people. They saw economic inte-

217

gration as a desirable economic strategy for small and medium-sized countries in a world with continuous technological and market change. Integration could increase and secure markets for a variety of a country's goods in the future, and hence mitigate the inevitable costs of adjustment to change.

The gains of economic integration include more efficient use of resources due to increased competition, specialization, returns to scale, increased investment, trade creation and diversion, as well as monetary stability. The opponents of integration for small countries would have to answer the question: How much is it worth to lose the market and potentials for gain in order to keep the right to pursue a domestic economic policy that is insulated from international influences? Practical economic experience in real life, especially in the post-cold war era, points to the stark reality that if a small country accepts or chooses a long-term protection policy, as opposed to liberalization or international economic integration, it chooses a long-term deterioration in its competitive position.

Technological developments, accompanied by major transformations in production organization, are underway throughout the world. Knowledge-intensive, rather than materials-intensive industries are setting the pace. On an increasing scale, traditional raw materials are being replaced by synthetics; and, to a greater extent, even production of raw materials is taking place on the basis of knowledge-intensive techniques. This does not mean that governments should ignore the production of raw materials when they have a comparative advantage, but it does mean that governments and the business community will have to pay careful attention when selecting new technologies appropriate to maximizing productivity. This can only happen within an economic integration context, where markets are large and economies of scale, which will facilitate restructuring at a higher level of efficiency and productivity, are certain to be realized and exploited.

218

International politics has also changed. The end of the cold war and the collapse of the centrally planned economies of Eastern Europe and the former Soviet Union are likely to have a two-fold impact on Africa in general and on East Africa in particular. First, Africa has been deprived of an alternative source of support. Second, restructuring of the economies of Eastern Europe and the former Soviet Union is already commanding closer attention, and absorbing a growing part of the concessional aid made available by the major Western countries. These countries have become keen competitors for investment capital and international trade, on account of their skilled workers, stronger infrastructures, and cultural ethnic affinities with most of the industrialised world. This is the great new challenge facing Africa now and into the twenty-first century. Failure to recognise this and adjust accordingly will certainly be catastrophic for the people of this continent.

In spite of slow progress and the severe set-backs that African states have experienced in their pursuit of economic integration in the post-independence era, they must persist in pursuing this goal until success is achieved. At independence, most African countries had such small and relatively unsophisticated capital stock that they were ill-equipped to pursue modern economic growth. Their labor force was largely unskilled, and production methods were based on traditional technologies. The small size of their economies and their restricted markets were also major handicaps to increased production. Economic integration was the only strategic policy that could remove the constraints of a limited market by increasing intra-African trade specialisation, allowing African countries to benefit from this process.

Models of association and economic relationship should be worked out that allow for free and equal participation of all states in building a regional and, eventually, a continental market. Different regional groupings such as ECOWAS (West

Africa), or SADCC (Southern Africa), or the newly formed Common Market for East and Southern Africa (which includes Egypt but excludes South Africa) need much firmer underpinnings in their political and economic realities if they are genuinely to stimulate intraregional trade. The groupings are riddled with interstate suspicion and concern about the dominance of the stronger economies such as those of Egypt and South Africa. For strong regional, and eventually continental, markets to develop, there must be a free flow of information, goods, and services between states. The fear of domination by the stronger economies such as South Africa, Nigeria, or Egypt should be off-set by the opportunities to all Africans that stronger inter-African cooperation can bring about.

By the same token, the stronger countries cannot focus exclusively on their own growth issues without storing up pressures from populations of neighbouring countries, pushed or pulled by the disparity of economic advancement and opportunity. It is in the interest of the stronger economies to help create opportunities in their neighbouring states to counterbalance the overwhelming pressure on a few regional metropolitan areas where high expectations put unbearable strain on existing facilities and on infrastructure and housing provision.

Regional and continental cooperation is also essential for water and hydroelectric power provision, sound and sustainable development of natural resources, and for combating disease, most notably HIV/Aids and malaria (both of which cannot be dealt with solely within a single country). The states need to build up good systems of communication, both road and rail, as well as new communications made possible by introducing information technology. This should make possible a leap-frog effect with the use of fiber-optic or wireless communication, avoiding the need for expensive and antiquated copper cables.

This type of change in policy must, however, discard

reliance on the old orthodoxy of received economic growth theories, because, to begin with, few of these studies, or the theories that sprang from them, could be termed objective. They were undertaken with more explicit political ends in the context of a world dominated by the bipolar conflict between the former U.S.S.R. and the U.S.A. and their respective allies in the "East" and "West". On questions related to the Third World, the new breed of specialists responded in grand measure to the ideological exigencies of the cold war between the superpowers. "Theories" about growth on examination often turned out to be no more than apologetics for one social system or another, having no roots in the reality of the Third World or of history.

To inject a note of caution here, however, while the above observation is largely true, judging by the failures that these theories engendered, not all writing on the Third World was of this tenor, and over the years a substantial body of important analytical and theoretical writing by scholars and writers in the high-income countries and from the Third World itself has demanded attention and has influenced thinking. At the same time the study of the Third World has become a subject in its own right. Tens of thousands of books claim authority on Third World issues, universities all over the world offer a huge range of courses on the Third World and support related research institutes.

6.6.2. Domestic Governance

It is perhaps of interest to revisit briefly the question of possible reinstatement of traditional forms of African democratic governance, if there is such a thing. Much has been written about Ghana under Jerry Rawlings and Uganda under Yoweri Museveni. In the former, a government that began in a military revolutionary tempo later turned democratic and moulded the idea of economic self-sufficiency combined with locally based democratic structures. Although Rawlings succeeded in democratically handing power over to another regime, i.e., under Kufuor, his economic policies were only marginally successful.

In Uganda, Museveni, who also came to power in a similar military revolutionary fashion after a long guerrilla war, tried the "no-party system" of so-called African democracy, which worked well for the first ten years, with a slight dose of authoritarianism. As the years went by, the Ugandan people, while appreciating the peace and economic prosperity that ensued after Museveni rose to power in 1986, realized that there is no better political system than multiparty democracy. The Western world had tolerated the Ugandan and Ghanaian models of governance, despite certain undemocratic features, on the grounds that they exhibited the beginnings of a model government that was not simply a wholesale colonial transplant, but one adapted to African culture and circumstances, crucially retaining governmental responsibility, economic probity, and commitment to open government. As time passes, however, it has also dawned on the West that democracy is democracy. The system may not be perfect, but the human race has not been able to devise anything better.

Political leaders everywhere are human beings and they are as subject to the kinds of pressures that confront all mere mortals. It will be interesting to watch and see whether Museveni will also hand over power peacefully as Rawlings did.

6.6.3. National Political Integration

National integration is also another important consideration. One of the biggest problems in countries that have been artificially created under colonialism, and that consist of a multitude of ethnic groups—both large and small—is how to achieve national integration and a national culture. Mwalimu Julius Nyerere achieved remarkable unity in Tanzania by insisting on Swahili as the national language and thereby creating a sense of national solidarity that superseded local ethnic identity.

Undoubtedly, it would be advantageous if leaders of every African country were to focus on the potential role of language, music, food, forms of dress, and other factors that might foster a sense of national identity through cultural solidarity, rather than have competition for political power as the dominant national agenda.

Second, there is the question of new social institutions. There is potential to explore new institutional forms that have greater "rootedness" in African culture and history, rather than looking to the Western corporate structure for the engine to drive economic growth. One example of such a new institutional structure would be the Family Association, based on the Lebanese model. (See Khalaf, 1971, pp. 235–250.) Long-term family commitment would probably make family associations more successful than cooperatives. Unlike the Lebanese model, however, it would be necessary to place a maximum size of, say, several hundred adults to prevent these family associations from becoming a hidden form of ethnopolitical mobilization. In various ways the government could encourage the people to form family associations as they may encourage savings and also have potential to deliver welfare benefits. They may also become the engine for business activity and growth in the informal sector, transferring into the formal sector when successful.

Another important consideration is the problem of corruption. In order to reduce corruption in the economy, the following seem essential policies to consider: first, keep government regulation of the economy to a minimum. All regulation invites corruption; second, reduce the number of civil servants, and increase their pay levels, so they do not need to bribe either to eat or to educate their children; third, avoid as much as possible employing expatriates, as their salary scales are outrageously high, causing jealousy and resentment even when they are working on so-called aid budgets.

It would seem that the key factors to accelerate national

integration, without losing the benefits of African cultural tradition, are the following: first, continuing efforts for a national language among all members of society to facilitate communication across ethnic boundaries, as Mwalimu Julius Nyerere achieved so successfully in Tanzania; second, political leaders demonstrating scrupulous transparency to ensure ethnic and regional fairness in distributing investment, education opportunities, and public-sector jobs; third, committing to statements of values for national law, and values that can be understood by all citizens and taught in all schools; and fourth, as far as possible, decentralizing economic and political power and decision-making so that local politicians can blame fewer decisions on the ethnic bias of central leadership; and fifthly, giving local politicians and business people the maximum degree of self-determination compatible with national unity.

7

What Role for the International Community?

7.1. Africa's Plight

The World Bank continues to paint a hopeless picture of Africa's situation: eight out of 100 infants do not live to see their fifth birthday; nine of every 100 boys and 14 of every 100 girls who reach school age do not attend school. Poverty is also evidenced in lack of political voice and in extreme vulnerability to ill health, economic dislocation, personal violence, and natural disasters. In addition, the scourge of HIV/Aids, the frequency and brutality of civic conflicts, and rising disparities between high-income and low-income countries have increased the sense of deprivation and injustice for many. How, then, can the wealthy Western world help African countries, in the context of an African Renaissance, to break the vicious cycle of poverty in which they are trapped? While some of the topics discussed in this book are at certain points acutely contentious, I have addressed them partly from the belief that constructive debate is the high road to clarity of thought, and partly from a similarly deep conviction that questioning familiar attitudes and orthodoxies concerning "Africa's problems" is now more urgent than at any previous time, even more than at the time of the Atlantic Slave Trade or of colonial invasion and subjection. I refer, of course, to the Western world's attitude towards Africa's predicament and its willingness to engage in a constructive, fair and humane development partnership. Because of the onset of globalization we are today all in the same boat in a sense that was never true before, even though some are still traveling first class and many others are still in steerage.

7.2. Misconceptions about "Donor Aid"

The great difference between "rich countries" and "poor countries" lies in the former having solved their economic growth problems and the latter having failed to do so; this is a view of the world that has governed current orthodoxy of policy and action, especially in wide segments of the "development industry." For many years the high-income world argued that Africa's economic growth strategy need only follow the same course as that of high income Western countries, and all would be well. The West knew best, and Africa needed only to follow. This was the great theme song of "development" in the 1960s, and much of it is still heard today. (See and compare the characteristic appraisal of British aid to Africa, sponsored by the official Overseas Development Institute, in Little 1964). Professor Basil Davidson, the renowned Western authority on African issues since the 1950s, has commented as follows:

> In their crudest forms, no doubt, such attitudes are an overhang of colonial paternalism. They go hand in

226

hand with others equally familiar, such as the identification of civilized progress with technological complexity, as though the truest measure of a society's improvement were to be found in the growth of its traffic jams. More subtly, these attitudes betray an oddly provincial belief that "the way we live in the West" is the way that everyone else ought to live, and that "our system" is the only right and proper future for mankind. (Basil Davidson, op.cit., pp. 3–4)

It was in the context of the above attitudes, so prevalent since the end of World War II, that the terms "donors" and "recipient" nations were coined to describe foreign aid relations, or the flow of financial resources from the West to Africa for development purposes. According to this view, all countries and multilateral financial institutions that participate in the Paris-based Development Assistance Committee (DAC) of the OECD are automatically referred to as "donors", which, in effect, means that they donate money to the poor nations of Africa to assist them in their development efforts. [Participating members of the Development Assistance Committee (DAC) of the OECD are: Australia, Austria, Belgium, Canada, Denmark, the European Commission, Finland, France, Germany, Ireland, Italy, the International Monetary Fund (IMF), Japan, the Netherlands, Norway, Portugal, Sweden, Switzerland, the United Kingdom, the United States, the United Nations Development Program (UNDP), and the World Bank.]

The problem here is a lack of distinction between "grants" and "loans." The word "donor", according to the Oxford Dictionary of current English, refers to "one who gives or donates something; one who provides blood for transfusion, semen for insemination or organ or tissue for transplantation." In other words, the term refers to someone who gives a gift or a grant. So the word "donor" is applied appropriately to NGOs such as

227

Oxfam, Christian Aid, and Médecins Sans Frontières, organizations that give grants to local projects. However, the term cannot rightly be applied to the major multilateral and bilateral institutions that give loans, however generous the terms and conditions may be. Careless use of this word "donor" by high-income Western countries, the so-called "international community," has given rise to a pathetic dependency syndrome that has made the African people by and large, and many of their leaders, believe that without money from the so-called Bretton Woods Institutions (namely, the World Bank and the IMF) their countries cannot achieve economic growth.

It is, therefore, distressing to hear an African leader heaping blame on the IMF and the World Bank for refusing to "give money" to his country, even to finance recurrent budgetary expenditure. It is distressing to see some African finance ministers present their annual budgets to parliament without the slightest reference to some of the most fundamental macro-economic indicators that are the pillars for any country's sustained economic growth. The gap between investment resources required to accelerate economic growth, and resources generated internally through their own domestic savings, is never mentioned, and yet it is such a crucial issue. The same is true of the gap between foreign exchange earnings acquired through trade and other means, and their needed level of imports. Bridging of these gaps through financial assistance from the IMF, the World Bank and other forms of bilateral assistance is admittedly crucial, but African governments cannot entirely rely on them because they are not grants. Heavy reliance on this form or source of funding not only increases Africa's external debts but also its economies' overdependence on external financial forces. As we shall see below, this form of financing is also diminishing most rapidly with the onset of the new economic order characterized by globalization and liberalization.

7.3. Bilateral and Multilateral Financial Cooperation

My contention here is that African countries must continue to insist on the increase of official development assistance that was originally meant to bolster bilateral aid on concessional terms. In other words, the emphasis on official development cooperation, both bilateral and multilateral, must remain a crucial component of the financial relationships between Africa and high-income countries for many years to come, despite the onset of globalization and liberalization philosophy. As a matter of fact, the earlier transfer of the philosophy of overseas development assistance (ODA) from the high-income countries to Africa was focused on the need for Africa to acquire concessional capital flows from both bilateral and multilateral sources to overcome the limited access they had to private capital markets. That is why low-income countries negotiated and won acceptance for a quantitative target of 0.7 percent of GNP as the level for high-income countries' assistance.

With the onset of globalization, African countries should now have unlimited access to the flow of private capital, in all its various forms, from Western capital markets as long as they adopt appropriate investor-friendly domestic economic and political institutions. However, as we shall see below, in spite of globalization and optimists' views about the efficacy of liberalization to solve low-income countries' thirst for economic growth capital, the outcome has been negative over the last ten years. This is because both experience and the rules governing financial investment have pointed towards private capital flows going where profits are highest, and not just where policies seem to be right. Experience has also shown that domestic policies of structural adjustment in Africa, even when vigorously applied under severe conditionalities, have not ensured that capital needs thereafter are met by market forces alone. That is why Third World countries, during the Durban conference in South Africa in September 1998, insisted that the emphasis on official financial cooperation, both bilateral and multilateral, must remain as an important policy in any Third World economic growth agenda, despite discouraging trends since the end of the cold war in 1989.

In a final report of the Ad Hoc Panel of Economists of the Non-Aligned Movement (NAM) in 1998 its chairman, Dr. Gamani Corea of Sri Lanka, former secretary general of the United Nations Conference on Trade and Development (UNCTAD), made the following far-reaching comments:

> The need for concessional flows is not confined to only the poorest of the poor countries. Many developing countries are not in a position, due to limits on their credit worthiness and other factors, to access private capital markets and hence to mobilize and direct private capital flows to sectors and activities of high priority. The attention of the developed countries needs to be drawn to the high risks, political and social, that are in prospect for the developing countries in the face of diminishing or stagnating flows of official development assistance. ...The developed countries have a stake in global and regional political stability and in ensuring that this is not jeopardized by diminishing capital flows to a large part of the world. (See *Elements for an Agenda of the South*, report of the Ad Hoc Panel of Economists to the Twelfth NAM Summit, Durban, South Africa, 1998, pp. 20–21, published by the South Center, April 1999, Chemin du Champ-d'Anier 17, 1211 Geneva, Switzerland, on behalf of the Non-Aligned Movement.)

In the context of an African Renaissance, the question of the maintenance, let alone increase, of capital flows to Africa through multilateral financial institutions, is even more problematic than bilateral official financial assistance whose constraints are dictated, for the most part, by political considerations. In the earlier period, the IMF was, for instance, supposed to support balance-of-payments requirements, the need for compensatory and supplementary financing of shortfalls in export earnings, the easing of the conditionalities accompanying various tranches of IMF lending, the need for giving attention to high-income countries in chronic surplus, and, not least, the international creation of liquid reserves and the channeling of such reserves through to low-income countries.

Although these stated requirements of Third World countries, of Africa in particular, were not adopted in full by these institutions, the political and economic climate of the 1960s and 1970s encouraged a degree of sensitivity to these concerns and to the need for some positive response, however measured. This was because the international political climate and the objectives of the major powers encouraged such responses.

In the more recent period, however, since globalization has replaced the cold war arrangements as the dominant organizing framework for international affairs, the scenario has changed markedly. Increasingly, high-income Western countries have begun to distance themselves from the earlier edifice of international economic cooperation, especially in the area of finance, and to turn to the advocacy of the policy requirements of this new doctrine. In brief, the highlights of this new doctrine emphasize the reliance on market forces spurred on by deregulation and a consequent reliance on the role of private actors. It is also paralleled by a scaling down of concessional official economic cooperation, both in relative and absolute terms, save for perhaps to the lowest-income countries, and a reluctance to expand the resources of the multilateral financial institutions, especially resources for concessional flows.

One of the issues that became closely associated with

African countries' access to official multilateral capital flows and debt relief is that of stringent conditionality applied by the IMF and the World Bank. Originally confined to requirements to ensure the soundness of projects seeking financing, the concept of conditionality—generally embodied in programs of structural adjustment—has come in recent years to embrace ever-widening dimensions. These extend from the overall macroeconomic policies of borrowing countries to domestic liberalization, deregulation, privatization and other areas—in fact, to virtually all important aspects of domestic policy. Conditionality has indeed become one of the major channels through which African countries have been induced to adapt to the requirements of the new international economic order known as globalization.

The implications of globalization in the new era has been spelt out in the following terms:

> As globalization deepens, new problems of undertaking national development in the context of an integrated world economy will become more prevalent. Even more than for the previous generations, open-economy models will be the rule. And whereas previous international policy issues revolved around trade policy, the next generation will have to devote more attention to determining the effects of international capital movements, migration, and technology transfer... . The previous provocations of dependency thinking and a New International Economic Order are passé. But there will be more controversy over whether globalization benefits the poor countries and whether it creates benefits for poor people within countries. The next generation will have to sort out the positive and negative impulses resulting from globalization. (Meier & Stiglitz 2001, p. 33)

There is much that is sound in the stipulations of macro-economic policy discipline, since these can contribute towards improvements in the domestic economic performance of borrowing African countries (especially with regard to reducing high-level official corruption). However, questions have arisen about the validity of these policy prescriptions that exhibit a high degree of uniformity despite significant differences in individual country situations. Criticisms have also been made of the neglect of the social and political implications when designing and imposing these packages. There are also questions relating to the ideological elements embodied in conditionality packages touching on such issues as the relative roles of the public and private sectors and of market forces.

The roles of the IMF and the World Bank will continue to remain crucial in multilateral international financial and monetary cooperation with Third World countries, and much more so with African countries in the context of the NEPAD (see below) and the African Renaissance. It was encouraging, then, that both the president of the World Bank and the managing director of the IMF paid visits to various African countries in early 2001 to solicit and, hopefully, listen to the views of African leaders on the policy strategies and requirements of African economic and social development. Their genuineness and sincerity will be measured by changes in the policy of these institutions towards Africa. Sweet words alone will not suffice.

Moreover, these two institutions and their regional counterparts in Asia, Africa, and Latin America must resist calling themselves "donors" because clearly they are not. They are essentially creditors or lenders of capital. Even loans at token interest rates of, say, half of one percent per year over fifty years must be recognized for what they are: not grants but *loans*, which must be repaid and where compound interest operates. Indeed, in regard to the external debt of Third World countries, these multilateral financial institutions were the last to participate in debt rescheduling, despite significant debts owed to them, claiming "preferred creditor" status. The term "donor–recipient relationship" has been used loosely in international financial circles. A new term must be found to replace it. Otherwise it will continue to give the wrong impression in Africa and will encourage a pathetic, yet unrealistic, dependency syndrome. This, of course, applies also to bilateral financial cooperation where credits and loans must be clearly spelt out and separated from grants.

With regard to the continued future of the IMF and World Bank, the following quotation is illustrative:

> ….because markets, technology and corporations are global in scope, while the jurisdiction of the nation-state is only local, there will be a need for new actions by the World Bank, the IMF, and the World Trade Organization (WTO). As the main constituents of the international public sector, they will have to devise new programs to ensure that the benefits of global integration are more equally shared, that competitive policymaking is avoided, and that problems of incomplete risk markets are mitigated as international integration becomes ever more complex. (Meier and Stiglitz, op.cit., p. 33)

In the light of the constraints that have emerged since the end of the cold war on the conventional forms of official capital flows to African countries, we believe that if an African Renaissance is to succeed, African governments will have to adjust their policies to the new era of globalization, while at the same time trying to negotiate the best financial cooperation packages from the existing bilateral and multilateral institutions.

As to the applicability of the IMF's analysis and the relevance of its policies to Africa, further technical and intellectual debate should be undertaken urgently, especially in the context of the onset of globalization. The demand by other Third World countries in Asia and Latin America for more transparency and accountability from the IMF and World Bank deserves strong support. These institutions demand transparency and accountability from African countries; we also need to demand the same from them, bearing in mind the domestic and wider impact of the policies the bank prescribes and imposes. ARI should mobilize African intellectual opinion and expertise, in cooperation with the newly established African Union and the Economic Commission for Africa, for a united and comprehensive discussion of these issues in their own intergovernmental fora, and formulate common views on how these matters could be better addressed.

7.4. Tackling Africa's debt

The scale of the debt problem calls for a "Debt Commission for Africa", to be established urgently, with the remit to consider debts on a case-by-case basis. For example, if a creditor had lent money to military dictator Idi Amin, and it was used to buy weapons to commit genocide, should the oppressed people of Uganda be expected to spend years repaying the loan? Surely justice requires that the debt be forgiven? To take another example, if a Western country had given trade credits to the late President Mobutu of Zaire in a situation when any reasonable person would have suspected these would be sent to his personal Swiss bank account rather than used to benefit his country, do the people of DRC now have a moral responsibility to repay the West? Surely not. Rather the bank or government has a moral responsibility to write off the debt as a matter of justice. Similarly, if the World Bank has lent money for a project recommended by its own experts, but it can be shown that it was never likely to be viable, whose responsibility is it to pay for the mistake?

A Debt Commission for Africa, consisting of international experts, should take on the task of reviewing loan records and deciding which debts should be written off as an issue of justice. However, in many cases, in my view, Africa does not have a *right* to have the debt written off. Africans signed the debt agreements; we must accept responsibility for those decisions or it will encourage the West to treat us as children. So, an act of generosity or "mercy" is required from Western creditors to cancel the outstanding debt.

A major concern to Western creditors is that African countries, if forgiven their debt, will immediately take on new debt. One way to avoid this possibility would be to require African governments requesting debt write-off to accept a provision that would state that all future debt would be written off every seventh year, over the next period of, say, twenty-one years. This would mean in practice that most Western aid agencies would no longer lend money to that African state, because they would fear that they would lose money in the next debt write-off year. International aid agencies or companies would only then provide capital in the form of risk capital (shares) in public or private sector companies, or as grants to government, and the country would be protected from further international debt slavery.

7.5. The Origins of NEPAD

At the onset of the Third Millennium, a few far-sighted African leaders were engaged in devising new ways through which a new international cooperation agenda could be forged between the continent and the outside world, and particularly with high-income Western countries. This issue became even more urgent with the realization that globalization, which was shaping world events, was now almost ten years old, yet Africans were not only unable to respond to the new situation, but the majority of them hardly even understood the forces at play. The twentieth century, and in particular its last two decades, was noted for the numerous scientific and cultural achievements that significantly improved the quality of life for people everywhere, with Africans alone left far behind.

Probably nothing, however, can be compared with the speed of change since the 1980s in how goods are manufactured; how people, ideas, and capital travel; and how nations and cities perform their roles. In other words, the last two decades of the twentieth century witnessed fundamental changes to our way of life; to our perception of our home, our workplace, and the world, and indeed to our future. Only Africans are living contentedly without, by and large, experiencing any of these changes. It is only in Africa where you find governments still comfortable with electricity and water rationing, and with telecommunication systems so archaic that they hardly function. And yet these are fundamental forces behind any society's modernization.

The birth, therefore, of the "Millennium African Recovery Program" (MAP) immediately after the U.N. millennium summit, which took place in New York in September 2000, was a welcome event for the continent. It was Presidents Thabo Mbeki of South Africa, Olusegun Obasanjo of Nigeria, and Abdelaziz Bouteflika of Algeria who spearheaded the earlier MAP plan, which was supported by the U.S.A., the EU, and Japan. The program has been described as Africa's version of the Marshall Plan—the U.S.-backed plan that lifted postwar Europe out of economic and social despair. In essence, these African leaders want the rich nations in the West to take a similar approach to their continent, and therefore they expect the G8 summit of industrialized nations to follow up their pledge

237

of support with tangible financial assistance based on sound, corruption-free programs.

The Millennium African Recovery Program has focused attention on a generous but realistic and prompt debt-relief program, especially for the HIPCs, enhanced flow of Official Development Assistance (ODA), barrier-free trade, and enlarged access to markets of the industrialized nations. In addition, there is the dramatic promotion of foreign direct investment, with an enabling Africa-wide desire for social peace, democratic governance, and a sustained fight against corruption.

In order to fulfil the requirements of the urgency and focus of this momentous opportunity, Mbeki, Obasanjo, and Bouteflika consolidated their efforts to form the Tripartite Consultative Group to oversee MAP in its immediate strategizing stage, with the involvement of the U.N. Economic Commission for Africa (ECA) and the African Union. This understanding empowered ARI to advise African governments to execute the program in close cooperation with major regional, national, and international institutions in Africa and abroad.

Inspired by the firm and shared conviction that African leaders have a pressing duty to eradicate poverty in their countries, MAP aimed to launch Africa on a path of sustained economic growth at the dawn of a new century. It sought to build on the momentum of change and progress in the continent, reflected in adoption of economic reforms, consolidation of democracy, and a new resolve in dealing with ethnic conflict, while recognizing that a new and effective partnership with the international community was essential to its success, even as it stressed the fact that the African governments and people had the primary responsibility for its implementation. In this regard, former president of South Africa Nelson Mandela could not have made the point more succinctly when he said:

Africa is beyond bemoaning the past for its problems. The task of undoing that past is ours, with the support of those willing to join us in a continental renewal. We have a new generation of leaders who know that we must take responsibility for our own destiny, that we will uplift ourselves only by our own efforts in partnership with those who wish us well. (Quoted from ECA's paper "Compact for African Recovery," prepared in May 2001 for consideration at the ECA Conference of African Ministers of Finance and Ministers of Development and Planning in Algiers, 8–10 May 2001)

In early 2001, President Abdoulaye Wade of Senegal also announced his OMEGA Plan for Africa, identifying the need to develop physical capital and human capital as the key prerequisites for sustained and balanced growth and arguing that investment needs in priority sectors to be brought under the purview of a single international authority. The OMEGA Plan, although slightly limited in its areas of concern, had the same vision and objectives as MAP, in the sense that both were inspired by the need to launch Africa on a path of sustained growth and development at the dawn of a new century and both were based on the premise that Africa must assume the primary responsibility for that effort. That is why at the extraordinary Summit of the OAU in Sirte, Libya, March 2001, African heads of state and government agreed that the MAP and OMEGA Plan be merged. President Wade has been touring Western capitals to drum up financial support for the OMEGA scheme.

The United Nations Economic Commission for Africa (ECA) adopted another important initiative, the Compact for African Recovery, aimed at operationalizing the MAP. This program can play a critical role within the international community, particularly within the framework of the U.N. General Assembly and its subsidiary organs and specialized agencies, in mobilizing the necessary financial resources and technical assistance required for its implementation. It should also play a leading role in bringing all the partner initiatives together within a single framework for the achievement of the MAP initiative.

In the course of 2001, MAP went through several changes, both in terms of name and objective: African leaders renamed it the New African Initiative (NAI) until 23 October 2001 when, at a meeting in Abuja, Nigeria, the name was finally changed to the New Partnership for Africa's Development (NEPAD). The international community has adopted this last formulation as the linchpin of their relationship with the African continent.

ARI will work in close cooperation with the ECA and the African Union in the implementation of the NEPAD objectives. Already the three organizations have cultivated cooperation at the highest policy level and working platform, and functional agreements are already in place. With its comprehensive objectives and work program based on its charter, the African Renaissance Institute is well-placed to work with African governments, intergovernmental organizations, NGOs, development institutions, both national and international, as well as the private sector.

The success of NEPAD will depend on three key factors: first, the willingness of high-income nations to open up their markets to African products, especially agricultural and manufacturing, and to cancel the crippling debts that low-income African countries owe to rich Western countries; the question of debt cancellation has always been difficult to sell. The G8 countries have expressed a desire to forgive some of these stifling debts, except those directly owed to the World Bank and the International Monetary Fund. However, the G8 countries have not made any significant efforts to turn their expressions of good intentions into positive action. We will explain the reasons below.

Second, one of the key agenda items is the support for African agricultural development as an engine of growth in the continent. This is critical because it will require intricate negotiations with the rich countries, since agriculture is heavily subsidized in the European Union, Japan, and the U.S., thus keeping out exports from low-income countries. "The lack of enthusiasm to lift trade barriers to African goods, especially agriculture, is another stumbling block. Trade barriers cost developing countries U.S.$ 20 billion a year, which was U.S.$ 6 billion more than they received in direct aid," said Niall Fitzgerald the chairman of Unilever. (See "African Recovery Plan Yet to Win Financial Backing," in *The People*, Monday, 25 June 2001, Nairobi, p. 14) The EU's Common Agricultural Policy (CAP) is particularly troubling, says Fitzgerald, observing that "the EU spent more money on cattle subsidies than many Africans have to live on. More than a dollar a day goes to support every cow in the EU herd. This compares with hundreds of millions of people in the developing world who are forced to live on less than one dollar a day." (Ibid, p. 14.)

Third, the most important consideration is that in return for the two fundamental concessions noted above, African countries must pledge to meet vigorous aims in good governance, democracy, human rights, peace, and the rule of law. Already, we are aware that the final version of NEPAD will strive to establish a coherent, focused strategy, and implementation program to tackle poverty and social development in Africa. Other goals include promoting democracy, respect for the rule of law and human rights, ending the many violent conflicts on the continent, eliminating the spread of HIV/Aids and other communicable diseases. Mfundo Nkhulu, a member of the technical team who participated in the drafting of the final version of the NEPAD charter, stated the following: "The NEPAD further calls for investment in information and communication technologies to access the knowledge economy and bridge the digital divide, diversifying production and exports through value added agriculture, and expanding tourism" (Ibid, p. 14).

Once all of the above proposals have been properly programmed and drawn up in such a manner as to obtain financial assistance, African countries can move singly and collectively to tackle their main problem of economic underperformance. We are encouraged that the British, Canadian and Japanese governments have expressed their willingness to help Africa and suggested how they are practically prepared to do so. This augurs very well for the realization of the objectives of NEPAD and also the African Renaissance within that program.

7.6. The Digital Divide

Africa's weakness in the area of the information superhighway, summed up as the "digital divide" between Africa and the Western countries, has greatly affected its participation in the globalization process. In a 7 August 2000 letter to me from a distinguished group of African intellectuals, representing lawyers, economists, businessmen, and bankers, they state the following on this subject:

> We believe that in order to attack realistically and in a durable manner the debt and development resource problems of the countries hit by severe poverty, much more is required than debt-forgiveness and debt alleviation. ...The fact is that in many of these countries, the use of modern methods that are becoming increasingly indispensable in the management of public assets in the very complex financial atmosphere of today is almost non-existent. So is the availability of skills for getting access to a lot of free

information that is available on the digitalized information channels today in the fields of agriculture, medicine, finance and trade. Without such information, it will be virtually impossible for these countries to manage their resources efficiently. This will affect not only those that they will save if their debts are reduced or written off, but also those resources that the generosity of the resource-surplus countries will be able to make to them in the form of aid, both bilateral and multilateral.

That is why many right-thinking people in Africa believe that to create a more favorable atmosphere in medium-and long-term poverty reduction, a radical approach to educate present and future Third World managers in the use of computer technology is indispensable. We also think that the volume of aid resources that needs to be deployed in this effort, compared with what is now required in the more usual areas of application of aid resources, is comparatively small. Viewed from this perspective, it is essential therefore to begin with a widespread program of computer training and familiarization in African schools and, along with that, to increase introduction of the computer into many fields of rural management.

In fact, the failure of financial institutions like the African Development Bank, in spite of its enhanced capacity to channel development resources to African countries, is because of the lack of attention given to modern methods of information management and communication between lenders and recipients of financial aid. Even corruption, also a major factor of these system failures, has had a devastating impact on financial institutions because of inadequate and outdated communication and control systems. Africa must therefore tackle the three major constraints in spreading this technology in order to make it the effective tool of economic development it can be.

The first constraint is the cost of acquiring computers and using them effectively, including using them for accessing information on the Internet. The second constraint is the surprisingly low level of familiarity that a majority of key African decision-makers have regarding the potential of the computer as a management tool. The third major constraint is the cost of communication.

We believe the first problem can be solved if African entrepreneurs or companies are trained and given opportunities to design and build cheap and effective computers locally, which would be widely available to much larger sectors of the population than is possible today. The objective would be to create computing facilities that would be within the reach of the educational budgets of most African governments. The target would be to have a computer training facility in every elementary school within seven years. In Africa, a country like South Africa has the technical capability to initiate such a project straightaway.

If African countries can succeed in this, in a few years we could have a generation of school leavers and graduates who are familiar with computers by the time they are absorbed into the production and management sectors of the economy. This should have the effect of radically increasing the demand for digital information. Such an increase in demand should, eventually, enhance the market and have the same impact on the prices of more sophisticated computer systems as has been the case in other parts of the world.

Solving the problem created by this sort of constraint should, we think, also pave the way for solving the two related problems noted above. An enhanced awareness and reliance on the computer as a management tool among Africa's decision-makers should be the natural result of training our present school children who will be tomorrow's decision makers. This, in turn would create two effects that should have a positive impact on today's poor communications systems: first, an increased demand for telephones should eventually reduce the unit cost of making telephones accessible to our populations; and second, Africa's decision-makers should be expected to become more communication-friendly than most of them are today.

That is why many of us in Africa were much encouraged when, in July 2000, former Japanese prime minister Yoshio Mori launched the Okinawa Charter on Global Information Society during the G8 Summit Meeting under Japan's leadership. The agenda required other world leaders to participate in this new global initiative aimed at narrowing the so-called "global digital divide," primarily targeting Africa which was recognized to be still far behind the cutting edge information communication technology. Every high-income nation was to adopt the principle of inclusion, meaning that everyone everywhere in the world should be allowed and enabled to participate in, and no one excluded from, the benefits of the global information society offered by the twenty-first century's potent forces of digital information and communications technology. This is because the ICT-driven economic and social transformation derives from its power to help individuals and societies to use knowledge and ideas.

Economic and structural change on a global scale underlies much of the far-reaching transformation of our time and has left hardly a single person or a single nation untouched. Waves of technological innovation accompany this transformation. These two tendencies have been mutually reinforcing, such that the world has become much more interdependent, and diverse globalization processes have been penetrating every nook and cranny of the world. These powerful and omnipresent changes have, also, seen the ascendancy of large cities, particularly megacities and world cities, in the global political economy. That is why African leaders and their representatives who frequent various meetings in the international fora should concentrate more on careful study of this global economic restructuring that has led to the world's economic integration, and thereafter they should find ways and means by which their continent can benefit, instead of only theorizing and debating about debt forgiveness or cancellation. While the question of debt relief is also extremely important for Africa and while everyone should support the Heavily Indebted Poor Countries (HIPC) Initiative, this alone will not solve Africa's problems unless massive corruption by some of its predatory leaders is eliminated. Otherwise debt relief will only facilitate more capital flight from some of the most affected African countries with dictatorial, poor, and unaccountable leadership.

In the days leading to the signing of the Okinawa Charter by the leaders of the G8 Summit in July 2000, the Japanese prime minister announced the Comprehensive Cooperation Package for Bridging the Digital Gap, with, as its centerpiece, the suggested allocation of U.S. $15 billion over five years for raising awareness of information communication technology opportunities, training for over 10,000 low-income country experts in ICT, and building its infrastructure and inter- and intra-regional networks. This was a major commitment, because it meant coalescing with the public and private sectors to bridge the global information and knowledge divide by bringing about global digital opportunity for the underprivileged and disadvantaged worldwide community in urban, rural, and remote areas.

It was intended, as one of the cardinal objectives of this proposal, that digital opportunities be created by leapfrogging conventional obstacles of infrastructural development, so as to meet the peoples' vital developmental goals, such as poverty eradication through wealth creation, health and sanitation development and improvement, security enhancement, life-long learning and training, and encouragement of more equitable and competitive trade.

An important aspect of the Okinawa G8 Summit was that this was the first time that representatives of the African countries of South Africa, Nigeria, and Algeria were invited as outside observers on the fringes of the meetings. Nevertheless, the invited heads of state and governments of these countries traveled to Japan, where they pleaded mainly for Africa's debt cancellation or forgiveness under the HIPCI lobbying arrangements. Also, in mid-January 2001, the prime minister of Japan visited South Africa, Kenya, and Nigeria, which offered a valuable opportunity for the opening of a decisive dialogue for concluding a firm partnership arrangement for implementing an Africa-wide comprehensive cooperation package for bridging the "digital gap."

The African Renaissance Institute, established in 1998, was unfortunately unable to seize this wonderful opportunity to advise African governments, through the OAU and ECA, in the immediate design of strategic plans for resource mobilization, both human and capital, in the execution of this idea, although there was an immediate need to establish an African-based "Digital Opportunity Task Force for Development Initiative in Africa" (DOTA), in order to take advantage of this Okinawa G8 offer. The lack of initiative by ARI was due to the fact that the institute was still finding its feet; it still needed to equip its functional institutional structures with a critical mass of top-flight technical policy analysts and managers who have the vision to grasp great opportunities of this kind. This indicates the urgent need for capacity-building within the institute.

While this is the immediate objective, the long-term objective must remain the achievement of substantially improved indigenous technical analysis and management of Africa's economic and social development processes. Building ARI's professional technical policy analysis and development management skills and institutions will, in turn, enhance utilization of Africa's already-existing resources and lead to creation of a forum for full and active African participation in the design and implementation of capacity-building programs, as well as improved coordination with our bilateral and multilateral financial partners. This will enhance greater focus, prioritization, and rationalization in the development of economic policy research and management capacity. This will inevitably and necessarily lead to substantial cost savings as well as to improved programs; and also to mobilized financial and technical resources to increase investment in Africa's human capital and institutions, both political and administrative, on a consistent and long-term basis.

7.7. The Impact of Globalization on Africa

The so-called cyberspace-driven "virtual world economy" of the twenty-first century is not an easy subject to grasp with brief explanation. The pervasive nature of globalization and its effect on Africa will naturally require a separate book on the subject for a proper understanding of it. In his authoritative book on globalization Thomas Friedman has described it in the following terms:

> Globalization is not simply a trend or a fad but is, rather, an international system. It is the system that has now replaced the old cold war system, and, like that cold war system, globalization has its own rules and logic that today directly or indirectly influence the politics, environment, geopolitics and economics of virtually every country in the world. (Friedman 2000, p. ix)

The problem is that, because of its material and intellectual poverty, Africa is always the last continent in the world to understand that times have changed, and that they need either to adapt very quickly or continue sleeping and perish for ever. For instance, the main moving forces behind the whole techno-logical story of globalization are the computer, the telephone, and the television. These three items are the cornerstones of the information age. Therefore, investment in information tech-nology is both a necessary and sufficient condition for under-standing and participation in the globalization age.

The ubiquitous nature of globalization presupposes a country's heavy investment in digital technology in general and in the Internet in particular. The World Wide Web not only allows people to access a vast storehouse of information from almost anywhere in the world, but also allows many types of businesses to become borderless. Nevertheless, how many people in Africa have access to the telephone even in urban areas? Need we mention rural areas, where 80 percent of the population lives, and where there is no access to electricity?

Moreover, the majority of the African population living in sprawling urban areas have no access to electricity either, because they are mainly unemployed slum dwellers. Those in the higher- and middle-income brackets are subjected to per-petual and irritating power rationing occasioned by high-level government corruption and ineptitude. The mere fact that Africans and their leaders are always quick to blame nature and the lack of rain for their economic backwardness, as the Kenyans did during the energy crisis of 1999–2001, is a clear testimony to the fact that they do not understand the signifi-cance of technology and its mastery.

Unless we in Africa can apply ourselves diligently with a view to controlling the forces of nature around us, we are des-tined to remain backward forever. The fact that there is drought does not necessarily mean that we should be rendered so help-less that we can have neither energy nor food! In many low-income countries there is a chronic shortage of telephones, let alone computers. In Brazil (a country far ahead of any African country, with the exception of South Africa, in terms of income per head), only about one person in ten has a fixed-line telephone, whereas for Africans the figure is only one in three hundred. In fact, there are fewer telephones in the whole of sub-Saharan Africa than in Manhattan, New York, and precious little infrastructure. That is why Friedman has written as follows about some of the poorly performing African countries:

> Poor countries such as Kenya and Zambia have fallen behind in the globalization age not because globalization failed them, but because they failed to put in place even the minimum political, economic and legal infrastructure to take advantage of globalization. Prosperity did not run away from them; they failed to make the choices that would encourage it to stay. Countries such as Uganda, Poland or South Korea have made the right choices and reaped the benefits. Nations don't fail to develop, per se; they fail to develop good government. (Friedman 2000, pp. 356–357)

Zambia, for instance, is one of the poorest countries in the world, with civil service salaries averaging between $50 and $70 a month, and yet an average monthly bill for water and electricity is $60. It is therefore difficult to imagine such a country ever benefiting from, let alone participating in, the globalization regime. In purely economic terms, what is the real meaning or definition of globalization? Two leading Western economists, Professor Joseph P. Stiglitz of Stanford University and formerly chief economist and senior vice-president of the World Bank, and Shahid Yusuf, research manager, Development Economics Research Group of the World Bank, describe the economic and social consequences of globalization in the following terms:

Globalization means the closer integration of the world economy resulting from increasing flows of trade, ideas, and capital and the emergence of multi-country production networks spawned by the investment activities of transnational corporations. Multinationals account for a large share of world production, and perhaps one-third of all trade is within firms. But globalism extends beyond economic interdependence to embrace the transformation of time and space as a result of the communications revolution and the spread of information technology. People are now more directly affected by distant events. By the same token, micro level actions can have macro level consequences. A change in the use of fuels or in the energy intensity of production in one part of the world can have significant effects on a host of countries. (Meier and Stiglitz 2001, p. 235)

It becomes vitally important, then, for Africans to understand the meaning and pervasive nature of globalization and its huge impact on our economies and therefore on our lives. It is primarily through globalization that countries can now obtain access to foreign direct investment, mainly by transnational corporations as a source of long-term capital flows to low-income countries. The demand for financial resource supply by low-income countries in Africa, Asia, and Latin America, where 80 percent of the world's poorest populations live, has become extremely competitive. To modernize, industrialize and urbanize, these low-income countries will require huge amounts of capital. Most of this capital will come, or must come, from domestic savings, but well-run low-income countries offering solid returns on investment will be able to supplement their domestic savings with resources from all over the globe. These low-income countries are also becoming the fastest growing markets for the products of multinational corporations, and an increasing volume of foreign direct investment will find its way to them, providing jobs for their workers.

It is necessary to have a clearer definition of, and hence a distinction between, foreign direct investment (FDI) and foreign portfolio investment (FPI). Private FDI consists of investment in physical capital and other production-related assets. It refers to those people building new production facilities, who undoubtedly helped to contribute to Asia's economic over-expansion and the resulting overcapacity that was the underlying reason for the deflation that haunted the region during the 1997–99 Asian economic crisis.

There is a distinction between FDI, conceptually at least, and FPI; the latter refers to purchasers of foreign liquid financial assets. They are the people who buy shares and bonds in overseas markets. They also contributed, in some measure, to exploding the Asian bubble by inflating local stock-market prices. In reality, the distinction is somewhat fuzzy, as financial transactions may involve elements of both. However, the higher liquidity of FPI underlies the presumption that it is more footloose than FDI.

We must, however, sound a serious warning here in so far as Africa is concerned. Although Gross Foreign Direct Investment by the financial markets of the leading industrial nations has increased more than thirty-fold since the 1970s, much of it has gone to fewer than a score of East Asian and Latin American countries. In other words, a negligible amount has found its way to Africa, because of the obvious political problems of governance and regulation that continue to bedevil the African continent. The transition from centralized and hierarchical government structures to multicentric and participatory forms of governance is emerging even more insistently within countries because of localizing tendencies occasioned by globalization. The end of the cold war extinguished the rivalry between the superpowers, removing an important source of geopolitical tension. It also removed one of the supports for centralized governments. Africa is probably the only continent where the majority of its leaders and peoples have been unable to grasp the meaning or the significance of these transformed international political circumstances and their impact on Africa's domestic economic transformation and development.

Another important point is that institutional and individual investors are also a major source of the growing volume of private portfolio capital and short-term capital flows that have overshadowed bank lending and investment in government paper. Mutual funds, hedge funds, insurance companies, and other investments, and asset managers as well now compete for national savings. Although this is true primarily in industrial countries, the consequences for low-income countries could be significant, because institutional investors are diversifying their portfolios internationally, enlarging the pool of potentially available financial capital. In 1997 they managed U.S.$20 trillion, of which on average 20 percent was invested abroad, i.e., about U.S.$1 trillion. This represents a ten-fold increase in the funds held by these institutions and a forty-fold increase in their investment abroad since 1980. In other words, the growth of foreign direct investment pales in comparison with worldwide private portfolio investment flows, which have multiplied to nearly 200 times their 1970 total. In fact, it has been said that these funds helped explode the Asian bubble of 1997 by inflating local stock-market prices although the Asian debt was the major contributory factor. My plea is that we in Africa must be aware and understand these global developments with a view to taking advantage of them.

In conclusion, let us be clear: I am not blindly extolling the virtues of globalization or the new fad of popular capitalism and shareholder democracy. I am quite aware of some new dangers to Africa of globalization; my purpose here is to help the African people understand that because the world has changed drastically, there is a powerful new economic force that is beyond their control, and they had better study it, adapt to it, and thereby avoid some of its negative tendencies. It will not be good enough just to react by criticizing the system, in partial or complete ignorance.

8

Hope for the Future

8.1. Mobilizing African Skills

In view of the fact that an African Renaissance is now upon us, we must be clear about our real problems, so that we can steer this great movement in the right direction. We must be careful that it is not hijacked from us, as is so often the case. The African Renaissance Institute has, therefore, an onerous task before it. Although it is an entirely private organization, it will require strong and steady geopolitical and geoeconomic support from the entire continent. Most important of all will be the determination of the leaders who have inspired this movement to ensure its success regardless of the obstacles placed in our way.

Even though the continent is currently rent apart by ethnic conflicts and civil wars, the Renaissance movement is still possible, as was the experience during the European Renaissance, which flowered at the exact period when violence and war was most widespread.

There is no doubt that the most crucial element in the African Renaissance movement is going to be the mobilization of the skilled and talented African, in and outside Africa, in key sectors of the social, economic, entrepreneurial, and scientific fields essential for the manifest transformation of African societies into long-term well-being.

This is why ARI's Executive Board has identified human resource development as its first priority. A nation's education and human resource development, not its capital or material resources, is the *sine qua non* that ultimately determines the character and pace of its economic and social development. Professor Frederick G. Harbison of Princeton University writes:

> Human resources constitute the ultimate basis for wealth of nations. ...Clearly, a country which is unable to develop the skills and knowledge of its people and to utilize them effectively in the national economy will be unable to develop anything. (Harbison 1973, p. 3)

With an in-built resilience and a driving passion to succeed, and the adoption and development of a work ethic that places a premium on investing in its people as a brain-industry, Africa can play a significant role in reshaping the world's industrial map, given its abundant and still largely untapped natural resources.

The best example of a country that followed the above dictum and registered gigantic economic success is South Korea. The country, that had low-level income and human resource development as recently as the 1950s, and with no natural resources to speak of in comparison with North Korea, relied primarily on its own human resources to lift itself by its bootstraps and become one of the most advanced countries in South-East Asia. Singapore is another example. Africa is in a far better position, for with its natural wealth it could make significant progress by the middle of the new millennium if its renaissance can succeed.

8.2. Africa in the Global Village

Our determination to achieve an African Renaissance is unshakeable, but at the same time we do not want to be oblivious to the obstacles ahead of us, not only in Africa but also in the international donor/creditor community. All these I have addressed in detail in this book. Nevertheless, as an African nationalist who has studied, worked, and lived in the West for over forty years and can therefore claim to understand both Africa and the West, I would grant that some of the world's concerns about Africa are legitimate and need to be addressed urgently. Whatever our views on globalization, the fact remains that it has made our socioeconomic world almost like a village, and so we ignore the criticisms of the rest of the world at our own peril.

Skeptics of an African Renaissance have pointed out that the presently developed and industrialized West took many centuries to achieve their current level or status of development and, therefore, Africa cannot hope to do any better; but the leaders of an African Renaissance are not saying that Africa will achieve its economic development instantly, or in ten years—only that it certainly will not take 400 years! At least we should make a purposeful and concerted effort, through collective commitment and forward planning, using the knowledge in science and technology that is now accessible—which was not available in the medieval and early modern ages—to move Africa towards the ranks of the world's industrial continents within thirty to forty years. This has been achieved by South Korea in the last century.

If Africa uses the new knowledge-intensive technologies,

such as electronics and biotechnology, in combination with technical training in computer science and information technology, then the sky is the limit. Brain will have replaced brawn. It is most encouraging that African leaders such as Thabo Mbeki have been for the last few years speaking openly—even evangelistically—about an African Renaissance in precisely these terms. In the postindustrial revolutions Africa has awakened to the realization that information is wealth, and that rapid and wide access to information is power. The computer has freed information, allowing it to play its proper role, and Africa is poised to use it, for information itself has become the key economic resource, the top factor of production—in fact more important than capital, labor, land, or raw materials.

We believe, like President Mbeki of South Africa, that Africa's time has come. The African Renaissance is upon us, and for those who have any doubts

> The moment has come when they should suspend their disbelief. Africa is readying herself for growth and development, fuelled by her own efforts and the profitable and safe injection of international private capital... [and therefore we should] ...do what we have to do together in order to achieve the sustained development of Africa. (Mbeki 1998, p. 11).

Our success, as Mbeki has said so many times, depends neither on the strength of our enemies nor on the obstacles placed in our way, but on the strength of our determination to succeed. Nothing could be more encouraging to present and future generations of Africans than that statement.

8.3. Bringing about an African Renaissance

There are, however, some important considerations: How do we spread the message of an African Renaissance, and who is to spread it? Where will the resources come from to facilitate this, for when we discuss resources, do we mean only financial resources, or human resources as well? A dream such as this does not simply happen; it must be made to happen. Even the European Renaissance used a number of well-planned and carefully orchestrated transmission mechanisms to spread the idea. We must do the same for Africa.

So, let us now try to answer the question of who will bring about an African Renaissance. It is important here to discuss the role of each of the following institutions: ARI, national governments, churches, financial and business organizations, universities and schools, professional organizations, cultural organizations, women's and youth organizations, and the judicial system.

Everyone has a role to play and each grouping must work out for itself how to contribute to an African Renaissance, as expressed in the values of hard work and integrity, in the development of the arts (painting, sculpture, design, music, poetry, literature), and in the development of science and technology, agriculture, business and financial growth. The establishment of the ARI creates the potential for a more systematic, yet informal, way to provide such a matrix within the African context.

The role of ARI is already spelt out in ARI's official documentation. However, it is worth emphasizing some aspects of ARI's role here. First, it should promote the ideas and ideals of an African Renaissance across the continent through high-level meetings of leaders and senior people. Second, it should negotiate with creditors where international bodies have more leverage than national governments to shift creditor priorities towards programs identified as contributing most effectively to an African Renaissance, for instance, to ensure a sustained investment in science and technology with priority to the agricultural sector. Third, ARI must encourage international attention to focus on the resources and opportunities that Africa offers for large-scale agricultural and mineral projects. Fourth, ARI can mediate between states in conflict situations, providing technical solutions and ensuring the necessary preconditions for an African Renaissance.

Another important consideration is the role of national governments. Material benefits can only come about through trust and the building-up of cultural commonality; not by imposing a centrally determined ideology, but by creating space for a civil society to develop that crosses and transcends state borders. The free market in goods and services goes hand-in-hand with a free market in culture and ideas. As well as threatening authoritarian, corrupt, and arbitrary regimes, however, this can also mean that harmful ideas and literature can be disseminated and lead to license and immorality. The best antidote to these is not censorship or repression, but the promotion of ethical values and the encouragement of those things that are genuinely conducive to the public good.

Public policy cannot function in an ethical vacuum; it needs to be undergirded and informed by a definite vision. In African terms I am referring to the centrality of *ubuntu*: that each is a person through their relationships with other people. People cannot be reduced to things or statistics; each person has an infinite value as a being created in the image of God.

Some specific roles for national governments might include the following: first, increase resource allocations and priority given to investment required for science and technology (e.g., lab equipment, materials, and books) and for scholarships for overseas training. Second, establish greater transparency regarding the regional allocation of government investment, educational opportunities, and public sector jobs.

Third, establish national awards for achievements in literature, music, and the visual arts, and for outstanding contributions to the care of the disadvantaged and to the development of interethnic relationships. Fourth, seek to limit the negative cultural impact of the business sector by evaluating the social consequences of the form and content of commercial advertising; the aim must be to ensure adequate controls to preserve traditional African social mores and values.

The history of Western civilizations has shown that the role of churches and other religious groups in the translation of Renaissance arts developments into science and technology development, and then into the political, economic, business and social life of nations, should not be underestimated. The political and cultural changes, particularly relating to limiting corruption and government control by the people, will depend in large part on a religious or ideological commitment among large numbers within the general population to reject corruption, to develop the concept of vocation where a job is seen as a calling from God, and to adopt a strong work ethic.

It is vital that Christianity, Islam and other religious and ideological belief systems provide the foundation of a strong quasi-political movement emphasizing personal integrity and purity, both in work and family life, as this is ultimately the only driving force capable of delivering the cultural context required for an African Renaissance. The role of churches and religious leaders is crucial; the church is by far the largest organization in Africa's "civil society". It must not be manipulated by politicians; rather it should be supported by politicians. Changes in self-perception and self-confidence flow from religious and ideological beliefs and are the key to all that follows.

In considering the role of universities and schools, some examples might include encouraging the study of the following: distinctive African patterns of relations at interpersonal and intergroup levels, for example, between old and young;

261

the roles and duties of relatives among different ethnic groups; how social networks operate, including different types of informal kinship networks; the link between social capital and health, and how to handle death. Other fruitful areas for investigation could include the arts: oral traditions, music, dance, painting, and sculpture within African traditions; scientific studies such as the medicinal qualities of plants used in traditional medicines; and, in partnership with local business leaders, potential commercial uses of raw materials found uniquely, or primarily, in Africa. An important priority within universities and schools should be providing good facilities for science and technology studies, including laboratory equipment, computers, books, and other materials.

An important aspect of the role of financial institutions and businesses in an African Renaissance could be to encourage and to facilitate new forms of family-based insurance, savings, and collective purchase rather than following the Western individualistic approach. Other initiatives might include providing greater financial support to informal sector activity based on extended family cooperation, and by encouraging new forms of professional business association to fight corruption.

As far as the role of the judicial system is concerned, one key development might be to re-establish the traditional role of local elders and "family group conferences" as an alternative to Western-style hearings in front of single magistrates or judges. A second initiative might be to review the forms of punishment adjudged by the courts so as to avoid social exclusion through prison systems based on the Western model, but rather seeking to ensure reintegration of the offender after the punishment.

In conclusion, I should point out that the African Renaissance offers no one solution to all of Africa's problems. Each African country has its own particular history, politics, agriculture, economic structure, and place within the international community. So, the central themes of this book should be adapted pragmatically by each country to its own particular situation; stressing one issue or need here, and stressing another there.

Our main concern and interest, however, will be how the world will assess whether or not there has indeed been an African Renaissance when they come to evaluate the idea in thirty or forty years' time. In our view, it would be wrong to measure the success or failure of an African Renaissance purely in terms of economic growth rates or of food production levels, important as these are. The success of an African Renaissance will also be shown by the quality of life of the African people, in terms of greater community and opportunity, improved access to healthcare and education, and a flowering of the literary, visual, and performing arts. In the final analysis, the degree of freedom and democracy under which Africans are living must also demonstrate whether or not the deeply desired African Renaissance has taken place.

Appendix A
African Renaissance Institute (ARI)

Foundation

Following Thabo Mbeki's speech in 1996, a few African strategists and intellectuals held consultations with a view to formulating pragmatic operational strategies for mobilizing and networking Africa's human resources in terms of intellectual wealth and enterprise for an African Renaissance in the third millennium.

The first meeting of the advisory think-tank of what was originally called the Institute for Africa's Economic Recovery and Development (later renamed the African Renaissance Institute) convened in Gaborone, Botswana, in August 1998. Ambassador (rtd.) Kapembe Nsingo of Zambia was appointed founding president and chairman of ARI's Executive Board, with overall responsibility for the management of the institute and the executive board. Five other founding executive directors, with regional responsibilities, were appointed: Ambassador (rtd.) Falilou Kane, Western and Northern Africa; Mr. Mwahafor Ndilula, Lusophone Africa; Professor Bax Nomvete (deceased), Southern Africa; Professor Washington A.J. Okumu, Central and Eastern Africa; Dr. Patrick Nkanza was appointed as head of the Institute of African Consultants. Professor Okumu was later appointed vice-president as well as vice-chairman of the Board, and Commissioner for Peace and Governance. Professor Thomas Odhaimbo was appointed a member of the board and Commissioner for Science and Technology. ARI acquired full legal status with the official registration of its statutes in October 1998 in Pretoria, South Africa.

It is vital to note that ARI is wholly owned and operated by Africans and is not a political movement. It does not claim to be a custodian of solutions to all of Africa's social and economic problems. The institute is nonpartisan to any political thought, system, or movement, beyond supporting the processes that are necessary to unlock our creative and resource potential. Its rationale and objectives are clearly stated in its statutes and executive summary.

ARI was established in the stark realization that the African continent is progressively and effectively being marginalized globally and through internal ethnically determined armed conflicts and, in some cases, the lack of sound and democratic governance. Few African states are making progress, while in many states there is little evidence of sustainable progress towards a higher quality of life. Africa's habitat remains poor and people are living under dismal and unacceptable social conditions. This marginalization of Africa, particularly economically, has become more pronounced after the end of the cold war. Most of the continent's economic structures are far from being resilient to external shocks, and manufacturing and food production remains inadequate to meet the needs of an increasing and relatively fragile youthful population. Debt and inflation persist in most African countries. Isolated cases of progress have often been unsustained; most of them appear unsustainable in the medium to long term. Research and development of appropriate technologies necessary for economic development is not adequately institutionalized. Insufficient (and sometimes inappropriate) technologies, production processes, and machinery are often imported at colossal costs. As we have already noted, there is a sharp rise in the continent's brain drain, incapacitating medium- to long-term development amidst growing management challenges occasioned by rapid global changes.

Appendix A

Structure

The African Renaissance Institute is, therefore, an institutional mechanism with an independent legal personality and mandate to carry out and implement an aggressive African development agenda. It is truly and uniquely a "hybrid" African institution in the sense that while it is mandated to work closely with governments and to seek their support and cooperation, it is neither controlled by or beholden to them. It is a fiercely independent private institute.

A small Secretariat in Gaborone is headed by a chief executive officer (CEO), who co-ordinates the institute's programs and liaises closely with the Council of Elders (comprising selected former heads of state and government who have pioneered various development initiatives of major significance to the rest of the continent in their own countries), the Council of Patrons (comprising carefully selected current heads of state and government who are spearheading transformation programs in their countries), the leadership of the National Chapters of the ARI, and the core programs of the institute. The core programs are organized under the umbrella of the respective commissions, each of them led by an executive director of ARI, who work in a decentralized manner throughout the continent and also closely interact with the national chapters. The initial commissions occupy the following eight fields:

- human resources development
- science and technology development
- economic recovery and enterprise development
- peace and governance
- infrastructure and communications development
- human settlements, energy, and the environment
- food, nutritional, and health security
- cultural rebirth.

Objectives

With its headquarters in Gaborone, Botswana, ARI has an extremely ambitious mission:

> [It aims to] establish the most effective way of mobilizing and networking Africa's human resources, intellectual wealth, and enterprise for an African Renaissance in the third millennium. It is designed to serve as a vehicle for Africa's thinkers, researchers, and development workers in all walks of life, across barriers of language, religion, and geographical borders, who are motivated by the quest for Africa's survival, recovery, and sustainable development. The ARI has been established to fully capture the visions, aspirations, creative endeavors and spirit of the African Youth, Woman and Man.

The African Renaissance Institute is determined to contribute to the determination and execution of Africa's own home-grown development agenda. In doing so, ARI will be a network of development activists, mobilized and organized, using the latest techniques and technologies, to optimize Africa's own capacity to resolve the age-old problems of: poverty and deprivation, technological backwardness, financial and economic dependency, macroeconomic management for global economic competitiveness, enterprise development vis-à-vis the constraints faced by local private sector enterprises, and, finally, the plight of youth, women, and growing unemployment.

Registered as a non-profit trust, ARI will operate with its financing, the ARI Trust Fund, basically derived from African sources, including those in the diaspora and friends of Africa.

As a private organization it is committed to contributing constructively to the continent's development process through working in collaboration with African governments, other African development institutions, and the private sector, in order to achieve the following nine priority objectives:

1. To undertake problem-solving research in seven priority areas: human resource development; science and technology development; economic recovery; governance and peace; infrastructure and communications development; human settlements, energy development and environmental protection; and, health and cultural affairs.

2. To build user-friendly and supportive databases containing significant findings or research on Africa's development endeavors. The data shall be generated from the archives of universities, research institutes, public and private companies, governments, nongovernmental organizations, multilateral financial institutions, regional organizations and other international organizations.

3. To assist African governments undertaking economic and recovery reforms. The institute shall provide independent counsel on reforms and problem-solving development strategies.

4. To facilitate regional and national dynamics for creating "real jobs" and to produce the critical material needs for the largest numbers of our people in the most cost-effective manner.

5. To monitor closely individual national economies and to provide early warning to governments of impending serious developments in their economies. The human resources of ARI shall therefore remain at the disposal of governments, public and private companies, constituting a pool of advisors who may be called upon to provide

objective diagnosis of problems that currently exist or those that may develop.

6. To cause the circulation of ARI's major assessments of the state of play of the continent's economic recovery program to be followed up through dialogue with bilateral, multilateral and other development agencies and organizations.

7. To put in place an inclusive participatory discussion process on the modalities for effecting Africa's economic recovery, involving community groups, public institutions, and the private sector.

8. To fight for the eradication of the false impression that "Africa has no problems" or that "all problems that exist are solely due to externally-induced or historical phenomena." The institute intends to develop an attitude of mind that is commensurate with the challenge for engendering the continent's self-reliant development and the creation of structures and policies requisite for Africa's competitive survival in the global economy.

9. To work towards "not feeling sorry for ourselves" and to deal with the real issues of backwardness that shall not vanish or go away through wishful thinking. Self-pity must be eradicated completely from the African psyche.

Appendix B
African Institute for Training and Research on Peace (AITROP)

Objectives

Through the African Renaissance, and with the help of the present enlightened leadership, we believe that Africa today has a unique opportunity to meet the global challenges that it faces. Securing peace, sustainable development, and democracy requires nations, in their common interest, to create a new system of global security and governance. We believe that the time is right for the African nations to take that great step forward now, living up to their common responsibility, to create within the context of the African Renaissance Institute, the African Institute for Training and Research On Peace (AITROP).

This will be a purely African center, run by Africans in cooperation with other such training centers that have been established in other parts of the world, such as:

- the Stockholm Initiative on Global Security and Governance
- the International Peace Academy (New York, U.S.A.)
- the Center for Security Studies and Conflict Research
- the Swiss Peace Foundation
- the Center for Development Research (Dhaka, Bangladesh)
- the Institute for African Alternatives (London, UK)
- the African Peace Research Institute (Lagos, Nigeria)
- the United Nations Center for Training and Research

- the Jimmy Carter Center (Atlanta, Georgia, U.S.A.)
- the Kissinger Associates (New York, U.S.A.)

The above list is not exhaustive; indeed, Holland, Germany, and Canada have undertaken other important research work on peace, from which Africa can learn a lot. These non-African organizations usually have adequate resources, both financial and human, to be able to accomplish their tasks, whereas African organizations of a similar nature always suffer from chronic lack of resources.

The creation of AITROP is necessitated by the fact that it is only Africa that lacks an independent, nonpartisan, pan-African institution dedicated to the promotion of peace and the prevention of conflicts through research and training, the preparation of draft concepts and communication.

To fill this gap AITROP intends to play an important and pioneering role in training and developing a continent-wide cadre of policy-makers and practitioners in the art of peace-making, peacekeeping and peace-building. It would be a place where peaceful foreign relations and the internal African requirements of peace and security policy would be discussed and publicized.

The main function of AITROP would be to help shape African peace and security policy through research and training, collecting and collating various peace accords, both African and non-African; conducting research on the causes of ethnic conflicts; offering recommendations and advice on the mediation of African disputes and conflicts; serving as a reference center for diplomats, military officers, members of the U.N. organizations systems concerned with peace issues, members of regional organizations, and officials of humanitarian and other non-governmental organizations.

In its training program AITROP should aim to fulfil the following interrelated objectives:

- to deepen the knowledge and expertise of Africans on critical policy issues relating to peacemaking, peacekeeping and peacebuilding;
- to provide opportunities for the African trainees to learn the techniques of diplomatic political negotiations at the various levels of negotiation and mediation from distinguished and internationally renowned Africans, especially the art of preventive diplomacy;
- to provide an opportunity for cross-fertilization of ideas between Africans and non-Africans in the art of diplomacy, mediation, and negotiation with people of different ethnic and cultural backgrounds.

We believe that the creation of AITROP will meet a critical need in the sense that, while the continent has so many ethnic conflicts, there are no Africans of repute who have had the support and proper backing, either within Africa or internationally, to undertake any mediation and/or negotiation tasks. With the exception of Julius Nyerere's mediation efforts on the Burundi ethnic conflict, most so-called mediators criss-crossing the African continent are non-Africans. While no one doubts their brilliance and qualifications, such people are often ignorant of the African ethos under which they are operating, added to which they often represent, wittingly or unwittingly, interests that may be in sharp contradistinction to African interests.

To ensure that African interests become an integral part of the formulation of policy at their inception regarding the modalities for the settlement of ethnic conflicts in Africa, AITROP would liaise closely with the U.N., the OAU and the European Union.

Peace and security will not be achieved in Africa unless national and international institutions are put in place to conduct in-depth research and analysis to highlight and eventually to deal with the threats that stem from failures in development, environmental degradation and lack of progress towards democracy. Injustices that prevail worldwide are a constant threat to the security of nations and peoples. Increasing economic and ecological interdependence have not been met by corresponding strengthening of global cooperation and governance. Working as an independent, non-partisan arm of the African Renaissance Institute, AITROP would fill a sorely required need in the African peace firmament. It would also, above all, bring some orderly coordination to the currently numerous *ad hoc* peace missions in Africa that only contribute to making conflicts much more intractable and complex. Not everyone can be a peacemaker or a mediator.

AITROP and OAU

It should be made abundantly clear that the relationship between AITROP and the Organization of African Unity's Mechanism for Conflict Prevention, Management and Resolution (hereinafter referred to as the Central Organ) must be close, so that continuous consultation and the establishment of a good working relationship can be put in place.

The difference, however, between the two organizations would lie in the fact that the Central Organ is an intergovernmental organization that places some limitations on it regarding freedom of action; while AITROP would be an independent, private, and nonpartisan think-tank with wide freedom for swift action, unencumbered by numerous bureaucratic official consultations before the lowest common denominator on decision-making is reached.

Although the OAU has been seriously weakened of late by divisions between the member states—mainly along black

African versus Arab lines that were most sharply exposed in differences over the wars in Western Sahara, Chad, Ethiopia, and Uganda—the collective principles that guided the Founding Fathers who met in Addis Ababa in May 1963 are still as relevant as ever. These African leaders were guided by their collective conviction that freedom, equality, justice, and dignity are legitimate aspirations of the African peoples and by their desire to harness the natural and human resources for the advancement of the continent in all spheres of human endeavor.

They were inspired by an equally common determination to promote understanding between the African peoples and to rekindle the aspirations of the African people for solidarity in a larger unity transcending linguistic, ideological, ethnic, and national differences. Even more important, they were fully convinced that to achieve these lofty objectives, conditions for peace and security must be established and maintained.

Although, stated above, the recent splits in the OAU have led the organization increasingly to avoid difficult political questions, and meetings now confine themselves largely to passing resolutions with little force on economic questions that are also rarely implemented, we believe that the OAU will still have a greater role to play in the future. What is badly needed is a re-examination of its proper role after the end of the cold war and the completion of the task of liberating the African continent.

This is a normal requirement for all great institutions in the world. We Africans must not be shy in re-examining the continued relevance of the policies of the institutions such as the OAU that we set up during the cold war. We must subject the OAU charter to intense scrutiny and to radical re-examination in the context of the emerging New World Order. Why can we not participate also in shaping and influencing the policies of such an order? We must not treat the OAU charter as a static, sacrosanct document. For instance, the diplomatic doctrine of noninterference in the internal policies of member states is not so strictly relevant now, particularly when a ruler violates the people's human rights on a massive scale and when there is no rule of law. These are issues where an African Renaissance can provide new and bold leadership and ideas.

Appendix C
African Foundation for Research and Development (AFRAND)

Establishment

In order to survive in this highly competitive world, the African Renaissance must endeavor to create a platform, or to support one that is already in existence, bringing together various commitments and initiatives to spearhead, expedite, and actualize the process of economic development in an Africa anchored firmly on a science culture and technological practice.

In this regard, we are fortunate that the idea of an African Renaissance has come at the right time, as if it were providentially inspired. This is because a meeting of African heads of state and government (known as the Presidential Forum on the Management of Science and Technology for Development in Africa), organized by the board of trustees of the Research and Development Forum for Science-Led Development in Africa (RANDFORUM) met in Maputo, Mozambique, in July 1994, under the chairmanship of President Joaquim Alberto Chissano, and established and launched a new body known as the African Foundation for Research and Development (AFRAND). This new body, with headquarters in Lilongwe, Malawi, was established as a research and development fund to finance science and technology programs in Africa by providing seed and venture capital to convert promising research results into technological products and social services.

277

The establishment of AFRAND was hailed as a milestone in Africa's development because for a long time Africa has lived off other people's technology, other regions' financial resources, and other continents' brainpower. In fact, this scenario of Africa's shameful dependence on other peoples and nations for nearly everything has not shown any sign of abating even after nearly four decades of independent statehood. World trade is now dominated by knowledge-intensive technologies, that arise from the translation of results from high-level research and technological development work. Such translation can only be realized when planned steps are taken:

- to create a culture of excellence and relevance in R & D;
- to foster an environment and program for capacity building and utilization in research and innovation;
- to put in place a mechanism for the effective translation of these R & D results into demand-driven, market-oriented technologies and processes.

At the founding of AFRAND, sixteen African states were represented by ten heads of state, two prime ministers, one deputy prime minister, and ninety-three official ministers. These states comprised Mozambique (host/chairman), Botswana (1993 host/chairman), Angola, Congo, Gabon, Malawi, Mauritius, and Namibia; Senegal, South Africa, and Tanzania; Uganda, Zaire, Zambia, and Zimbabwe. Numerous multilateral and national development institutions attended, including the African Development Bank (ADB), Preferential Trade Area of Eastern and Southern Africa, being turned into a Common Market for Eastern and Southern Africa (PTA/COMESA), African Regional Industrial Property Organization (ARIPO), United Nations Economic Commission for Africa (ECA), and the Association of African Universities (AAU). There were

more than 400 participants, a significant proportion representing the private sector and community-level leadership.

Role in the African Renaissance

Since AFRAND has already been established and is supposedly
a going concern (although currently there is not much heard
about it) there is no need for us to reinvent the wheel. It would
merely be a question of revisiting the foundation to determine
ways and means in which it can serve the noble cause of the
African Renaissance in the new millennium. If its apparent dor-
mant state is due either to lack of resources or of managerial
capabilities, then these and any other issues and/or obstacles
must be urgently addressed.

Note, however, that AFRAND is a unique body that is not
intended to be another bureaucratic organization like many
other such bodies in Africa and elsewhere. It is a fund in the
sense that it is not meant to support basic research *per se*; but its
mandate lies principally in transforming R & D results into key
technological products and social services that Africa needs.
Debt-for-Science Swaps covering the entire range of African
states were to act as its endowment fund source. This was also
considered a more realistic way of tackling the African debt
conundrum, because Africa should not believe that its more
than U.S. $200 billion unpayable debt will be written off,
despite the massive efforts of the Jubilee 2000 pressure group.
The African Development Bank was supposedly responsible
for banking and investment for AFRAND, assuring prudence
and financial competence.

Lastly, AFRAND's founders wanted to design it in such a
way that less politics should be injected into the organization,
and thus to prevent its emulating the demise of most other
such bodies. So, AFRAND is a hybrid body in the sense that it

was established under an Intergovernmental charter in order to give it a pan-African legal framework; but it will at the same time function as an independent, self-sustaining body with its own autonomous governance and directorate. Perhaps all these structures should be re-examined to determine whether they are truly meeting their original objectives.

Appendix D

Table 4. Chronology of Conflict in Africa

Year	Country	Name of Conflict	Type of Conflict
1948–1994	South Africa	Anti-apartheid struggle	Internal
1955–1972	Sudan	First civil war	Internal
1960–1965	DRC (Zaire)	Post independence war	Internal
1960–1964	Rwanda	Ethnic strife	Internal/Ethnic
1961–1974	Angola	Independence war	Independence
1962–1974	Guinea Bissau	Independence war	Independence
1964–1975	Mozambique	Independence war	Independence
1965–1980	Zimbabwe	Struggle for majority rule	Independence
1966–1990	Namibia	Liberation war	Independence
1966–1969	Nigeria	Biafra civil war	Internal
1966–1996	Chad	Civil war	Internal
1966	Namibia	Caprivi strip secession	Internal/Regional
1970–1974	Burundi	Ethnic strife	Internal/Ethnic
1974–1991	Eritrea	War for Independence	Independence
1974–1978	Ethiopia	Revolution	Internal
1975–1991	Mozambique	War with Renamo	Internal
1976–1983	Ethiopia	Ogaden war	Internal
1977–1978	Ethiopia/Somalia	Somali war	Interstate
1978–1991	Ethiopia	Civil War	Internal
1978–1979	Uganda/Tanzania	Amin invasion	Interstate
1978	Ghana	Rawlings coup	Internal
1979–1996	Central African Republic	Coups and civil strife	Internal
1980–1984	Uganda	Obote overthrow/civil war	Internal
1982–	Senegal	Casamance	Internal
1983–	Sudan	2nd Civil war	Internal
1984–1989	Somalia	North West Secession	Internal
1989–1997	Liberia	Civil war	Internal
1990–1994	Rwanda	Civil war and genocide	Internal/Ethnic
1990–	Sierra Leone	War with RUF	Internal/Regional
1991–	Somalia	Civil war	Internal/Factional
1992–	Angola	2nd War with UNITA	Internal
1993–	Burundi	Civil war	Internal/Ethnic
1997–2000	Congo (Brazzaville)	Civil war	Internal
1997	DRC	Civil war	Regional
1998	Ethiopia–Eritrea	Border conflict	Interstate

Based on University of Michigan database, Federation of American Scientists–Military analysis network and "The World Guide 2000"

Source: *The Causes of Conflict in Africa: Consultation Document* (DFID, 2001), p. 23.

Appendix E

Table 5. Key Indicators for Africa

Source: *The Causes of Conflict in Africa*: *Consultation Document* (DFID, 2001), pp. 24–25.

Country	Gross national product (GNP) Dollars 1999	GNP per capita Avg annual growth rate % 1998-1999	Public Expend. Health % GNP 1990-98	Public Expend. Educ'n % GNP 1997	Milit. Expend. % GNP 1997	External Debt Millions of $'s 1998	External Debt Present value % of GNP 1998	Overseas development assistance Dollars per capita 1998	Overseas development assistance % of GNP 1998
Algeria	1,550	1.3	3.3	5.1	3.9	30,665	66	13	0.9
Angola	220	-37.4	3.9	—	20.5	12,173	279	28	8.1
Benin	380	2.2	1.6	3.2	1.5	1,647	46	35	9.2
Botswana	3,240	3.0	2.7	8.6	5.1	548	10	68	2.3
Burkina Faso	240	2.7	1.2	1.5	2.8	1,399	32	37	15.5
Burundi	120	-2.5	0.6	4.0	6.1	1,119	72	12	8.8
Cameroon	580	2.2	1.0	—	3.0	9,829	98	30	5.0
Central African Republic	290	1.9	1.9	—	3.9	921	55	34	11.6
Chad	200	-4.1	2.4	1.7	2.7	1,091	38	23	10.0
Congo Dem. Rep.	–	–	1.2	–	5.0	12,929	196	3	2.0
Congo Rep.	670	4.8	1.8	6.1	4.1	5,119	280	23	3.9
Cote d'Ivoire	710	1.1	1.4	5.0	1.1	14,852	122	55	7.6
Dominican Republic	1,910	6.2	1.6	2.3	1.1	4,451	28	15	0.8
Egypt	1,400	4.0	1.8	4.8	2.8	1,964	29	31	2.3
Eritrea	200	0.8	2.9	1.8	7.8	149	11	41	19.7
Ethiopia	100	0.8	1.7	4.0	1.9	10,352	135	11	10.0
Ghana	390	4.8	1.8	4.2	0.7	6,884	55	38	9.6
Guinea	510	2.1	1.2	1.9	1.5	3,546	69	51	9.8
Kenya	360	0.1	2.2	6.5	2.1	7,010	45	16	4.2

	Gross national product (GNP)	GNP per capita	Public Expend. Health % GNP	Public Expend. Educ'n % GNP	Milit. Expend. % GNP	External Debt		Overseas development assistance	
	Dollars 1999	Avg annual growth rate % 1998–1999	1990–98	1997	1997	Millions of $'s 1998	Present value % of GNP 1998	Dollars per capita 1998	% of GNP 1998
Lesotho	550	-3.0	3.7	8.4	2.5	692	42	32	5.7
Madagascar	250	2.3	1.1	1.9	1.5	4,394	89	34	13.5
Malawi	190	4.4	2.8	5.4	1.0	2,444	77	41	24.4
Mali	240	2.7	2.0	2.2	1.7	3,202	84	33	13.5
Mauritania	380	2.0	1.8	5.1	2.3	2,589	148	68	17.8
Morocco	1,200	-1.0	1.3	5.0	4.3	20,687	54	19	1.5
Mozambique	230	6.6	2.1	—	2.8	8,208	74	61	28.2
Namibia	1,890	0.6	3.8	9.1	2.7	—	—	108	5.8
Niger	190	-1.1	1.3	2.3	1.1	1,659	55	29	14.4
Nigeria	310	0.5	0.2	0.7	1.4	30,315	74	2	0.5
Rwanda	250	4.8	2.1	—	4.4	1,226	34	43	17.3
Senegal	510	2.3	2.6	3.7	1.6	3,861	58	56	10.8
Sierra Leone	130	-9.8	1.7	—	5.9	1,243	126	22	16.2
South Africa	3,160	-0.9	3.2	7.9	1.8	24,712	18	12	0.4
Tanzania	240	3.1	1.3	—	1.3	7,603	71	31	12.5
Togo	320	-0.3	1.1	4.5	2.0	1,448	68	29	8.6
Uganda	320	4.8	1.8	2.6	4.2	3,935	35	23	7.0
Zambia	320	0.4	2.3	2.2	1.1	6,865	181	36	11.4
Zimbabwe	520	1.8	3.1	3.8	3.8	4,716	69	24	4.7

References

Achebe, C. 1984. *The Trouble with Nigeria*, London: Heinemann.

Brandt Commission 1980 "North–South, A Program for Survival", 1980. *Report of the Independent Commission in International Development Issues*, London.

Brown, L.R. 1996. *State of the World 1996*. London: Earthscan.

Buchanan, K. 1975. *Reflections on Education in the Third World*. Nottingham, England.

Burke, P. 1998. *The European Renaissance: Centers and Peripheries*. Oxford: Blackwell.

"The Causes of Conflict in Africa": Consultation Document, 2001. Department for International Development, London.

Clarke, D. 1998. *Slaves and Slavery*. Rochester, England.

Cooke, P. and K. Morgan 1998. *The Associational Economy*. Oxford: Oxford University Press.

Davidson, B. 1975. *Can Africa Survive?* London: Heinemann.

Davidson, B. 1994. *The Search for Africa*. London: James Currey.

Dualeh, H. 1994. *From Barre to Aideed: Somalia: The Agony of a Nation*. Nairobi, Kenya: Stellagraphics.

Enriquez, J. 1999. "Too Many Flags." *Foreign Policy*, Autumn/Fall, pp. 30–50.

Falola, T. 1995. "Africa in Perspective." Unpublished article, 14 February.

Fieldhouse, D.K. 1992. "How Africa Lost Its Past." *Times Literary Supplement*, London.

Friedland, W.H. and Rosberg, C.G. (eds.) 1964. *African Socialism*. Stanford, CA: Stanford University Press.

Friedman, T.L. 2000. *The Lexus and the Olive Tree*. London: Harper Collins.

Galbraith, J.K. 1992. Article in *Observer*, London.

Goudie, A. 1977. *The Future of Climate*, Predictions Series, Vol.5. London.

Griffiths, I.L.L. 1987. *An Atlas of African Affairs*. London: Routledge.

Hadjor, K.B. 1988. *Nkrumah and Ghana*. London: Kegan Paul International.

Hadjor, K.B. 1993. *Dictionary of Third World Terms*. Harmondsworth: Penguin Books.

Hadland, A. and J. Rantao 1999. *The Life and Times of Thabo Mbeki*. Rivonia: Zebra Press.

Harbison, H.A. 1973. *Human Resources as the Wealth of Nations*. New York: Oxford University Press.

Kalambuka, H.A. 2001. "The Arab Factor in the East African Slave Trade," *Daily Nation*, Nairobi, 24 May.

Khalaf, Samir. 1971. "Family Associations in Lebanon," *Journal of Comparative Family Studies*, Vol. II, No 2, pp. 235–250.

Lake, F. 1966. *Clinical Theology*. London: Darton, Longman and Todd.

Lele, U. and S. Stone 1989. *Population pressure, the Environment, and Agricultural Intensification: Variations on the Boserup Hypothesis*, MADIA working paper.

Little, I.M.D. 1964. *Aid To Africa*. Oxford: Pergamon Press.

Lijphart, A. 1977. *Democracy in Plural Societies*. Binghampton, N.Y: Yale University Press.

Mbeki, Thabo *et al* 1998. *The African Renaissance*, Konrad-Adenauer-Stiftung, Occasional Papers Series, Johannesburg.

Meier, G.M. and J.E. Stiglitz 2001. *Frontiers of Development Economics*. Oxford: Oxford University Press.

Meredith, M. 1984. *The First Dance of Freedom—Black Africa in the Postwar Era*. London: Hamish Hamilton.

Mohiddin, A. 1981. *African Socialism in Two Countries*. London: Croom Helm.

Mutua, A.N. "Africans to Blame for the Leaders They Have," *Daily Nation Commentary*, Nairobi, 20 June 2000.

Nkrumah, K. 1970. *Class Struggle in Africa*. London: Panof Books Ltd.

Obasanjo, O. and A. Mabogunje (eds.) 1992. *Elements of Democracy*. African Leadership Forum, Nigeria.

Plato. "Early Socratic Dialogues," ed. Trevor J. Saunders. Harmondsworth: Penguin, 1987.

Porter, M.E. 1998. "The Adam Smith Address: Location, Clusters and the New Microeconomics of Competition," *Business Economics*, 33, 1 January, pp. 7–13.

Redhead, B. 1984. *Political Thought From Plato to Nato*. London: Ariel.

Reilly, K. (ed.) 1988. *Readings in World Civilizations*. New York: St. Martin's Press.

Report of the Ad Hoc Panel of Economists to the Twelfth NAM Summit, Durban, South Africa, 1998, pp. 20–21, *Elements for an Agenda of the South*, published by the South Center, April 1999, Chemin du Champ-d'Anier 17, 1211 Geneva, Switzerland, on behalf of the Non-Aligned Movement.

Sagay, J.O. and D.A. Wilson 1978. *Africa: A Modern History (1800-1975)*. London: Evans Brothers.

Sandbrook, R. 1986. *The Politics of Africa's Economic Stagnation*. Cambridge: Cambridge University Press.

Scott, J.C. 1976. *The Moral Economy of the Peasant*. New Haven, Conn: Yale University Press.

Segal, R. 2001. *Islam's Black Slaves: A History of Africa's Other Black Diaspora*. New York: Farrar, Straus and Giroux.

Simpson, E.S. 1987. *The Developing World: An Introduction*. Harlow: Longman.

Skidelsky, R. 1996. *The World After Communism—A Polemic for Our Times*. London: Papermac.

Soyinka, W. 1996. *The Open Sore of a Continent: A Personal Narrative of the Nigerian Crisis.* Oxford: Oxford University Press.

Stavros, L.S. 1971. *The World since 1500.* Upper Saddle River NJ: Prentice Hall.

Tevoedjre, A. 1979. *Poverty: Wealth of Mankind.* Oxford: Pergamon.

Thomas, A. *et al.* 1994. *Third World Atlas.* Buckingham: Open University Press.

Todaro, M.P. 1987. *Economic Development in the Third World.* London: Longman.

Vitousek, Peter M. *et al.* 1997. "Human Domination of Earth's Ecosystems," *Science,* 25 July, 494–99.

Weber, M. 1947. *The Theory of Social and Economic Organization.* New York: The Free Press and the Falcon's Wing Press.

Weber, M. and Roth, G. 1968. "Personal Rulership, Patrimonialism and Empire Building in the New States," *World Politics,* 20: 2.

Williams, E. 1993. *Capitalism and Slavery* (first published 1944). London: Deutsch.

Wolf-Phillips, L. 1979. "Why Third World?," *Third World Quarterly,* 1: 1, 105–116.

Index